Instagram®

WITHDRAWN

by Jenn Herman, Corey Walker, and Eric Butow

for **dummies**®

A Wiley Brand

Instagram® For Dummies®

Published by: **John Wiley & Sons, Inc.,** 111 River Street, Hoboken, NJ 07030-5774, www.wiley.com

Copyright © 2020 by John Wiley & Sons, Inc., Hoboken, New Jersey

Published simultaneously in Canada

No part of this publication may be reproduced, stored in a retrieval system or transmitted in any form or by any means, electronic, mechanical, photocopying, recording, scanning or otherwise, except as permitted under Sections 107 or 108 of the 1976 United States Copyright Act, without the prior written permission of the Publisher. Requests to the Publisher for permission should be addressed to the Permissions Department, John Wiley & Sons, Inc., 111 River Street, Hoboken, NJ 07030, (201) 748-6011, fax (201) 748-6008, or online at http://www.wiley.com/go/permissions.

Trademarks: Wiley, For Dummies, the Dummies Man logo, Dummies.com, Making Everything Easier, and related trade dress are trademarks or registered trademarks of John Wiley & Sons, Inc., and may not be used without written permission. Instagram is a registered trademark of Instagram, LLC. All other trademarks are the property of their respective owners. John Wiley & Sons, Inc., is not associated with any product or vendor mentioned in this book.

LIMIT OF LIABILITY/DISCLAIMER OF WARRANTY: WHILE THE PUBLISHER AND AUTHOR HAVE USED THEIR BEST EFFORTS IN PREPARING THIS BOOK, THEY MAKE NO REPRESENTATIONS OR WARRANTIES WITH RESPECT TO THE ACCURACY OR COMPLETENESS OF THE CONTENTS OF THIS BOOK AND SPECIFICALLY DISCLAIM ANY IMPLIED WARRANTIES OF MERCHANTABILITY OR FITNESS FOR A PARTICULAR PURPOSE. NO WARRANTY MAY BE CREATED OR EXTENDED BY SALES REPRESENTATIVES OR WRITTEN SALES MATERIALS. THE ADVISE AND STRATEGIES CONTAINED HEREIN MAY NOT BE SUITABLE FOR YOUR SITUATION. YOU SHOULD CONSULT WITH A PROFESSIONAL WHERE APPROPRIATE. NEITHER THE PUBLISHER NOR THE AUTHOR SHALL BE LIABLE FOR DAMAGES ARISING HEREFROM.

For general information on our other products and services, please contact our Customer Care Department within the U.S. at 877-762-2974, outside the U.S. at 317-572-3993, or fax 317-572-4002. For technical support, please visit https://hub.wiley.com/community/support/dummies.

Wiley publishes in a variety of print and electronic formats and by print-on-demand. Some material included with standard print versions of this book may not be included in e-books or in print-on-demand. If this book refers to media such as a CD or DVD that is not included in the version you purchased, you may download this material at http://booksupport.wiley.com. For more information about Wiley products, visit www.wiley.com.

Library of Congress Control Number: 2019913050

ISBN 978-1-119-59393-5 (pbk); ISBN 978-1-119-59400-0 (ebk); ISBN 978-1-119-59399-7 (ebk)

Manufactured in the United States of America

V10013909_091319

Contents at a Glance

Introduction 1

Part 1: Getting Started with Instagram 5
CHAPTER 1: Instagramming Like a Pro 7
CHAPTER 2: Installing Instagram Everywhere 11
CHAPTER 3: Setting Up Your Profile 25
CHAPTER 4: Navigating Instagram 41
CHAPTER 5: Why Isn't This Working? 57

Part 2: Getting Creative with Instagram Content 75
CHAPTER 6: Taking and Posting Great Photos 77
CHAPTER 7: Recording and Posting Great Videos 103
CHAPTER 8: Personalizing Your Post 119

Part 3: Connecting with a Community on Instagram 137
CHAPTER 9: Finding People to Follow 139
CHAPTER 10: Interacting with Other Instagrammers 155
CHAPTER 11: Direct Messaging with Others 167

Part 4: Telling Tales with Instagram Stories 197
CHAPTER 12: Exploring Instagram Stories 199
CHAPTER 13: Creating Instagram Stories 217
CHAPTER 14: Adding Style to Your Stories 245
CHAPTER 15: Sneaky Story Sharing 265
CHAPTER 16: Using Instagram Highlights to Keep Your Content Alive 277
CHAPTER 17: Going Live on Instagram 291

Part 5: Becoming a Pro at IGTV 299
CHAPTER 18: Understanding IGTV 301
CHAPTER 19: Creating an IGTV Presence 307

Part 6: The Part of Tens 317
CHAPTER 20: Ten Things Not to Do on Instagram 319
CHAPTER 21: Ten Types of Great Instagram Photos 325

Index 339

Table of Contents

INTRODUCTION 1
About This Book. 1
Foolish Assumptions. 2
Icons Used in This Book 2
Beyond the Book 3
Where to Go from Here 3

PART 1: GETTING STARTED WITH INSTAGRAM 5

CHAPTER 1: Instagramming Like a Pro. 7
Figuring Out What You Need to Get Started 7
Discovering How to Add Posts to Your Instagram Account 8
Connecting with Others on Instagram 9
Exploring the Excitement of Instagram Stories. 10
Creating Videos with IGTV 10

CHAPTER 2: Installing Instagram Everywhere 11
Installing Instagram Wherever You Want to Use It. 11
Installing the app on your iPhone. 12
Installing Instagram on your iPad 12
Installing the app on Android 15
Installing on a Windows PC 15
Installing on your Mac (sort of) 17
Exploring Instagram on the Web. 19
Starting to Gram Instantly 21

CHAPTER 3: Setting Up Your Profile 25
Personal Profile Practices. 25
Choosing a username and name 27
Deciding on a profile photo. 30
Writing a Dazzling Bio. 32
Deciding what information to include 32
Formatting your bio 34
Considering layouts for your bio. 35
Adding a web address to your bio 35
Taking Advantage of a Business Profile Upgrade. 37
Setting Your Account Privacy Settings 39

CHAPTER 4: Navigating Instagram. 41
Scrolling through the Feed. 41
Making Sense of the Instagram Algorithm 44

Exploring the World of Instagram..................................47
    Finding and viewing the Explore page 47
    Searching for what makes you happy 47
Checking Your Notifications...................................53

CHAPTER 5: **Why Isn't This Working?** 57
Installation Issues 57
    Dealing with compatibility issues 58
    Checking your space.......................................58
    Unfreezing an installation on your iPhone or iPad..........63
    Finding a missing app on your iPhone or iPad 63
    Resolving issues on an Android device 63
Log-In Difficulties..64
    Checking your username 64
    Fixing password issues....................................64
    Dealing with a disabled account 67
Finding Relief for Common Problems 67
    Instagram won't share 67
    Getting Instagram to notify you 69
Nothing Is Working . . . Now What?..........................70
    Reporting a problem on your iPhone or iPad 70
    Reporting a problem on your Android smartphone or tablet 71
Getting Rid of Error Messages.................................71
    Can't add a comment 71
    Can't delete comments....................................72
    Can't refresh feed 72
    Can't follow anyone else..................................73

PART 2: GETTING CREATIVE WITH INSTAGRAM CONTENT 75

CHAPTER 6: **Taking and Posting Great Photos**................77
Taking Your Best Shot...77
Improving Your Best Shot 79
    Applying a filter 81
    Tweaking with the editing tools...........................83
    Saving your changes (or not)..............................89
Enriching Your Photo 89
    Describing your photo 90
    It's good to have options 91
Posting Your Photos: Ta Da!...................................94
Uploading Photos from Your Camera Roll.......................96
Uploading Multiple Photos to One Post........................98
    Selecting multiple photos.................................98
    Applying filters and adding photos.......................101

Editing photos individually. 102
Adding information and sharing your photos. 102

CHAPTER 7: **Recording and Posting Great Videos** 103
Recording Videos. 103
Filming with a smartphone or tablet 104
Recording multiple video clips. 108
Deleting video clips 108
Checking out your video. 108
Improving Your Video. 109
Applying a filter 110
Changing the cover frame 110
Adding details. 111
Posting your video. 113
Uploading a Stored Video. 114
Uploading Multiple Videos from an iPhone or iPad. 116

CHAPTER 8: **Personalizing Your Post** 119
Determining How Long Your Captions Should Be 119
Formatting Your Caption 122
Including Calls to Action in Your Caption. .123
Tagging People in Your Posts 124
Adding Locations to Your Posts. 126
Taking Advantage of Hashtags 128
Knowing where to place hashtags in your post 128
Identifying how many hashtags is ideal. 130
Finding the right hashtags for you 130
Saving hashtags for repeated use. 132
Creating a new hashtag 134

PART 3: CONNECTING WITH A
COMMUNITY ON INSTAGRAM. 137

CHAPTER 9: **Finding People to Follow** 139
Where Are My Peeps?. 139
Syncing your contact list. 140
Finding New Friends 141
Exploring the Explore function 142
Searching the Search feature 143
Letting Instagram suggest users to you. 145
Deciding Whom to Follow Back. 147
Viewing and following your followers. 147
Reciprocating a follow or not. 148

Finding Your Tribe 149
    Finding or creating a community you vibe with 150
    Deciding whether Instagram pods are beneficial 152

CHAPTER 10: **Interacting with Other Instagrammers** 155
Interacting with the Posts in Your Feed 155
Replying to Comments on Your Own Posts .158
    Responding to comments from the Notifications tab 158
    Responding to comments from the post itself 160
    Deciding to delete a comment 160
Keeping Instagram Healthy by Reporting the Bad Eggs 163
    Reporting a commenter 164
    Reporting from an iOS device 164
    Reporting from an Android device 164
    Blocking a commenter 165

CHAPTER 11: **Direct Messaging with Others** 167
Starting a New Direct Message 168
Sharing Photos and Videos via Direct Message 173
Sharing GIFs 181
Using Voice Messages 184
Creating a New Group Message 186
Replying to a Direct Message 188
Using Live Chat in Direct Messages 188
Navigating Your Inbox 191
Getting Rid of Unwanted Messages 194

PART 4: TELLING TALES WITH INSTAGRAM STORIES 197

CHAPTER 12: **Exploring Instagram Stories** .199
Finding Stories to Watch 199
Interacting with Stories You Watch 204
    Forwarding through the things you don't like 204
    Going back to the things you want to see again 204
    Pausing a story to see more 205
    Reacting to a story 205
    Understanding Story Limitations 207
    Upload criteria limitations 208
    Playing-time limitations 208
Accessing the Story Camera 210
    Editing your settings 212
    Changing the camera from regular to selfie mode 215

CHAPTER 13: Creating Instagram Stories 217

Planning a Story from Start to Finish 217
Deciding What to Share 218
    Sharing your less-than-perfect stuff. 218
    Showcasing your personality and lifestyle. 219
Adding a Story Photo 221
Adding a Story Video. 227
    Filming with the stories camera 227
    Experimenting with all the camera options. 228
    Uploading a video from your camera roll 234
Adding a Text Post. 236
Saving Your Story. 238
    Saving before publishing 238
    Saving after publishing (within the 24-hour active window). 238
    Automatically saving all your stories 238
    Accessing your archives 241

CHAPTER 14: Adding Style to Your Stories 245

Jazzing Up Your Story Post Using Stickers 245
    Location, mention, and hashtag stickers for search
    and notifications 246
    GIFs, sliders, emojis, and more 251
    Questions, polls, quizzes, chats, and more 253
    Countdown and Music stickers to intrigue your followers 256
    Picture in picture for the fun of it 256
    Deleting stickers that don't work. 258
Personalizing Stories with Doodles. 259
Saying More with Text 262
    Changing your font option. 262
    Removing your text boxes 263

CHAPTER 15: Sneaky Story Sharing 265

Sharing Another Story to Your Own Story. .265
Sharing Some Stories to Select People. 267
    Sharing via a direct message 267
    Sharing to your Close Friends list 268
Sharing Regular Instagram Posts to Your Stories. 272
Changing Your Story into a Regular Instagram Post 274

**CHAPTER 16: Using Instagram Highlights to Keep
Your Content Alive** 277

Getting Acquainted with Highlights 277
Creating a New Highlight Gallery 279
    Adding a highlight from your profile 279
    Adding a highlight from an active story 279

Naming and customizing your highlight .282
Setting a cover image for your highlight 282
Creating a custom cover image. 282
Adding Content to a Highlight. 285
Sharing a current story. 285
Finding an archived story. 285
Deleting a story from a highlight. 287
Coming Up with Fun Ideas for Highlights 289

CHAPTER 17: **Going Live on Instagram** 291
Getting Started with Live Videos. 291
Knowing When to Go Live 294
Developing a Game Plan 294
Interacting with Live Guests. 295
Inviting a Guest onto the Live Broadcast. 296
Saving Live Broadcasts and Sharing Them 298

PART 5: BECOMING A PRO AT IGTV. 299

CHAPTER 18: **Understanding IGTV**. 301
Finding IGTV within Instagram. 301
Finding IGTV within the IGTV App 303
Understanding How IGTV Videos are Formatted 305
Tapping Into Whose Videos You're Seeing. .305

CHAPTER 19: **Creating an IGTV Presence**. 307
Setting Up an IGTV Channel. 307
Using your mobile device to set up IGTV. 308
Using your computer to set up IGTV 309
Uploading Videos to IGTV. 309
Using your mobile device to upload. 309
Using your computer to upload 311
Creating Quality Content for IGTV. 314
Making your videos shine. 314
Using the video description to your advantage 314
Responding to Comments on Your Videos .315

PART 6: THE PART OF TENS. 317

CHAPTER 20: **Ten Things Not to Do on Instagram** 319
Using the Same Name as Your Username. .319
Picking an Irrelevant Username 320
Using a Bad Profile Photo. 320

Not Including a Bio 321
Ignoring Instagram Stories. 321
Not Using Captions 322
Hashjacking 322
Tagging People Who Are Not in the Photo 322
Following Everyone Who Follows You 323
Using Automated Tools to Follow or Like Others. 324

CHAPTER 21: **Ten Types of Great Instagram Photos** 325
The Human Element. 325
Adorable Animals 326
Bold Colors. 328
White Space 329
Make It Blue 329
Flat Lays 332
Long Angles 333
Lifestyle. 333
Rule of Thirds. 336
Organic Environments 336

INDEX. 339

Introduction

Are you excited about learning how to use Instagram? We hope you are! Because we love Instagram, and we're excited to show you how to use it and how to have fun with it! Instagram is all about entertainment and creating enjoyable content. Because you've chosen this book, we know you're ready to get started creating an Instagram account you enjoy!

More and more people are joining Instagram every day. But with that growth comes a lot of noise and saturation from people who don't quite understand how to use the platform effectively. After reading this book, you'll have the tools and tactics necessary to build a successful Instagram profile.

About This Book

This book helps you use Instagram successfully. Instagram really is as simple as uploading a photo — and that was how the platform was initially designed. But you can do so many things with each photo or video — like adding filters, writing creative captions, and having conversations in the comments. And, as Instagram adds more features to the platform, such as multi-image posts and stories, understanding how to create this additional content is just as important.

We take you through every step of setting up your profile, creating and uploading content to Instagram, writing descriptive captions, finding hashtags that help you get more exposure, building your followers, and using all the fun features built into Instagram.

You don't have to read this book from beginning to end — in fact, you can use the Table of Contents and Index to find the information you're most interested in right this very minute. You don't even have to read every word. If you're short on time and just want to know what you need to know to get the job done, you can skip anything marked with the Technical Stuff icon, as well as sidebars (the text in gray boxes).

Finally, within this book, you may note that some web addresses break across two lines of text. If you're reading this book in print and want to visit one of these web pages, simply key in the web address exactly as it's noted in the text, pretending as though the line break doesn't exist. If you're reading this as an e-book, you've got it easy — just click the web address to be taken directly to the web page.

Foolish Assumptions

We made a few assumptions when writing this book. We assume that you

>> Have a smartphone

>> Have photos and videos you want to share

>> Don't want to look like an amateur, even if you're new to using Instagram

>> Are committed to devoting time and energy to build a presence on Instagram

>> Want to be a part of the Instagram community

If these assumptions are correct, then this book is for you! We're confident that the tactics and information in these pages will help you achieve your goals.

Icons Used in This Book

To make sure you don't miss important details, we use the following icons throughout this book. Here's what the different icons mean:

TIP

Anything marked with the Tip icon is a small piece of expert advice that will save you time and make your experience on Instagram easier.

REMEMBER

This book is a reference, which means you don't have to commit it to memory. There won't be a test on Friday! But, every once in a while, we tell you something so important that we think you should file it away with other important information, like your best friend's birthday and the name of the newest royal baby.

TECHNICAL STUFF

Most of this book is all about telling you what you need to know to use Instagram, and nothing more. But every once in a while, our inner geeks emerge, and we get a little technical. When this happens, we flag it with the Technical Stuff icon. If you're in a hurry, or you just don't care about this kind of thing, you can skip anything marked with the Technical Stuff icon without losing the point of the subject at hand.

WARNING

When you see a Warning icon, you're not at risk of blowing up your Instagram account or doing anything irreparable, but you can rest assured that some helpful advice is at hand — advice meant to prevent any headaches or minor snafus.

Beyond the Book

In addition to what you're reading right now, this book also comes with a free, access-anywhere Cheat Sheet that provides a handy list of Instagram lingo, size limits for photos and videos on Instagram, and steps for sharing posts and profiles. The Cheat Sheet also includes Instagram limits for everything from usernames to bios to the number of posts you can like in an hour and more. To view the Cheat Sheet, simply go to www.dummies.com and type **Instagram For Dummies Cheat Sheet** in the Search box.

Where to Go from Here

The first few chapters dive into how to set up a new Instagram account. If you already have an Instagram account, you can skip the first two chapters, but we encourage you to check out Chapter 3 because it contains information on how to set up an effective profile. Don't worry, you can easily update or edit anything you've already started!

If you run into trouble, check out Chapter 5, which is dedicated to troubleshooting Instagram issues. And if you're looking for inspiration, read Chapter 21.

We would love to hear from you about your experience with this book. Did you find it helpful? Was there something else you wish we had covered? Are you enjoying using Instagram now? Please feel free to email us. You can reach Jenn at jenn@jennstrends.com, Eric at ceo@butow.net, and Corey at corey@themarketing specialist.com.

It's time to jump into all the fun of Instagram that we've been talking about! Enjoy the book!

1

Getting Started with Instagram

Chapter **1**

Instagramming Like a Pro

Welcome to the exciting world of Instagram! This is an incredibly fun and interactive social media app that allows you to connect with more people and brands around the world — all through the power of images and videos.

If you're overwhelmed by the idea of Instagram or how to use it effectively, have no fear! This book is designed to cover all areas of Instagram to bring you up to speed on what works, how it works, and what you need to do to make it work for you.

So, let's dive right into all the basics you need to get started.

Figuring Out What You Need to Get Started

To get started, Instagram is a mobile app, designed for use on smartphones and tablets. It isn't designed for use on a computer, even though there are ways to access Instagram on a laptop or desktop.

So, the first thing you need is a smartphone. Instagram works best on iOS devices (like an iPhone or iPad) and Android devices. These days, smartphones come equipped with well-designed cameras (both front and rear facing) to allow you to take high-quality images and videos directly from the device.

The next thing you need is the Instagram app, of course! In Chapter 2, we explain all the steps to find, download, and set up the Instagram app on your phone. When you're ready for that step, head over to Chapter 2.

Discovering How to Add Posts to Your Instagram Account

There are actually quite a few ways to upload content to Instagram.

First, you can add photos or videos to your *feed* (the part of your profile where all your photos appear). These uploads can only be done via your mobile device, not a computer. And there are multiple formats you can use for uploading, including square, portrait, and landscape orientations, for both photos and videos. We cover how to upload photos and videos in Chapters 6 and 7.

You can also add photos and videos to your stories. Stories expire 24 hours after you upload them. They're displayed as circles at the top of your feed and denoted by a colored ring around a profile photo of anyone who has active stories on his or her profile (see Figure 1-1).

FIGURE 1-1: Instagram stories are displayed at the top of your home feed. Anyone with an active story has a ring around his or her profile photo.

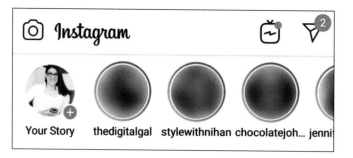

Stories can also only be uploaded via your mobile device, and they have limitations — videos can't be more than 15 seconds long. We cover Instagram stories in Chapters 12, 13, and 14.

Finally, you can upload videos to IGTV. This is a separate channel within the Instagram family of apps that allows you to create and watch long-form video. Videos on IGTV must be at least 15 seconds long and, for some accounts, can be up to 60 minutes long. Videos under 10 minutes in length can be uploaded via your mobile device or computer, but videos longer than 10 minutes can only be uploaded via a computer. Currently, larger accounts and verified accounts have the ability to upload videos over 10 minutes in length, but Instagram plans to remove time limits to videos in the future. Chapters 18 and 19 are devoted to IGTV.

Connecting with Others on Instagram

One of our favorite reasons for loving Instagram is that it's a great platform to connect with more people. Fortunately, there are plenty of ways to stay connected!

You can follow as many accounts as you like, up to 7,500 accounts (but we can't imagine actually following that many people!). You'll want to start by following the friends, family, celebrities, brands, and other accounts that you enjoy. When you follow someone on Instagram, the content they post to their accounts will appear in your feed, allowing you to see their posts and interact with it. You can simply double-tap a post to like it, or you can tap the heart icon to like it. You can also leave comments on people's posts to share your thoughts or add into the conversation on their posts.

We talk much more about finding the right people to follow and how to interact with them in Chapters 9 and 10.

You'll also be able to see the stories of people you follow and you can watch and interact with their stories directly. When you choose to reply to someone's story, the reply is sent as a direct message (DM) to that person's inbox. This keeps the conversation private between the two of you rather than publicly visible to anyone looking at that content.

Speaking of DMs, you can send private messages to one or multiple people via Instagram as well. Again, this keeps your conversations strictly between those in the chat and allows for more means to communicate. You can share photos, videos, and text messages via DMs. You can even do a live video chat with people in DMs if you want to. We cover all of the details on messaging in Chapter 11.

Exploring the Excitement of Instagram Stories

Instagram stories are such a hot topic that we dedicate a whole part of this book to this subject. Instagram stories combine videos and photos to tell a sequence of posts as a "story." Videos can be 3 to 15 seconds in length, and photos play for 7 seconds. You can easily tap to navigate forward or backward through a story or swipe to change whose story you're viewing. If this sounds overwhelming, don't worry! We've got you covered in Chapter 12.

One of the main attractions to stories is the ability to customize the content in so many different ways. Stories have a variety of "stickers" that allow you to add emojis, GIFs, polls, questions, music, and so much more. You can also doodle and draw or add text to stories. There are a variety of camera effects that allow you to take different styles of videos for added fun and intrigue. And, of course, there are filters! It wouldn't be Instagram without filters. Chapters 13 and 14 dive deep into all these features for you.

In addition to creating stories, you can also broadcast live video in the story section of Instagram. These live videos can be up to 60 minutes in length and they disappear after 24 hours just like your other story posts. But we won't leave you hanging! Chapter 17 gives you all the information you need to host a successful live broadcast.

Creating Videos with IGTV

IGTV was launched in June 2018 as another component of Instagram. Originally, the videos had to be formatted to a vertical orientation in order to be uploaded. And all videos auto-played through the sequence in which they appeared in your feed.

Instagram encountered growing pains with this feature, however, and had to make some changes over time to make IGTV more user friendly and more accessible. Now, even though IGTV is still a separate component of Instagram, you can see IGTV videos in the feed and the Explore page. The IGTV home page now displays all videos of those you follow and those they recommend for you in one scrolling feed, rather than auto-playing in a set sequence. This gives you more freedom to choose which videos you want to see.

IGTV will continue to be a presence on Instagram and is a clever way to share longer-form videos with your followers. Because there are so many aspects of IGTV that differ from the other Instagram features, we dedicate all of Part 5 to IGTV.

Chapter **2**

Installing Instagram Everywhere

The good people at Instagram realized long ago that many people use Instagram with all their computing devices, not just smartphones. If you haven't installed Instagram yet, this is the chapter you need to read.

We start by explaining how to install the Instagram app on smartphones, tablets, and computers. Next, we explain how to use Instagram on the web, in case you're using a computer. Finally, we show you how to launch the Instagram app on your computer or device so you can scratch that itch and start Instagramming!

Installing Instagram Wherever You Want to Use It

Instagram was designed for a smartphone, but you don't have to use it there — you can use it on your laptop or desktop or tablet, if you want. Just be aware that the full functionality of the Instagram mobile app isn't quite there on a computer.

For that reason, we start by showing you how to install Instagram where it was originally intended to be used: on your phone.

Installing the app on your iPhone

The first version of Instagram, which was available for download on October 6, 2010, was for iPhone users. It was a wise decision: The popularity of the iPhone combined with Instagram's ease of use when it came to sharing photos resulted in more than one million registered Instagram users by the end of 2010.

It's easy to download Instagram from the App Store to your iPhone:

1. **On your iPhone, tap the App Store icon.**

2. **Tap the Search icon at the bottom of the screen.**

3. **Tap the Search box, at the top of the screen, and start typing the word** Instagram.

   After you type the first few letters, Instagram appears at the top of the results list.

4. **Tap Instagram in the results list.**

5. **Tap Get.**

   If you're prompted to sign in to the App Store, do so and then tap Buy.

6. **Tap Open.**

   The app appears on the screen, as shown in Figure 2-1.

The next time you want to open Instagram, just tap the Instagram icon.

Installing Instagram on your iPad

Instagram has yet to create a native app for the iPad, which is another one of life's great mysteries (but not at the level of where missing socks go). However, you can use the iPhone app on the iPad.

Here's how to install Instagram on an iPad:

1. **Tap the App Store icon.**

2. **Tap the Search icon in the lower-right corner of the screen.**

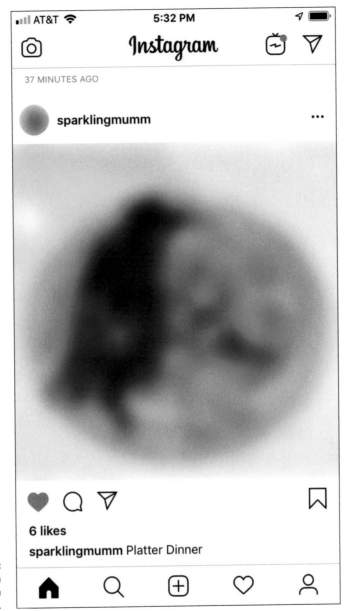

FIGURE 2-1:
The Instagram
app on an
iPhone.

3. **Tap the Search box, at the top of the screen, and start typing the word** Instagram**.**

   After you type the first few letters, Instagram appears at the top of the results list.

4. **Tap Instagram in the results list.**

5. **Tap Get (see Figure 2-2).**

If you're prompted to sign in to the App Store, do so and then tap Buy.

6. **Tap Open.**

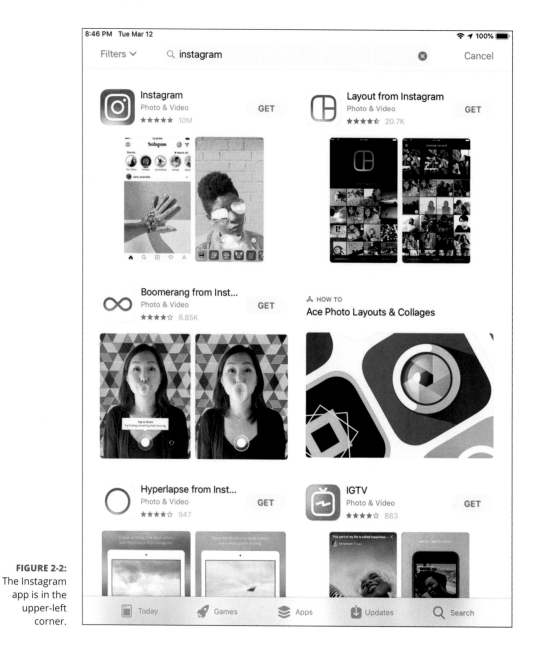

FIGURE 2-2:
The Instagram
app is in the
upper-left
corner.

Installing the app on Android

After Instagram was satisfied with the development of its app on the iPhone, staffers turned their attention to developing Instagram for the Android platform. On the first day the app was released, in April 2012, more than a million users downloaded it.

Here's how to install Instagram on your Android smartphone or tablet from the Google Play Store:

1. **Tap the Play Store icon on the Home screen.**

   If the Play Store icon isn't on a Home screen, tap Apps on the Home screen and then tap Play Store in the Apps screen.

2. **Tap the Search box at the top of the screen, and start typing the word Instagram.**

   Instagram appears in the results list.

3. **Tap Instagram in the results list.**

   The app information screen shown in Figure 2-3 appears.

4. **Tap Install.**

5. **Tap Open.**

Installing on a Windows PC

The Windows version of Instagram is a Windows 10 app. As any Windows 10 user knows, Microsoft is trying to make Windows the best of both worlds by offering apps that can run on both Windows on computers and the Windows Mobile 10 operating system. (Good luck trying to find anyone using Windows Mobile 10 on a smartphone.)

Windows PC users can install the Instagram app from the Windows Store or the Instagram website. Here's how to install the app from the Windows Store:

1. **Click the Start icon in the taskbar.**

2. **Click Microsoft Store in the list of programs or click the Start tile in the Start menu.**

3. **Click Search in the upper-right area of the screen.**

4. **In the Search box, type** Instagram.

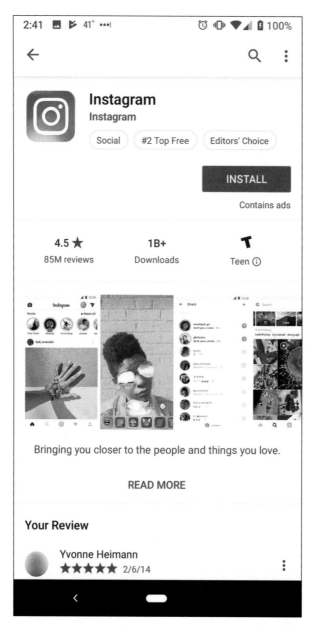

FIGURE 2-3:
Tap Read
More to (you
guessed
it) read
more about
Instagram.

5. **In the list that appears below the Search box, click Instagram.**

6. **Click the Install button, as shown in Figure 2-4.**

    After the Windows Store installs the Instagram app on your computer, the Install button in the Store window changes to Launch.

7. **Click Launch to start the app.**

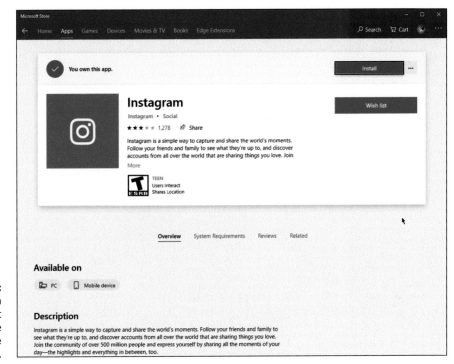

FIGURE 2-4:
Click Install in
the upper-right
area of the
Microsoft Store
window.

Installing on your Mac (sort of)

Instagram doesn't have a Mac version of its app available to download, as you'll discover if you search for Instagram in the App Store. If you try to download the app from iTunes by clicking Get on the Instagram app page, you'll see the Get button change to Downloading for a few seconds, and then the button will change back to Get.

The only way you can access Instagram is on its website. And if you use a web browser other than Safari, you'll only be able to view, like, and comment on photos and videos. Fortunately, you can bamboozle the Instagram website into thinking you're accessing the website on the iPhone so you can upload photos.

REMEMBER

You can only upload photos from your Mac from the bamboozled Instagram website. You can't take photos, shoot videos, or upload videos.

Here's how to trick Instagram into thinking you're on an iPhone when you're really on a Mac:

1. **Open Safari on your Mac.**

2. **Choose Safari ➪ Preferences or press Command+, (comma).**

3. **Click Advanced in the menu bar at the top of the window.**

4. **Click the Show Develop Menu in Menu Bar check box, shown at the bottom of Figure 2-5.**

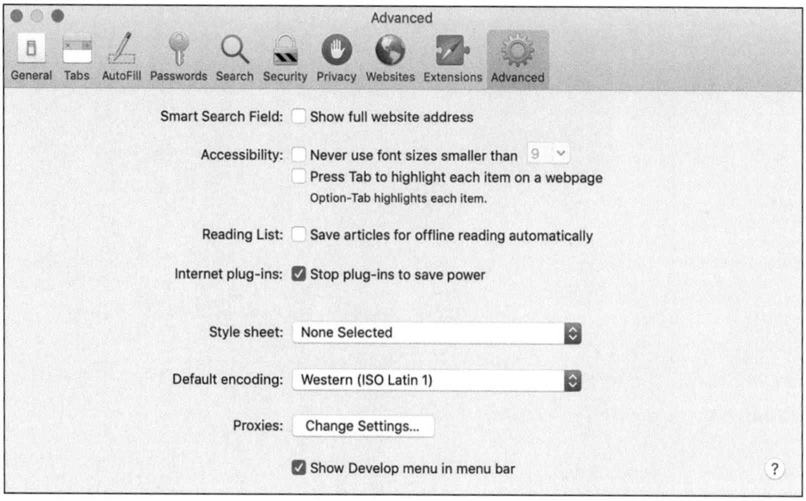

FIGURE 2-5:
Display the Develop menu in the Safari menu bar by clicking the check box at the bottom.

5. **Close the window.**

The Develop option now appears in the menu bar.

6. **Click Develop, move the mouse pointer over User Agent, and then click Safari–iOS 12.1.3–iPhone in the side menu.**

7. **Open the Instagram website and log in.**

The Instagram home screen appears, as shown in Figure 2-6.

8. **Click the plus icon.**

The File window opens so you can navigate to your desired folder and add photo(s) to your Instagram profile.

After you upload your photos, you'll find that the photo-editing options in Safari are more limited than those in the iPhone app. (And remember that you can't upload videos to Instagram on Safari.)

If you'd rather upload photos to Instagram using an app, check out Flume and Uplet, two apps listed in an article by Lewis Painter on the Macworld UK website describing the process we've just outlined here (www.macworld.co.uk/how-to/mac-software/instagram-for-mac-3641569/). A discussion of third-party apps is beyond the scope of this book, so check out that Macworld UK article for more information.

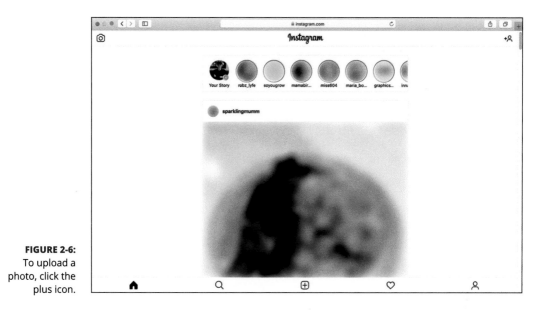

FIGURE 2-6:
To upload a
photo, click the
plus icon.

Exploring Instagram on the Web

If you're away from your smartphone or you just like browsing Instagram on your desktop or laptop computer, you can do that, but you have less functionality there.

Go to www.instagram.com in your computer's web browser. From here, you can log in to Instagram in one of two ways:

>> **Use your Facebook account.** Click Log In with Facebook. (If your browser doesn't have your Facebook account information stored in a cookie, the Facebook window appears on your screen so you can type your username and password.) Then click or tap the Log In As button.

>> **Use your Instagram username and password.** Scroll to the bottom of the screen and click the Log In link next to "Have an account?" Then type your Instagram username and password in the appropriate fields and click Log In.

REMEMBER

If you haven't created an Instagram account yet, bookmark this page and read Chapter 3 to learn how to create an effective profile.

After you log in, you see the home page with the latest photos and videos from users you follow. The top of the screen, shown in Figure 2-7, features the

Instagram logo at the left, the Search box in the center, and three icons to the right of the Search box:

>> **Compass icon:** Opens the Discover People page so you can view a list of other users whom Instagram thinks you may want to follow. To follow a user, click the Follow button.

>> **Heart icon:** Displays a list of notifications, such as when someone comments on one of your photos or videos.

>> **Person icon:** Displays your Profile page.

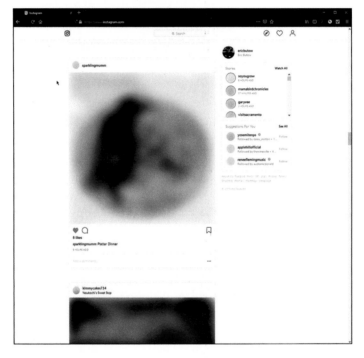

FIGURE 2-7:
The Search box is at the top of the page.

If you're on the Discover People or Profile pages, you can return to the home page by clicking the Instagram icon (camera) or the Instagram logo.

Scroll down the screen to see photos and videos from other Instagram users you follow. Below the photo, you can click the heart icon to like the photo. You can also add a comment by clicking Add a Comment (see Figure 2-8), typing the comment, and then pressing Enter.

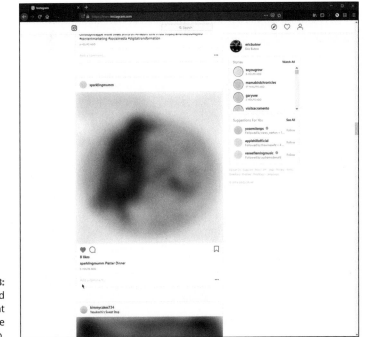

FIGURE 2-8:
You can add
a comment
below the
photo.

Note the icon with three dots to the right of the person's username. Click this icon to open a pop-up menu that enables you to

» Report the photo or video as inappropriate.

» Unfollow the user.

» Open the post in its own web page.

» Embed the photo on a website.

» Share the post on your Facebook feed, in a message on Facebook Messenger, in a tweet on Twitter, or in an email message.

» Copy the post link to your clipboard so you can add it to a website or email message.

» Cancel the action and close the menu.

Starting to Gram Instantly

If you're using Instagram on an iPhone, iPad, or Android device, you can start the app by tapping its icon, as shown in Figure 2-9.

FIGURE 2-9:
The Instagram icon appears in the upper-right corner of the screen on this iPhone.

If you're using Instagram on an iPhone or iPad for the first time, you'll be asked to turn on Instagram notifications in the Please Turn On Notifications window. If you don't turn them on, you won't know, for example, if one of your followers likes a photo you posted. Turn on Instagram notifications by tapping OK in the window. Next, you see the Instagram Would Like to Send You Notifications window. This seems redundant, but Instagram is asking you to send your notifications with sounds and alerts. If you want to do this, tap Allow in the window. Otherwise, tap Don't Allow in the window.

TIP

You can always modify your notifications settings in the Settings section of the Instagram app. Just go to your profile, tap the three lines in the upper-right corner, and tap Settings.

If you're using an Android smartphone or tablet, you won't see a notification window. Instead, you'll see your home screen so you can log in. Turn to Chapter 5 for instructions on how to change the notification settings in Instagram for Android.

To open Instagram on your Windows PC, click the Start icon in the taskbar and then click Instagram in the apps list, as shown in Figure 2-10. Alternatively, you can click the Instagram icon in the Start menu.

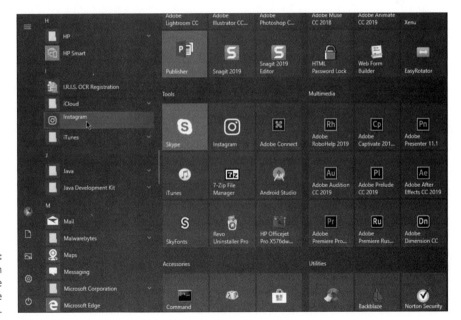

FIGURE 2-10:
The Instagram app is in the I section of the apps list.

When you sign into the app on an iPhone, iPad, or Android device for the first time, it will ask you to log in using your Instagram username and password or your Facebook account. If you don't have an Instagram account, click the Sign Up link at the bottom of the window. The signup screen asks you to log in with Facebook or create an Instagram account by clicking the Sign Up with Phone or Email link. From there, you'll be able to use the signup wizard to create an account.

TIP

Want to launch Instagram from your taskbar? Simply right-click the Instagram icon in the taskbar, and click Pin to Taskbar.

Chapter **3**

Setting Up Your Profile

After you install the Instagram app on your mobile device, the first major task you face is setting up your profile. Your profile should accurately represent you.

In this chapter, we show you how to set up the different components of your profile, including a username and name and a bio. We also explain how to set up a business profile, in case the account you're creating is for, well, a business. Finally, we end the chapter by showing you how to select your privacy settings.

Personal Profile Practices

Your Instagram profile is not only your first impression to potential followers and new visitors but also your consistent message to your existing audience. Your profile should be recognizable as your style and representative of what you want people to see about you. Figure 3-1 shows you what a standard personal profile looks like on Instagram.

Instagram profiles are composed of the following five components: username, name, profile photo, bio, and web address.

Choosing a username and name

Your username and name are two of the most important components of your Instagram profile because they're the only two searchable criteria of your profile. When users type a keyword or name in the Search field on Instagram, the app looks at only the username and name fields of accounts to determine if an account is relevant to that search query.

REMEMBER

The username is the string of characters at the top of the profile. The name is the bold text below the profile photo. If you want your account to be found by a keyword or phrase, be sure to include it in either the name or username for your account.

Choosing the best username

When you set up a new Instagram account, you're required to choose a username. Your Instagram username is how you're recognized on Instagram: All activity, from the content you post to how you engage with others, is associated with your username. The username is at the top of the profile (refer to Figure 3-1).

Your username is delineated with the at (@) symbol when referring to you as a user. The web address (technically known as the *URL*, short for *Uniform Resource Locator*) for your Instagram account is

```
http://instagram.com/yourusername
```

When you interact on Instagram, the username appears as

yourusername

An Instagram username is limited to 30 characters and must contain only letters, numbers, periods, and underscores. You can't include symbols or other punctuation marks as a part of your username.

TIP

Choose a username that represents you or your name, is recognizable, and, if possible, distinguishes what you do. Your username may be simply your name or nickname. If you're already established on other social media, like Twitter, you might want to choose the same username on Instagram as you use on other sites, so that your current audience can easily find you.

During the registration portion of your Instagram account, you're prompted to select your username. If the username you selected is available, a check mark will appear. If someone is using the username you entered, an X will appear in the username field. Keep selecting alternatives until you find an available username.

TIP

If the username you want to use is unavailable, you can use alternative options by adding periods or underscores to the username, by using abbreviations, or by adding another word.

If you're signing up for a new Instagram account using the website, Instagram will populate an available username for you. You're welcome to use this suggested name, but we don't recommend it, because it's generic and it won't represent you or be nearly as creative as one you come up with yourself.

TIP

Always check what your username looks like as one long word. If you wanted your username to be "christoper u", it would read as "christopheru" which may get misread as "chris to pheru" or "christophe ru" or other versions. Instead, include an underscore or a a period to separate words, like "christopher_u".

TECHNICAL STUFF

There is little you can do to have an existing username transferred to your account if it's in use or was previously registered by another user. If another account is using your registered trademark as its username, visit https://help.instagram.com/101826856646059 for information on how to file a claim of trademark violation.

After you select a username, all content linking to your profile is associated with the username's URL. If you want to change the username at some point, your URL would change and you would need to update all backlinks and links to that profile accordingly. This is why it's best to choose the right username when setting up your profile.

If you want to change your username, follow these steps (see Figure 3-2):

1. **Go to your profile on Instagram on either your mobile device or your computer.**

2. **Tap or click Edit Profile.**

3. **In the Username field, type the new username.**

4. **Save your changes.**

   To do so, tap the check mark, Done, Save, or Submit button (depending on the device you're using).

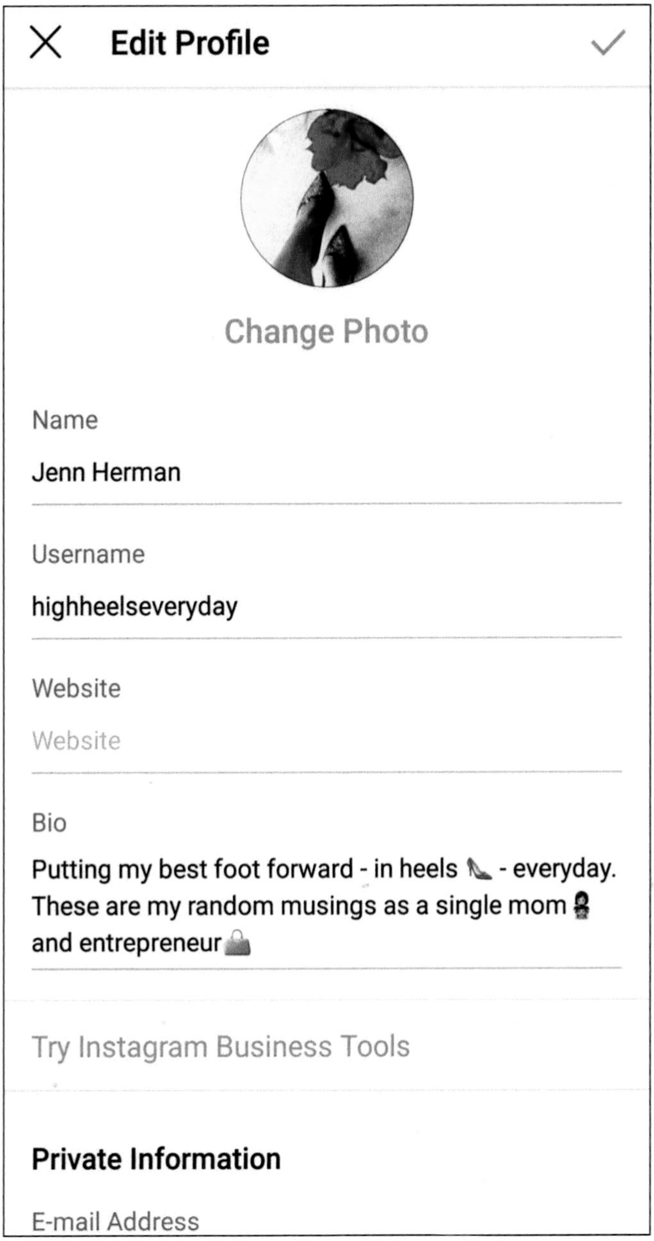

FIGURE 3-2:
Editing your
username
and name
information.

Choosing the best name

Your Instagram name is visible only when someone visits your profile directly. The name appears in bold below the profile photo (refer to Figure 3-1). You can use your actual name or a nickname as your name on Instagram.

Your profile will perform better in searches and look less amateurish if the name and username are different. Having a name that's different from your username provides double the opportunity for keywords and searchable criteria in the Instagram app. Power users on Instagram take the time to craft good username and name components.

Unlike your username, which is one word, your name should be in proper sentence structure with capital letters and spacing. Your name (like your username) is limited to 30 characters, including spaces.

TIP

You can be found in more searches on Instagram if you include a keyword or phrase in your name or username or both. If you didn't put a defining keyword in your username, you should include one in your name field, in addition to your actual name.

The name on your profile is not tied to your URL or other defining aspects of Instagram, so you can change it without your username being affected. Consider adding or changing keywords, as necessary, to appeal to your target audience on Instagram.

If you want to change your name, do the following:

1. **Go to your Instagram profile, and tap or click Edit Profile.**

2. **In the Name field, type the new name.**

3. **Save your changes.**

   To do so, tap the check mark, Done, Save, or Submit button (depending on the device you're using).

Deciding on a profile photo

The *profile photo* on your account, as well as your username, is associated with all your activity. When you post anything to Instagram or engage with other users in any way, your profile photo is visible.

Your profile photo should represent you and be recognizable to others. If you actively use other social media platforms, you may want to use the same photograph for your Instagram profile as you already use on other platforms. That way, you create cohesion across your online media and assure your followers that they found the correct account when searching for you. The account of @lorettagavin in Figure 3-3 is a good example of having a profile photo that stands out, is easy to recognize, and represents her as a person.

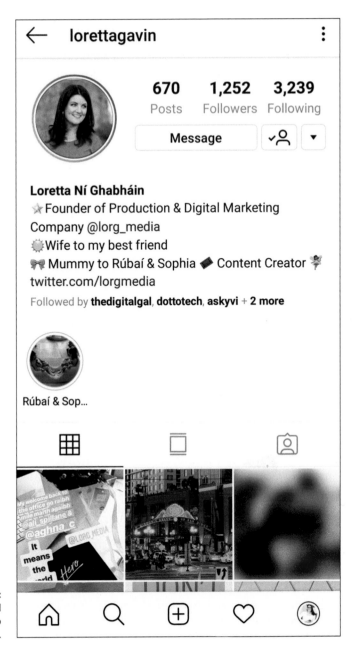

FIGURE 3-3:
A good
profile photo
represents you.

TIP

Profile photos on Instagram are cropped to a circle, so your photo should fit properly within that crop. Don't use a logo or an image that loses valuable content when cropped to a circle.

The profile photo on your profile page appears larger than anywhere else on Instagram. When interacting with others, the profile photo is a thumbnail (small) version. Choose an image that isn't too busy, overwhelming, or cluttered with text, because the image will become difficult to decipher as a thumbnail.

The best profile photos have a clear object of focus, contain a simple background, and are sized at least 550 x 550 pixels. The ideal image size is 1,080 by 1,080 pixels for a square image. (If you upload a photo that's too small, it may appear *pixelated*, which is what happens when a low-resolution image is enlarged too much and the individual square pixels become obvious, making the image blurry.)

Writing a Dazzling Bio

Your bio is a short description on your profile that tells people about you. This description is similar to a 30-second elevator pitch — it's how you convince new visitors to follow your account.

Most people will read your bio only the first time they visit your profile. Your bio is the first impression you give to new viewers and should accurately convey the message you want to share.

Deciding what information to include

Before you start writing your bio, choose at least two or three key aspects of your life to highlight. These should be traits that will connect emotionally, in some way, with your those you want to attract, such as the example shown in Figure 3-4.

You need to determine the voice and style of your bio. If you're the next Amy Schumer, your Instagram bio should reflect that irrevent, hilarious style through words and relevant emojis. In contrast, if your identity is more straight-laced and serious, your bio shouldn't be silly and humorous.

REMEMBER

Even if your profile is meant to connect with friends and family, sharing your personality and purpose in the bio will help clarify that to people who may find you.

The Instagram bio is limited to 150 characters, including spaces. The bio is designed to be one single paragraph of information, but you can use formatting techniques to add spaces and line breaks.

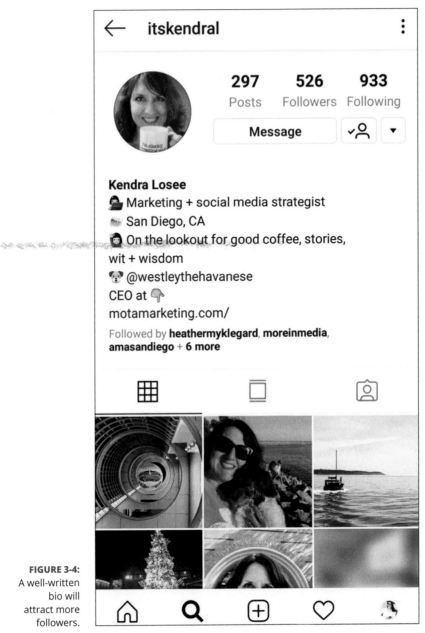

FIGURE 3-4:
A well-written bio will attract more followers.

TIP

Because Instagram was designed to be used on a mobile device, it's best to format your bio on a mobile device so that you retain the correct alignment. No matter what formatting you create, your bio on a desktop or computer device will always be one long paragraph spanning the width of the browser, unlike the vertical alignment seen on mobile devices.

Make use of emojis and symbols from your mobile device's keyboard to create visual appeal in your bio. To add emojis, open the emoji keyboard on your mobile device — just tap the smiley-face icon at the bottom of your keyboard.

Instagram is a visual platform, and having emojis in the bio helps yours stand out from other users. You have many emojis to choose from. If the traditional funny face and cartoonish emojis don't translate to your style, use simple emoji symbols such as squares, diamonds, triangles, and arrows to add color and visual content without detracting from your professional style.

Formatting your bio

You can edit or create your bio by tapping the Edit Profile button in your Instagram profile. On the Edit Profile screen (refer to Figure 3-2), go to the Bio field and insert the text for your bio. Save any changes when you're finished.

Android users can format a bio completely in Instagram. If you want to include line breaks and spacing, tap the Return or Enter key (on the keyboard of your mobile device) at the end of the line. Make sure that you don't have an extra space after the final character on the line and that the last character on the line is not an emoji. If you have an extra space or an emoji as the final character, the space breaks you inserted with the Return or Enter key will not appear in your published text.

iOS users can format a bio in Instagram, but line breaks will not be retained. Instead, it's best to open the Notes app on your device and use it to craft your bio description, including all formatting. Then copy the bio, open Instagram again, select Edit Profile, and paste the description in the Bio field. As with Android users, you must ensure that no extra space appears after the final character on the line and that the last character on the line is not an emoji.

You can edit and rewrite your bio as often as you want. We recommend reviewing your bio every six months to verify that the information is still accurate and relevant.

Considering layouts for your bio

Instagram has traditionally had the profile photo on the left side of the profile and the bio directly beneath it. As Instagram has added more features, like IGTV and Story Highlights, the profile section has gotten longer and taken up more space. To alleviate this problem, Instagram began truncating the bios with a "... more" link. Tapping the "... more" link will open the full bio, as shown in Figure 3-5.

Additionally, Instagram started rolling out new profile layouts with the profile on the right side of the profile and a more condensed spacing to allow for better positioning of the bio content. You may see any variation of the bio formats shown in Figure 3-5.

FIGURE 3-5: Instagram has been testing and rolling out new profile layouts.

Adding a web address to your bio

Most people use web addresses in their bios when they're using their Instagram profiles for business purposes. But there may be occasions where you want to share a website link even on your personal profile.

Perhaps you want to send people to your YouTube vidoes, or to your personal gallery of photos on Flickr, or to a reservation link for an upcoming party. In any of these situations, or others, you can include the URL for that destination in the link location in your bio.

TECHNICAL STUFF

TRACKING YOUR SOCIAL MEDIA TRAFFIC

To accurately track your Instagram traffic, you need to do more than upload a direct link to your website. If someone clicks the link in your bio from Instagram on the desktop, Google Analytics records it as referral traffic from Instagram. When someone taps the link in Instagram on a mobile device, a new browser is opened. Google Analytics doesn't properly track that traffic for you. Instead, it considers opening the new browser *direct* traffic, not social media referral traffic.

Although Google Analytics is tracking that traffic for you, it's categorizing it alongside all other direct traffic to your site, not as a clickthrough from Instagram. As a result, you may look at your website traffic and be convinced that Instagram is not driving any significant traffic, when it may be sending much more traffic than you're aware of.

To correct this problem, use a link shortener that provides trackable data on the number of clicks. The link shorteners Bitly (https://bitly.com), Google URL Shortener (https://goo.gl), and Rebrandly (www.rebrandly.com) are the most reliable and safe options. Each provides a data analysis of each link to allow you to track how many clicks you're generating.

To use a link shortener, follow these simple steps:

1. **Find your long-form URL (the direct link from your website) and copy it.**

2. **Open the link shortener website of your choice.**

3. **Paste the long-form URL in the link shortener website.**

   The link shortener generates a short link.

4. **Customize the short URL to match your branding or page.**

5. **Copy the short URL and paste it as your URL in your Instagram bio.**

Most link shorteners generate a link with random letters and numbers, such as http://bit.ly/2X4y6. This doesn't look professional, and visitors may find the link confusing or question the link's validity. You can customize the link to reflect your brand. For example, if your long-form URL is http://jennstrends.com/blog, the short-form one may be http://bit.ly/JTBlog or http://bit.ly/JennsTrendsBlog.

The only place that you can place a clickable link on Instagram, as a personal profile, is in the bio. You can't include clickable links in regular posts or stories. If you have any reason to send people to a website link, you'll need to place that link here in the bio.

From the Edit Profile button on your Instagram profile, there is the option to list a URL link. Simply copy and paste or type in the link address in this field.

Your URL can be updated or changed as frequently as you like. You may have a default web page for your profile but change it to coincide with a promotion or campaign you're running on Instagram. After that campaign is complete, you can change the link back to your default or simply delete it if you don't have anything to drive traffic to.

On a personal profile, you won't get Instagram analytics regarding how many people clicked the link in your bio. If you wanted to use this feature for business and drive traffic for your business, you would want to upgrade to a business profile on Instagram (see "Taking Advantage of a Business Profile Upgrade," later in this chapter).

Taking Advantage of a Business Profile Upgrade

In late 2016, Instagram introduced business profiles to Instagram. Before this feature rollout, all profiles on Instagram looked identical. Now brands have the capability to stand out from regular accounts and can benefit from a variety of features available only to business profiles.

By upgrading to a business profile on Instagram, you get features such as the following:

>> Easy-to-access contact buttons that make it easy for your customers to email you, call you, or get directions to your location

>> An industry listing that informs visitors what you do as a business

>> In-app analytics to best monitor what is and isn't working in your content strategy

>> The ability to boost posts from your Instagram profile and run ads on Instagram

>> The ability to manage your Instagram comments and engagement through your Facebook page

REMEMBER

You're allowed only one clickable link (in your bio). The contact button feature means people can call, text, or email you, or get directions to your business location, providing you additional ways to connect directly with your customers and close more sales!

To upgrade to a business profile, do the following:

1. **Log in to Instagram on your mobile device, and tap Edit Profile.**

2. **Tap the Switch to Professional Account option (see Figure 3-6).**

3. **Choose Business and follow the prompts to select your Category and email contact info.**

4. **If you have a Facebook page to connect your account to, select it from the Pages you're logged into. If you don't have a Facebook page, tap Don't Connect to Facebook Now.**

5. **Update or add information as necessary.**

   For example, if your information does not populate a phone number but you would like to include the Call contact button, you can add your phone number to that field in the Contact Options screen.

   You can edit this information at any time, in case you want to add or delete a contact option later.

6. **Save your information.**

   Tap the check mark in the upper-right corner of the Contact Options screen.

Your Instagram account is now set up as a business profile! After upgrading your account, your new business profile appears to anyone visiting your profile.

REMEMBER

Even though you have these additional features as a business profile, your profile characteristics, such as your username, name, bio, and URL, remain the same.

TECHNICAL
STUFF

In addition to a Business account, you can opt to have a Creator account. This type of account has a few more options for insights and analytics but does not currently cooperate with third-party tools, so you won't be able to use a scheduling tool or social media management tool to manage your Instagram account if you have a Creator account.

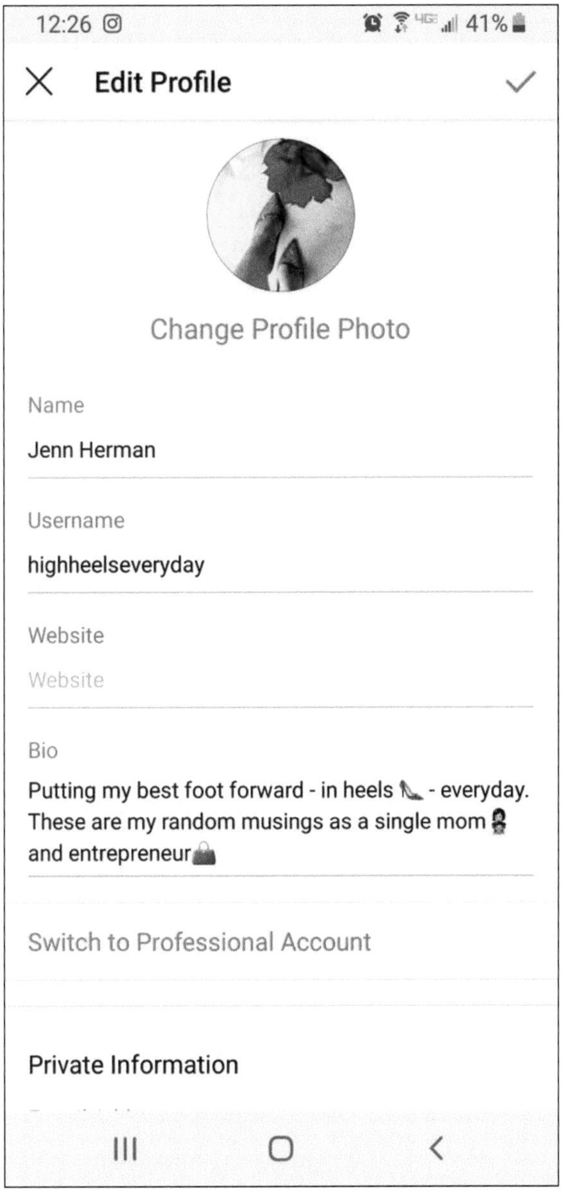

12:26

Edit Profile

Change Profile Photo

Name

Jenn Herman

Username

highheelseveryday

Website

Website

Bio

Putting my best foot forward - in heels 👠 - everyday.
These are my random musings as a single mom 👩
and entrepreneur👜

Switch to Professional Account

Private Information

FIGURE 3-6:
Upgrade to
a business
profile by
selecting the
Switch to
Professional
Account
option.

Setting Your Account Privacy Settings

When you set up a new Instagram account, it will default to a public account, meaning anyone on Instagram can find you and see your content. Many Instagram users are okay with this, but if you want to keep your account more private, you can.

When your account is private, other users will be able to see your username, name, profile photo, and bio, but they won't be able to see any of your posts.

To edit your privacy settings, follow these steps (see Figure 3-7):

1. **Go to your Instagram profile, and tap the three-line button in the upper-right corner.**

2. **Tap Settings at the bottom of the screen.**

3. **Tap Privacy.**

4. **Tap Account Privacy.**

5. **Tap the toggle button for the option to make your account private.**

FIGURE 3-7:
Making your account private.

When you make these changes, anyone who is currently following you won't see anything different on your profile, but anyone who is not currently following you will no longer see your account posts. If someone wants to follow you, he'll need to request to follow you. You'll receive that request and you can approve or deny that person the ability to follow you.

Chapter **4**

Navigating Instagram

Afer you've installed Instagram and set up your profile page (refer to Chapter 3), it's time to start seeing what Instagram is all about! There are millions of accounts waiting for you to explore. You'll be amazed at the variety and specificity available to you with just a few taps on your mobile phone. Are you a fan of Australian shepherds? There are 5.8 million posts about them. Like azaleas? You'll find 113,000 posts are out there waiting for you! Not to mention all the people who may become part of your online tribe when you find you have similar interests (or even if you don't).

In this chapter, we explain what's in your feed and how the Instagram algorithm decides what to show you. Then we fill you in on the Explore page and the variety of different ways to search for people, hashtags, and places. Finally, you get the skinny on your notifications and what you should do with them.

Scrolling through the Feed

If you're familiar with other social media platforms, like Facebook or Twitter, you're probably used to having a "feed." The Instagram feed is found by tapping the house at the lower-left corner of your screen, as shown in Figure 4-1. There, you can scroll through to see posts from the accounts and hashtags you're following (plus ads and accounts Instagram suggests). However, it's important to note that the Instagram feed is extremely personalized for each individual user. Even if two people followed the exact same accounts, they would get different feeds because they would interact with the content from those accounts in different ways. You can find out more about the way content is shown to you when we talk about the Instagram algorithm in the next section.

FIGURE 4-1:
The Instagram feed is accessed by tapping the house at the lower-left corner of your screen.

Your feed is the hub of your interactions with people. It allows you to access the following (see Figure 4-2):

FIGURE 4-2:
Your Instagram
feed gives
you access to
all areas of
Instagram.

A. New Instagram stories from the people you follow at the very top of your feed

B. The ability to create new Instagram stories by tapping the camera at the top left of the screen or by swiping right on any post in your feed

C. IGTV by tapping the TV screen icon to the right of the Instagram logo

D. Direct messages by tapping the paper airplane at the upper right of the screen

E. Posts from the people and hashtags you follow, ads, and suggested posts from Instagram

F. The Explore page by tapping the magnifying glass at the lower right of the screen

G. The ability to create a new post by tapping the plus sign at the lower middle of the screen

H. Notifications by tapping the heart at the lower right of the screen

I. Your profile by tapping your profile photo at the lower far right of the screen

Making Sense of the Instagram Algorithm

Ahhhh, the mysterious Instagram algorithm. Everyone has a theory about the way it works, but Instagram finally shared how content is ranked in each individual user's feed in 2018. Instagram uses three major factors to determine what's shown:

» **Interest:** Instagram is looking at the content you interact with to determine what you want more of. If you always like or comment on content from certain accounts, that's a high level of interest. If you always like a certain type of content (like dogs or cars or food), then more of that type of content will appear higher in your feed. (Yes, Instagram uses artificial intelligence and other factors to determine what's in the content and determine if you have an interest in it.) Similarly, if you always watch videos, video content will rank higher in your feed than photos or graphic images. Interest or relevancy is based on the prediction of how likely you are to actually interact with the content placed in front of you.

» **Timeliness:** The recency of the posts from those you follow is an important factor in what you see. Instagram puts more emphasis on recency of posts to ensure you see content that is more fresh.

>> **Relationships:** Instagram cares about who you interact with the most. Which accounts do you always comment on or like their posts? Or which accounts do you regularly visit via their profiles? These indicators mean you probably really want to see their content, and chances are, these people are your friends or family, so their content appears higher in your feed.

There are a few other factors that play into the algorithm, such as the following:

>> **Frequency:** How often you use Instagram and log in determines how much of the content in your feed gets sorted. For example, if you log in every hour, that's not a lot of content that needs to be sorted. So it looks fairly chronological and you see pretty much everything. But if you only log in once a week, a ton of content has been uploaded by everyone you follow, so that content gets some serious ranking and sorting to put the most relevant content at the top of your feed, and you may not see every post from everyone you follow.

>> **Following:** Obviously, if you follow more accounts, that means there's a lot more content in your feed. The more content there is, the more it's sorted and ranked. So, following less people means you see more stuff from the people you care most about.

>> **Usage:** This ties into both of the preceding points. If you're on Instagram for hours a day, the algorithm digs further into the content sources to give you fresh content at the top of your feed. If, however, you only log on for ten minutes a day, you're just going to see the highlights that Instagram thinks are most relevant to you. It's like watching the evening news: If you watch the first five minutes, you get all the day's highlights. But if you keep watching the whole broadcast, you get all the stories and the juicy little extras they throw in throughout the segment.

TIP

Want to make sure you never miss a post by a certain person or business? You can get a notification each time they post new content by going to one of his posts, tapping the three dots to the right of his name, and then tapping Turn on Post Notifications (see Figure 4-3). You can also mute, unfollow, or share from this area.

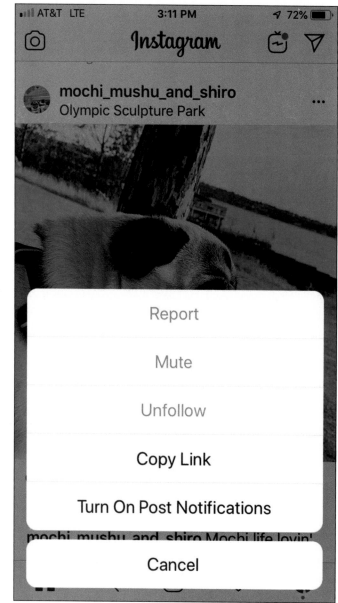

FIGURE 4-3:
Get notifications about new posts from accounts that are important to you by turning on post notifications.

Exploring the World of Instagram

If you're having trouble finding all the accounts you want to follow, Instagram has a solution for you. The Explore page offers photo and video posts, Instagram stories, shopping posts, and IGTV videos all tailored to you by the algorithm. It factors in accounts you're already following and interacting with, and shows you content that is similar or related in the hopes that you'll tap on it.

Finding and viewing the Explore page

Here's how to use the Explore page:

1. **Tap the magnifying glass at the bottom of any screen.**

   Several photos, videos, and stories are presented, as shown in Figure 4-4.

2. **Tap any photo or video that interests you.**

   Now you can scroll down to see the rest of the Explore page.

3. **If you'd like to see more posts from an account, tap the Instagram username at the top of any post that interests you.**

4. **Look around the page. If you want to follow that account, tap the blue Follow button at the top of the user's profile page.**

TIP

If you'd rather explore new content by specific topics, there's a way to do that, too. Referring back to Figure 4-4, at the top of the Explore page, you see several buttons starting with IGTV. Tap any of the buttons that interest you, or scroll left to see more topics.

Searching for what makes you happy

Another great way to find new content is by using the Explore page to search Instagram. Instagram offers four ways to search: Top, Accounts, Tags, and Places.

To try out the Search feature, tap the magnifying glass on any page. The Explore page appears, as described in this chapter. Tap the Search field at the top of the page. On the iPhone, Top, Accounts, Tags, and Places are now available for your choosing. On Android, only icons are shown to represent these sections.

FIGURE 4-4:
The Explore page displays stories, videos, and posts you might like. You can also search by topic using the buttons at the top of the Explore page.

Searching by top

The *Top feature* (see Figure 4-5) shows you suggested accounts, followed by accounts that someone you follow also likes, followed by accounts you most recently interacted with. To find new content you'd like, search for a keyword that interests you. For instance, typing **real estate** presents several accounts that have *real estate* in their usernames or in their profile titles. Scroll through those that are interesting, and follow those you like!

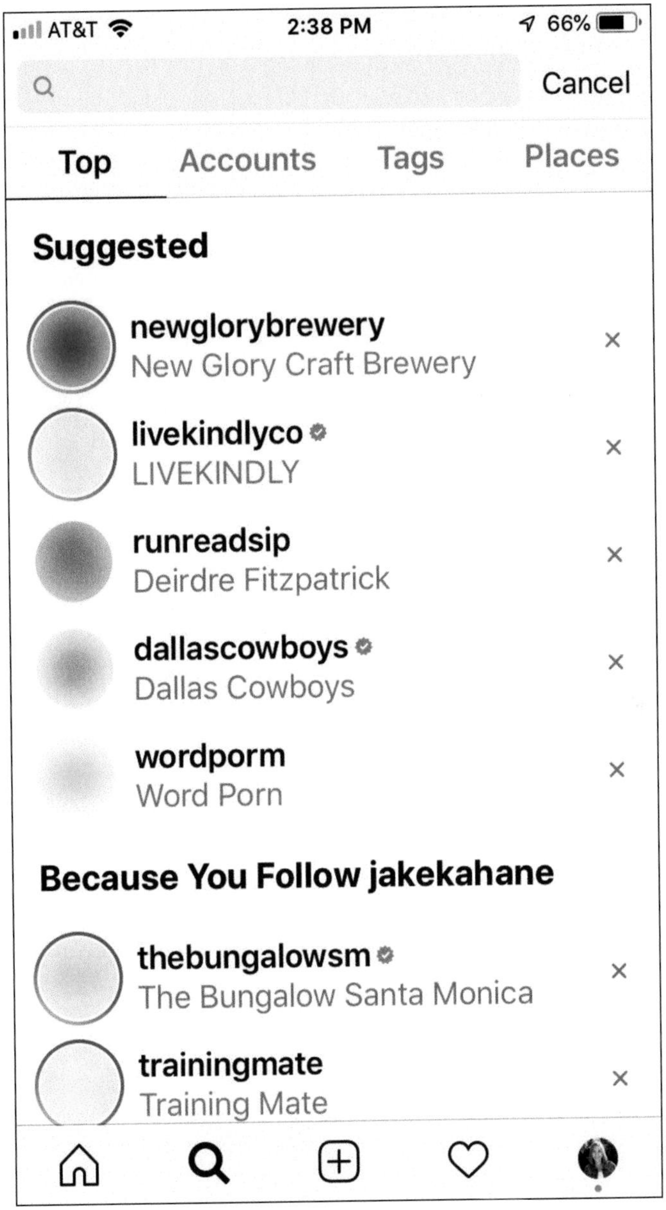

FIGURE 4-5:
Search by top to see suggested accounts from Instagram and accounts with which you've recently interacted.

The screen shows an Instagram search interface with tabs: Top, Accounts, Tags, Places.

Suggested

- newglorybrewery — New Glory Craft Brewery
- livekindlyco — LIVEKINDLY
- runreadsip — Deirdre Fitzpatrick
- dallascowboys — Dallas Cowboys
- wordporm — Word Porn

Because You Follow jakekahane

- thebungalowsm — The Bungalow Santa Monica
- trainingmate — Training Mate

Searching by accounts

The *Accounts feature* (see Figure 4-6) can be used in a similar manner to the Top feature, but you may also choose to search by someone's name. Try searching for friends, businesses, and colleagues by name. Tap on the account and scroll through to view the content and decide if you'd like to follow that account. If the accounts are private, you'll need to request access to follow.

Searching by hashtags

The *Tags feature* (see Figure 4-7) allows you to search by hashtag. Start simply by choosing a basic hashtag you're interested in and see what appears. For example, if you're interested in scuba diving, start with #scubadiving. If you get too many results to be useful, add something more specific, such as #scubadivingbahamas. Unlike the first two categories, search results for your hashtag don't show specific accounts, but rather the searched hashtag and a list of similar ones. You must then tap the specific hashtag to see a feed of posts, and you can choose from Top or Recent. Scroll through the accounts and tap the ones that call out to you. Then follow the ones that seem active and engaging.

Searching by places

The *Places feature* enables you to search by location. If you're trying to find people or businesses currently near you, the easiest way to start is to tap Near Current Location on the iPhone or Nearby Places on Android. Several nearby locations pop up for you to choose from. Tap a location near you, and then all the posts marked with that location pop up. Additionally, at the top of the results feed, there is a Stories icon; tap that icon to watch Instagram stories that have been tagged with the location. Also, if the location is a business that has its own Instagram account, the account will be labeled Related Business and listed above the feed on Android; you can see it by clicking View Information above the map on iPhone. Having access to this information can be especially helpful if you're traveling and want ideas for restaurants or shops to visit. Tap some posts that catch your eye, and follow the ones you like. If you'd like to discover information about a location you aren't currently in, stay on the Places tab and use the Search bar to enter a location, as shown in Figure 4-8.

FIGURE 4-6:
Search by
accounts to
find accounts
by name.

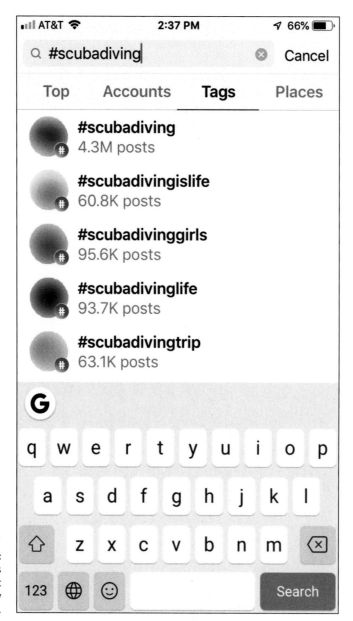

FIGURE 4-7:
Search by tags
to find content
organized by
hashtag.

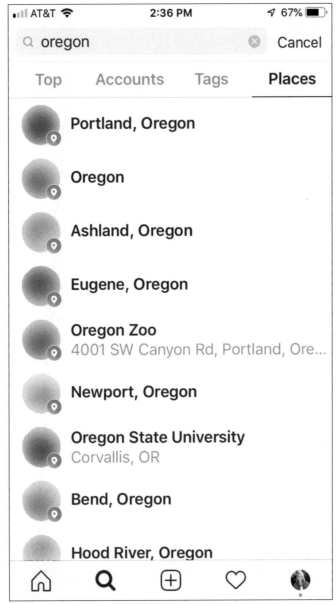

FIGURE 4-8:
Search by
places to
search for
accounts that
have tagged a
location near
you currently
or a location
you enter via
the Search bar.

Checking Your Notifications

If you participate regularly on Instagram, posting content, following new people, making comments and more, you'll start getting notifications. Notifications are accessed by tapping the heart at the bottom of your screen while on any page within the main Instagram app (not stories or IGTV).

To see notifications that apply to activity affecting your account, make sure you're on the tab marked You after you tap the heart (see Figure 4-9).

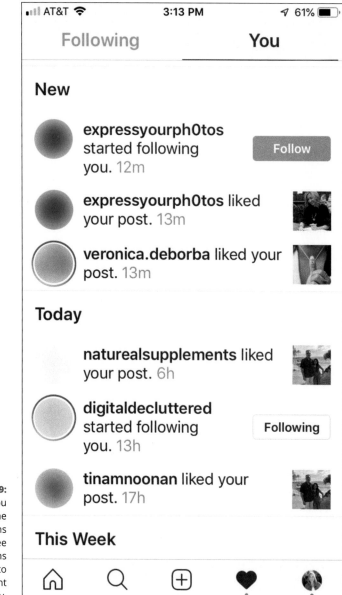

FIGURE 4-9:
Tap the You tab on the notifications page to see notifications applying to your account only.

The notifications shown on the You tab of the Notifications page are from people that have recently

>> Followed you

>> Liked one of your posts

>> Commented on one of your posts

>> Tagged you in a post

TIP

If you've been on Instagram a while, you'll also get notifications for Memories that say, "See your post from X years ago today." Clicking the thumbnail will open the old post in Instagram stories so you can share it.

To go to a new follower's account, tap her name from the Notifications page.

To see the post that someone liked, commented on, or tagged you on, tap the thumbnail of the photo from the Notifications page.

If you scroll further down the page, Instagram suggests other people to follow that the algorithm deems interesting to you.

The Following tab of the Notifications page shows you the activity of some of the accounts you follow (see Figure 4-10 for examples).

TIP

You can get push notifications on your phone if you'd like to see who's commenting and liking your page in real time. To turn on Push Notifications, follow these steps:

1. **Go to your profile and tap the three lines at the top right of the screen.**

2. **Tap Settings.**

3. **Tap Notifications and choose which activities you'd like to get notifications about, or use the Pause All slider to not get any push notifications.**

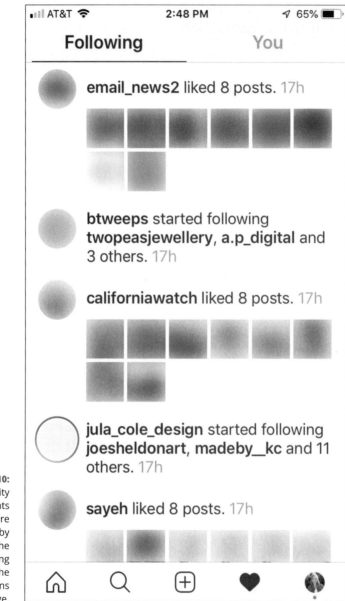

FIGURE 4-10:
See activity
of accounts
you are
following by
tapping the
Following
tab on the
Notifications
page.

Chapter **5**
Why Isn't This Working?

Nothing in this world is perfect, and Instagram is no different. Sometimes weird (and frustrating) quirks happen with the app and you may find it difficult to do certain things while using it. Fear not! Help is on the way . . . just keep reading.

In this chapter, we take you through some of the more common issues that users report running into with Instagram and give you steps to correct (or at least get past) them.

REMEMBER

The latest version of iOS for the iPhone and iPad (version 12.3.1) and Android Nougat (version 7.0) were used to create the instructions for this chapter. If you have a different version of iOS or Android, your mileage may vary.

Installation Issues

When Instagram won't install for you, we've got your back. Instead of panicking, read on to discover the common reasons why Instagram won't install and suggestions for resolving them. If they don't work, take a few deep breaths because we've thought of that, too, in the "Nothing Is Working . . . Now What?" section, later in the chapter.

Dealing with compatibility issues

If you're receiving compatibility error messages, it may be time for you to upgrade your operating system before you install Instagram because the app requires iOS 10 or later on an iPhone or iPad. (You can also use it on an iPod Touch, but the instructions are the same as for the iPhone.)

For Android users, the Google Play Store entry for Instagram states that compatibility is dependent on the smartphone or tablet you're using. When you download Instagram, the Google Play Store automatically checks your smartphone or tablet to ensure that it's compatible.

That said, Instagram notes that some Android users receive a "Device not compatible" message. If you receive this message, you should clear all Google Play Store data stored on your smartphone or tablet and then try to install Instagram again. Here's how:

1. **On the Android's home screen or the Apps screen, tap the Settings icon.**

2. **Tap Applications.**

3. **Swipe up and tap Google Play Store in the All Apps list.**

   The Application Info screen appears.

4. **Tap Storage.**

   The Storage screen appears, as show in Figure 5-1.

5. **Tap the Clear Data button.**

6. **Tap Delete in the pop-up window that appears.**

Now you can return to the Google Play Store and try to install Instagram again. If that doesn't work, go to the bottom of the Instagram page within the Google Play Store website and then click the `android-support@instagram.com` link. Now you can send an email message to Instagram so you can tell them what the exact problem is and receive a response from the Instagram team.

Checking your space

If you use your smartphone or tablet a lot, you know that storage issues are a bane of your existence. (If it's your only bane, well done.) You can check the memory usage to see how much memory space Instagram is eating up.

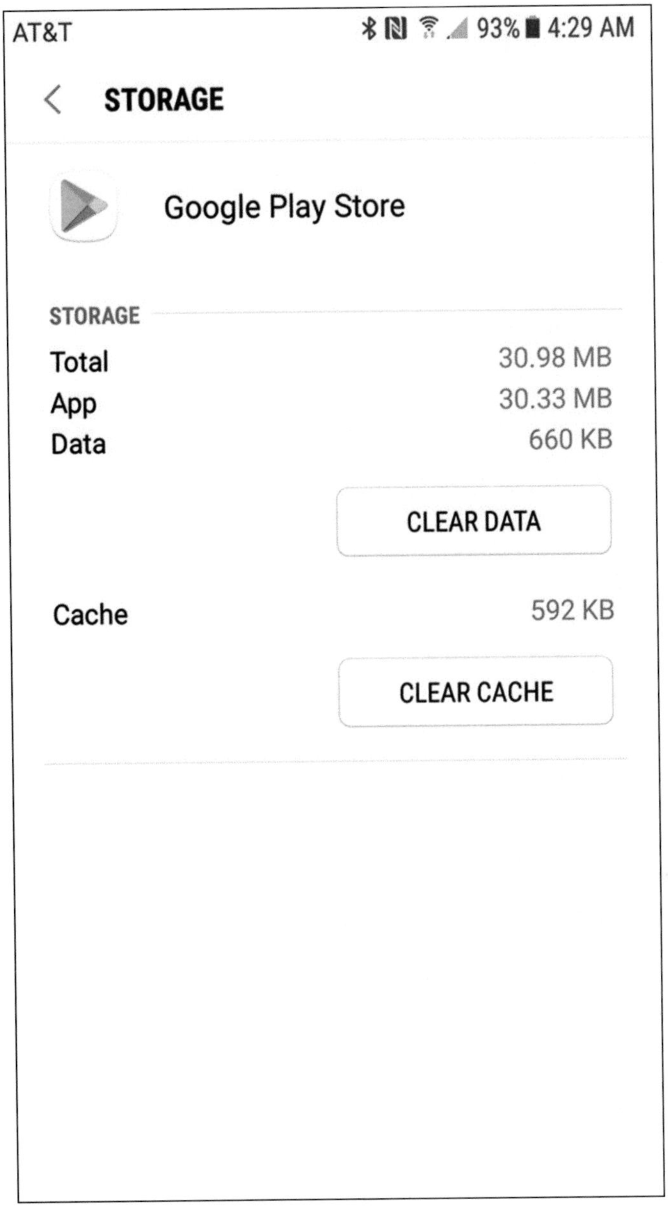

AT&T   ✻ 🅽 🛜 ▲ 93% 🔋 4:29 AM

<   **STORAGE**

▶   Google Play Store

STORAGE

Total	30.98 MB
App	30.33 MB
Data	660 KB

CLEAR DATA

Cache	592 KB

CLEAR CACHE

FIGURE 5-1:
Clear your
Google Play
Store data
here.

iPhone and iPad

You can find out how much storage space Instagram is using on your iPhone or iPad by following these steps:

1. **On your phone's home screen, tap Settings.**

2. **Swipe up on the screen if necessary, and then tap General in the settings list.**

   The General screen appears.

3. **Tap iPhone Storage or iPad Storage.**

   The iPhone Storage or iPad Storage screen appears.

4. **Tap Instagram. (You may need to swipe up first.)**

   In the Instagram screen that appears, the Documents & Data entry shows you how much storage space Instagram is using, as shown in Figure 5-2.

TIP

If you think Instagram is taking up too much space and the app is affecting the performance of your iPhone or iPad, tap Offload App to free up storage space but save your photos and profile data. If that doesn't help, reinstalling Instagram might. Instagram will save your data so that everything will still be there when you reinstall.

To reinstall Instagram, tap Delete App in the Instagram screen. Then repeat the steps in this section to see whether reinstalling freed up any storage space.

Android smartphone and tablet

As with the iPhone and iPad, it's easy to find out how much memory the Instagram app is using on your Android smartphone or tablet. Here's how:

1. **On the home screen or the Apps screen, tap Settings.**

   The Settings screen appears.

2. **Tap Applications.**

3. **Swipe up until you see the Instagram entry in the All Apps list.**

4. **Tap Instagram.**

   The Application Info screen appears.

5. **Tap Storage.**

   The total storage appears in the Storage screen, as shown in Figure 5-3.

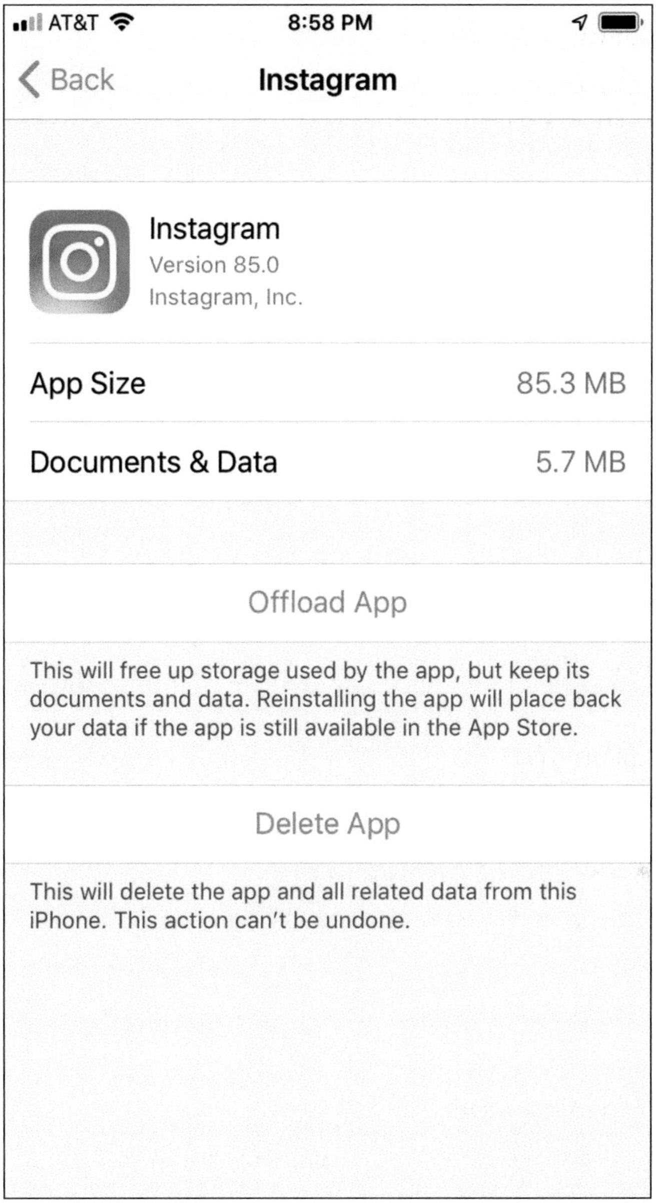

FIGURE 5-2:
The storage
space that the
Instagram app
is taking up
appears to the
right of the
Documents &
Data entry.

To clear all the memory that the Instagram app is using without clearing all the app's data, tap the Clear Cache button.

If you think Instagram is taking up too much space and the app is affecting the performance of your smartphone or tablet, tap the Clear Data button on the Storage screen. Then tap Delete in the pop-up window that appears in the center of the screen.

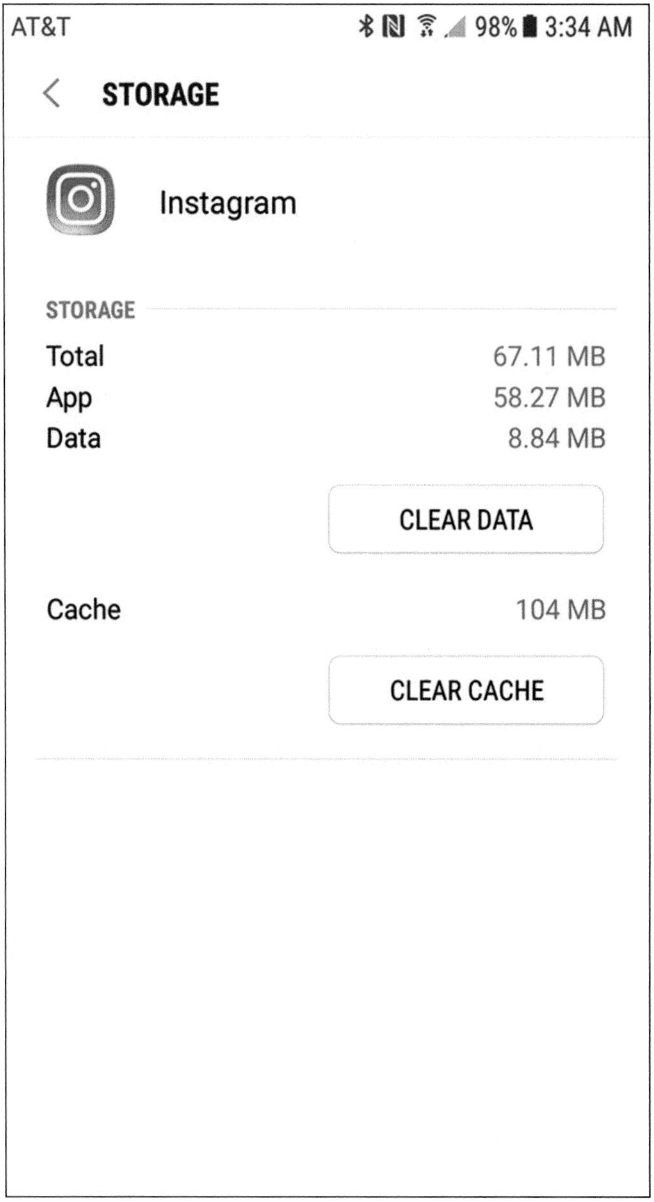

AT&T ✳ 🄽 📶 98% 🔋 3:34 AM

< **STORAGE**

Instagram

STORAGE
Total	67.11 MB
App	58.27 MB
Data	8.84 MB

CLEAR DATA

Cache   104 MB

CLEAR CACHE

FIGURE 5-3:
The storage
space on an
Android device.

Android clears your Instagram profile data stored on your smartphone or tablet, any photos or videos you've taken in the Instagram app that you haven't posted to your feed, as well as all the memory that the Instagram app is using. If the app is open, it closes automatically.

If you've already posted photos or videos to your Instagram account, your posts remain in your feed. Photos and videos you've saved on your smartphone or tablet are also safe.

Unfreezing an installation on your iPhone or iPad

If the Instagram app freezes during installation and you've given the App Store a reasonable amount of time to install the app, try a cold restart of your iPhone or iPad by turning the device off and then back on.

After you restart your iPhone or iPad, try installing the Instagram app once more. If this doesn't work, you'll have to contact Apple Support, which is easy to access from the Apple website. Just go to `http://support.apple.com`.

Finding a missing app on your iPhone or iPad

If the App Store says Instagram is installed but you don't see it on your iPhone or iPad, connect your phone to your computer and sync your apps using iTunes on your computer.

If iTunes won't cooperate, it's time to contact Apple Support (`http://support.apple.com`).

Resolving issues on an Android device

If you have problems installing the Instagram app on an Android device, there may be a connectivity problem between the Google Play Store and your smartphone or tablet.

In this case, you need to go through the Google Play troubleshooting wizard, which takes you step-by-step through solving the problem. If the wizard can't help, Google will give you options for contacting its support staff members so they can dig deeper. You can access the wizard at `https://support.google.com/googleplay/troubleshooter/6241347?hl=en`.

Log-In Difficulties

If you can't log in to the Instagram app, one of several issues may be the culprit. You may have a problem with your username or password, or Instagram may have disabled your account. We'll be your guide in resolving all these problems so you can start Instagramming.

Checking your username

If Instagram won't accept your username, you may have typed the username incorrectly. This may seem silly or even insulting, but ensure that your username is typed correctly. If your username has repeated characters, it's easy to miss one of those characters as you type.

REMEMBER

Did you add the @ symbol to your username? That symbol is used only to tag people in a comment in Instagram. So ditch the @ when you type your username.

If you still can't add your username, you may have changed your username. When you change your username or any other account information, you get an email message from Instagram informing you that your information was changed.

If you didn't get one of those messages in your email inbox or in your junk email folder, ask one of your friends or colleagues to log into Instagram, look at your profile, and find out if the username was changed. If your friend or colleague knows how to take a screenshot, have that person take a screenshot to send to you. After you review it, you can send it to Instagram if needed.

TIP

Do you suspect that your account was hacked? Instagram has suggestions for getting more help to secure your account at `https://help.instagram.com/149494825257596`. This page also contains a link to contact Instagram and explain what's happening.

Fixing password issues

If you've forgotten your Instagram account password, here are some suggestions for finding it or, as a last resort, resetting it so that you can get back to scratching your Instagram itch.

REMEMBER

If you're using your Facebook username and password to log in to Instagram, you'll have to open Facebook to reset your password.

Checking your password

If you use a password manager app, open it to see your username or password in Instagram or Facebook. If you're using your Facebook account to log in to Instagram, you may want to log in to Facebook (or log out and log back in) to find out if your Facebook password is working properly.

Password management apps can become cranky from time to time and not work properly, so if you find that your Facebook or Instagram password doesn't work when you type it, you have several options to fix the problem:

» Restart the password management app.

» Restart your computer, smartphone, or tablet, and then try logging back in to Instagram to see whether the password management app works properly.

» Uninstall and reinstall the management app. Before you do this, write down all your accounts, usernames, and passwords — keeping them in a secure location, of course.

Finding your saved Instagram signup message

When you sign up or change your account information, you receive an email message that contains a link to log into your account, as well as the email address you used to log in. Be sure to click the link in the email message so you can log in with the email address Instagram expects you to use. (The link includes your password so you don't have to enter it.)

REMEMBER

If you don't see the Instagram email in your inbox, check your junk email folder. If you find the message, you can tell your email app that messages from Instagram are not junk.

Logging in with a code sent by email

If you don't have the email message you received from Instagram and you can't remember the password (or you can't find it in your password management app), you can log in with a six-digit code sent to the email address associated with your account. Simply follow these steps:

1. **Open the Instagram app, and then tap Forgot Password (iOS) or Get Help Signing In (Android).**

    The screen shown in Figure 5-4 (iOS) or Figure 5-5 (Android) appears.

2. **Tap Username or Email (iOS) or Username, Email, or Phone (Android), and then type your Instagram username or email address.**

FIGURE 5-4:
Getting password help on an iPhone.

FIGURE 5-5:
Getting help on an Android smartphone.

3. **Tap Next.**

   You'll receive an email from Instagram in a few minutes.

   If you mistyped your email address when you signed up for your account, you won't receive an email message in your inbox. In this case, reset your account information using the phone message detailed in the next step.

4. **Type the six-digit confirmation code you received in the email.**

   The Instagram New Password web page appears in your browser.

   If you haven't received a confirmation code within a few minutes, tap the Request a New One link on the screen.

5. **Tap Next.**

Logging in with a code sent to your smartphone or tablet

If you don't have access to your email account, Instagram can send you a six-digit code on your smartphone or tablet (provided your tablet has a data plan). Here's how:

1. **Open the Instagram app, and then tap Forgot Password (iOS) or Get Help Signing In (Android).**

   iOS users see the Trouble Logging In screen (refer to Figure 5-4). Android users see the Log In Help screen (refer to Figure 5-5).

2. **Tap Phone (iOS) or Username, Email, or Phone (Android) and then type your phone number.**

3. **Tap Next.**

4. **(Android) Tap Send an SMS.**

5. **Tap the six-digit code in the Confirmation Code box.**

6. **Tap Next.**

Dealing with a disabled account

Instagram won't tell you that your account has been disabled for violation of its Community Guidelines until you try to log in and you see a message telling you that your account is disabled.

Now what? Enter your username and password, and then follow the onscreen instructions to try to appeal the decision. There are no guarantees that your account will be reinstated.

Finding Relief for Common Problems

If you run into problems uploading photos or videos, sharing with other Instagram users, or receiving notifications, read on to get some suggestions for finding solutions fast (and what to do if you can't).

Instagram won't share

Instagram has noted that problems exist when sharing your photos and videos with Facebook and Tumblr. You may encounter problems sharing your Instagram posts on Twitter, too.

You may have problems sharing your Instagram posts on Facebook, Twitter, or Tumblr for the simple reason that your preferred social network is down. In that case, you just have to wait until it fixes the problem.

If you verify on another smartphone, tablet, or computer that Facebook, Twitter, or Tumblr is operating normally, the link between Instagram and the other site may have become disconnected. You can reset the link from a smartphone or tablet app by following the instructions in this section.

REMEMBER

If you still can't connect after you reset your links, the Instagram or Facebook app may have become corrupted. In that case, it's best to remove both apps and then reinstall them. Facebook and Instagram save your data, so you won't have to log in to both apps after you reinstall them.

Here's how to reset your linked Facebook, Twitter, or Tumblr accounts:

1. Tap the Profile icon in the lower-right corner of the screen.

The screen shown in Figure 5-6 (iOS) or Figure 5-7 (Android) appears.

2. Tap the menu icon (iOS) or the three dots icon (Android).

3. Tap Settings at the bottom of the screen.

4. Tap Account.

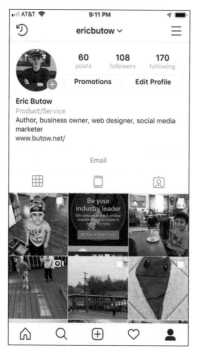

FIGURE 5-6:
The Profile screen on an iPhone.

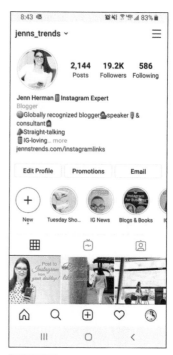

FIGURE 5-7:
The Profile screen on an Android smartphone.

5. **Tap Linked Accounts.**

   The Share Settings screen appears.

6. **Tap Facebook, Twitter, or Tumblr.**

7. **Tap Unlink Account.**

8. **Tap Yes, Unlink in the pop-up window that appears in the center of the screen.**

   Instagram and the other app (Facebook, Twitter, or Tumblr) are now unlinked.

9. **Tap Facebook, Twitter, or Tumblr.**

   This step reconnects the accounts. Try sharing your Instagram post again.

Getting Instagram to notify you

If you turned on notifications in the Instagram app but don't see notifications on your smartphone or tablet, check whether the Instagram app is sending you notifications.

Checking notifications on your iPhone or iPad

Here's how to check and set your Instagram notifications on your iPhone or iPad:

1. **On the iPhone or iPad home screen, tap Settings, and then tap Notifications.**

   The Notifications screen appears.

2. **In the apps list, swipe up and tap Instagram.**

3. **If the Allow Notifications entry is off, slide the switch from left to right.**

   If the slider is green and the switch is to the right side, notifications are on.

By default, Instagram notifications appear in Notification Center and on the Lock screen. You'll also see a Badge App icon and hear a sound when you receive an Instagram notification.

Checking notifications on your Android smartphone or tablet

Here's how to check and set Instagram notifications on your Android smartphone or tablet:

1. **On the home screen, tap Apps, then tap Settings, and then tap Applications.**

   The Applications screen appears.

2. **In the apps list, swipe up and tap Instagram.**

3. **Swipe up the Application Info screen until you see the Notifications option in the list.**

   If notifications are on, you'll see the word *Allowed* below the Notifications option. If they're off, the word *Blocked* appears.

4. **If notifications are off, tap the Notifications option and then turn on notifications.**

   You can also instruct Instagram to show notifications silently and make notifications a priority. When notifications are a priority, the notification will sound and turn on the screen when the Do Not Disturb feature is on.

Nothing Is Working . . . Now What?

When all else fails, you need to contact Instagram to report the problem. Instagram will need the following information to help you:

» The type of smartphone or tablet you're using

» The operating system and version you're using on your smartphone or tablet

» When the problem occurs and how often it occurs

You can report a problem in the Instagram app on your iPhone, iPad, Android smartphone, or Android tablet.

Reporting a problem on your iPhone or iPad

If you're using Instagram on an iPhone or iPad, follow these steps to report a problem:

1. **Tap the Profile icon.**

2. **Tap the menu icon.**

3. **Tap Settings at the bottom of the screen.**

4. **Tap Help.**

5. **Tap Report a Problem.**

   The Report a Problem window appears.

6. **Tap Something Isn't Working.**

   The Feedback screen appears.

7. **Write your report.**

8. **Tap Send, in the upper-right corner.**

Reporting a problem on your Android smartphone or tablet

Here's how to report a problem if you own an Android smartphone or tablet.

1. **Tap the Profile icon.**

2. **Tap the three lines icon.**

3. **Tap Settings.**

4. **Tap Report a Problem.**

   The Report a Problem window appears.

5. **Tap Report a Problem.**

6. **Write your report.**

7. **Tap the Send icon.**

Getting Rid of Error Messages

As with any app, you'll occasionally get error messages in the Instagram app on your iPhone, iPad, or Android device. And like any app, you may not understand why you're getting those error messages. In this section, we list four common error messages and how you can get around them.

Can't add a comment

If you receive an error message that states that you can't add a comment, one of these reasons may apply:

>> You can't include more than five tags in a comment. (You tag other Instagram users by typing the @ symbol before the username.)

>> You can add no more than 30 hashtags in a comment.

- » You can't post the same comment multiple times in one post.

- » Instagram filters out certain words and phrases, such as profanity, to meet its Community Guidelines.

- » You haven't updated Instagram recently to ensure that you have the most recent version.

If none of these reasons applies to you, close and restart the Instagram app. The next step is to turn your smartphone or tablet off and on, and then launch the Instagram app. Still not working? You need to contact Instagram for support, as described in the preceding section.

Can't delete comments

As of this writing, Instagram has a problem telling its users that a comment has been deleted. This problem arises if you try to delete a comment and get an error message that says the comment can't be deleted.

One potential solution is to close the Instagram app, restart it, and then view your post on the screen to see whether the comment is still there. If it is, you can close the Instagram app and clear all Instagram data as described earlier in the "Checking your space" section. That should clear out the deleted comment from your post.

If the comment is still there and you still get the error message when you try to delete the comment, your best option is to ignore it. By the time you read this, we hope that the problem will have been fixed or at least hidden effectively.

REMEMBER

You can delete only comments you've posted and comments from others about your posts.

Can't refresh feed

When you refresh your feed screen by swiping down, sometimes you won't see new posts. That could simply mean none of your followers has posted anything recently. However, if you can't refresh your feed over a period of time, it could be due to one of the following:

- » Your Wi-Fi signal is weak, or you're in an area with heavy Wi-Fi network usage, thus weakening the connection.

>> You've reached the limits of your carrier's data plan. You'll need to find a Wi-Fi network or shell out money for more data in your plan.

>> Instagram is having some issues. You'll just have to be patient.

If all else fails, report the problem in the Instagram app as described in the preceding section, and see whether Instagram can figure out what's wrong with the app.

Can't follow anyone else

If you receive a message that says you can't follow anyone else, check your profile to see how many other Instagram users you're following. If it's 7,500, you won't be able to follow any other accounts.

Most people will never reach the 7,500 limit. If you receive this error message and you are below (even well below) the limit, report the problem in the Instagram app so you can work with Instagram Support to solve the mystery.

REMEMBER

There is no limit to the number of Instagram users who can follow you.

WARNING

Instagram has an unadvertised limit to the number of people you can follow per hour and per day. Our best conservative estimate is that Instagram users can follow 30 per hour and have 800 follows per day, so we recommend that you adhere to these limits. If you exceed one or both limits, you'll have to wait until the top of the next hour or the beginning of the next day to follow someone. However, some users may be allowed to exceed these limits based on different account factors. You can learn more about Instagram limits and the factors that affect these limits at www.socialmediaexaminer.com/instagram-shadowban-what-marketers-need-to-know.

2

Getting Creative with Instagram Content

Master the art of taking great photos.

Discover the best video-making tactics.

Write captions to tell your story and use hashtags to get your story out there.

> » Using the photo-editing tools in Instagram
>
> » Adding descriptions and more
>
> » Creating a post with one photo or multiple photos

Chapter **6**

Taking and Posting Great Photos

I n this chapter, you find out how to take photos with Instagram, use editing tools to make your photos look their best, and then share photos stored on your iPhone, iPad, or Android smartphone or tablet with your followers and on other social networks.

REMEMBER

You can upload photos only in the Instagram app on your smartphone or tablet, not from the Instagram website.

All figures in this chapter were taken using the iPhone app, because that's Instagram's native platform. Don't worry, Android users — we note any differences between the iPhone and Android apps throughout.

Taking Your Best Shot

Before you can post a photo on Instagram, you need to tell the app where to get the photo. In this section, we cover taking a photo. For details on selecting from your existing photos, see the "Uploading Photos from Your Camera Roll" section, later in this chapter.

When you first log in to Instagram, you'll see your feed on the screen. Tap the plus (+) icon at the bottom of the screen. When prompted, allow Instagram access to your phone's camera. Next, you'll see the Photo screen shown in Figure 6-1.

FIGURE 6-1:
Now you can
take your
picture.

The good news is that you have to go through this process only once. The next time you open Instagram and tap the plus (+) icon, you won't have to enable camera access.

Note the following elements in the Photo screen:

>> **Viewer:** The viewer appears in the top part of the screen.

>> **Switch cameras icon (two circular arrows):** The switch cameras icon is in the lower-left corner of the viewer. Tap the icon to switch between your smartphone's front and back cameras.

>> **Flash icon (lightning bolt in a circle):** The flash icon appears in the lower-right corner of the viewer. Tap the flash icon to toggle the following flash modes:

- *Off:* This mode is the default. The icon circle appears hollow.

- *On:* The circle is white and the lightning bolt appears hollow.

- *Auto-detect:* The circle is hollow with an *A* inside.

>> **Shutter button (large gray circle in the bottom half of the screen):** The shutter button is what you tap to take a picture.

>> **Cancel button (iOS) or X (Android):** In the upper-left corner, tapping this button returns you to your Instagram feed.

When you're ready to take a photo, tap the shutter button. Your phone makes a camera shutter sound, as it does when you use the phone's Camera app.

Improving Your Best Shot

The photo you've just taken appears in the viewer of the Filter screen, as shown in Figure 6-2. The screen contains the following four sections, from top to bottom:

>> The *top menu bar,* with a < (back) icon on the left, the Lux icon in the center (which you learn about later in this chapter), and the Next link on the right

>> The *viewer,* which displays your photo

>> A row of *filter thumbnail images* so you can see what your photo will look like with a filter applied

>> The *bottom menu bar,* with a Filter menu option (selected by default) and the Edit option

FIGURE 6-2:
The Filter
screen.

Not interested in editing your photo? Simply tap the back icon in the upper-left corner to save your photo. Instagram saves your photo automatically and displays the camera screen so you can take a new photo if you want.

Applying a filter

Below your photo in the viewer is a row of filters. Each filter includes a thumbnail image so you can see the filter's effect on your photo.

Swipe from right to left in the row of thumbnail images to view all 23 filters, from Clarendon to Nashville. (Normal is the default image, without a filter.) Tap a filter thumbnail image, and the photo in the viewer changes to show you the photo with that filter applied.

REMEMBER

To return to the original photo, tap the Normal thumbnail (refer to Figure 6-2). To continue processing the photo with a filter, either tap Edit at the lower-right corner of the screen to edit your photo further, or tap Next in the upper-right corner of the screen to add a description to your photo. (You learn how to add a description in the "Enriching Your Photo" section, later in this chapter.)

What happens when a filter is not quite to your liking and you'd like to tweak it? You can change the intensity of any filter (except Normal) by tapping the filter thumbnail image again. A slider appears; move it to the left and right to change the intensity. The photo in the viewer changes to reflect the selected intensity. The default intensity for each filter is 100. (And yes, we checked each one.)

In iOS, a white box appears to the right of the slider. Tap this box to add a white frame around the photo. If you don't like having the white frame, tap the box again.

When you've set the intensity to just the right amount, tap Done (iOS) or the check mark (Android). If you're still not satisfied and want to return the photo to its original intensity, tap Cancel (iOS) or the X (Android).

REMEMBER

Keep in mind that any filter settings will revert to the default after you leave this screen.

TIP

If you want to see how the photo with a filter compares to the original photo, tap and hold down on the viewer to view the original photo. Release your finger to see the photo with the applied filter.

Managing filters

Are there too many filters or are your favorite ones are too far down in the list? No problem. Swipe to the end of the filter list, and you'll see a Manage icon. Tap the icon to open the Manage Filters screen, shown in Figure 6-3, where you can perform three tasks: Change the order of filters in the row, add filters, and disable filters.

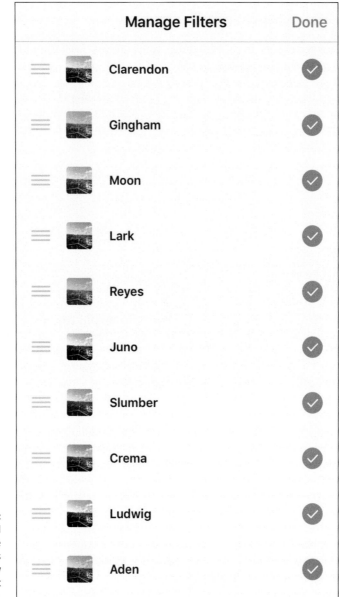

FIGURE 6-3:
Swipe up and
down in the
Manage Filters
screen to view
the entire list
of filters.

The filters on the Manage Filters screen appear in the same order as they do in the Filter screen. You can change the order of filters as follows:

1. **Tap and hold down on a filter name in the list.**

   The filter name gets larger after you hold down on the name for about a second.

2. **Move the name in the list.**

   As you move the filter name, other filter names helpfully move out of the way so you can see where your selected filter will appear in the list.

3. **When the filter is where you want it, release your finger.**

   The filter name appears in your desired location in the list.

That's all there is to it! To return to the Filter screen, tap Done (iOS) or the check mark in the upper right (Android).

When you swipe up and down in the list of filters on the Manage Filters screen, you may see several filter names that don't have check marks to the right of the filter name. These filters are disabled, but it's easy to add any of them to the Filter screen: Simply tap a filter name that doesn't have a check mark to the right of the name. A check mark is added, which means the filter is active. Tap Done, and you return to the Filter screen, where you see your new filter in the row of filters.

If you decide that you don't want to include one or more filters in the Filter screen, you can disable it by tapping the filter name in the list on the Manage Filters screen. The check mark to the right of the name disappears. (To add it back, just tap the disabled filter name again.) When you're finished, tap Done (iOS) or the check mark in the upper right (Android).

Tweaking with the editing tools

When you've finished experimenting with filters, view Instagram's editing tools by tapping Edit (iOS) or Edit/Filter (Android) at the bottom of the screen. (Some Android users may see a wrench icon instead.) A row of editing tools appears below the viewer, as shown in Figure 6-4.

Swipe from right to left in the row of editing tools to see all 13 tools. Tap a tool to open it below the viewer.

FIGURE 6-4:
The tool name
appears above
each tool icon.

What you see below the viewer depends on the tool you tapped. For example, when you tap the Brightness tool, a slider appears so you can increase or decrease the photo's brightness. No matter what tool you use, the photo in the viewer reflects the changes you make and a gray dot appears below the tool icon.

Here's what you can do with each tool:

>> **Adjust:** You can adjust your photo in several ways by using the Adjust tool. Instagram automatically adjusts your photo to center it before you make any adjustments. A row of three icons and an associated slider bar appear below the photo, as shown in Figure 6-5, so you can make the following changes:

- Change the vertical or horizontal perspective of the photo by tapping the left or right icon, respectively, below the photo. After you tap the icon, it's highlighted in black. The slider bar is a series of vertical lines. Swipe left and right in the slider bar to see the change reflected in the photo. As you slide, the highlighted icon above the slider bar is replaced with a box that shows you the change amount measured in degrees.

- If the object in your photo appears tilted, tap the straighten icon in the middle of the icon row. Then swipe left and right in the slider bar to tilt the photo so that the object appears straight. As you swipe in the slider bar, a box appears in place of the straighten icon and shows you the number of degrees you're tilting the photo.

- Rotate the photo 90 degrees counterclockwise by tapping the rotate icon in the upper-right corner of the screen. Keep tapping the rotate icon to continue to rotate the photo in the viewer.

- Crop the photo to a specific area by first zooming in (touch the photo and spread your thumb and index finger apart) in the viewer. Then hold down on the photo and drag it in the viewer until you see the part of the photo you want to post on your Instagram feed. If you decide you don't want to crop the photo, zoom back out to the photo's original size by pinching your thumb and index finger together in the viewer.

TIP

You can overlay a grid on the photo to help you center it. On the iPhone and iPad, the grid icon appears at the upper-left corner of the screen. Tap the grid icon to change the size of the grid. On an Android device, tap the photo until you see the size of the grid you want. If you tap the grid icon or photo often enough, you'll remove the grid entirely.

>> **Brightness:** In the slider bar below the viewer, slide the dot to the left to darken the photo or to the right to make the photo brighter. As you move the slider bar, the photo in the viewer darkens or brightens accordingly.

>> **Contrast:** In the slider bar, make the light areas of your photo even lighter by sliding the dot to the left. Make the dark areas even darker so the focus is on the lighter areas of your photo by sliding the dot to the right.

FIGURE 6-5:
Use the slider bar in the Adjust screen to change the photo's perspective.

>> **Lux tool:** At the top center of the Filter and Edit screens is an icon that looks like a magic wand. Tap it to open the Lux tool, which you can use to quickly change the exposure level and brightness instead of using the separate Brightness and Contrast editing tools. Move the slider to change the exposure level and brightness. When you're finished, tap Done to save your changes, or tap Cancel to discard them.

If you want to undo any edits you've made, tap the Lux icon and then move the slider to its default location, 50. (The default setting for the Brightness and Contrast editing tools, however, is 0.) When you're done, tap Done.

» **Structure:** This tool enhances the details in the photo, such as adding color in an area that appears washed out in the original. In the slider bar, slide the dot to the right to see how the tool increases the details of the photo in the viewer. If you think the photo is too detailed, slide to the left to make the photo fuzzier.

» **Warmth:** In the slider bar below the viewer, slide the dot to the right to make the colors warmer by adding orange tones or to the left to make the colors cooler by adding blue tones.

» **Saturation:** In the slider bar, slide the dot to the right or left to increase or decrease, respectively, the intensity of all colors in your photo.

» **Color:** You can change the color of your photo's shadows or highlights or both, as well as change the intensity of the tint. Eight colors are available: yellow, orange, red, pink, purple, blue, cyan, or green, as shown in Figure 6-6.

  - *To change the color of shadows in your photo:* Tap Shadows, if necessary (it's the default), and then tap one of the color dots.

  - *To change the highlight color:* Tap Highlights, and then tap one of the eight color dots, which are the same colors as those used for shadows.

  - *To change the tint intensity for the shadow or highlight color:* Tap the color dot twice. In the slider bar that appears below the viewer, slide the dot to the left or right to decrease or increase the intensity, respectively. When the intensity looks good to you, release your finger from the dot and then tap Done (iPhone or iPad) or tap the check mark (Android) to return to the Color page.

» **Fade:** Do you want your photo to look like it's been sitting in a shoebox for years . . . or decades? In the slider bar, slide the dot to the right to fade the color from your photo or to the left to add color.

» **Highlights:** In the slider bar, slide the dot to the right to increase the brightness in bright areas of the photo. Slide to the left to darken the bright areas in the photo.

» **Shadows:** In the slider bar, slide the dot to the right to lighten the dark areas in your photo. Slide to the left to darken the dark areas.

» **Vignette:** This tool allows you to darken the edges of the photo so people will focus on the center of the photo. In the slider bar, slide the dot to the right to darken the photo edges.

FIGURE 6-6:
Tap the color
dot to select a
color for your
photo shadow.

» **Tilt Shift:** You can blur the outer edges of your photo and keep the center in clear focus so people will automatically look at the focused area. Tap Radial below the viewer to blur all four edges of the photo and keep the center focused in a circular shape. Tap Linear to blur just the top and bottom edges of the photo.

You can change the size of the "unblurred" area of the picture by tapping the center of the photo with your thumb and forefinger. Then spread them apart to make the area larger or together to make the area smaller. Tap Off if you don't like the changes and want to keep your entire photo in focus.

>> **Sharpen:** This tool sharpens features that aren't visible in the original photo, such as the texture on a wall. In the slider bar, slide the dot to the right and left to make the photo less and more fuzzy, respectively.

After you finish making changes to your photo, apply your effect by tapping Done (iOS) or the check mark (Android). Or discard the effect by tapping Cancel (iOS) or the X (Android).

Saving your changes (or not)

When you've finished using the editing tools and filters, you can do one of three things:

>> **Discard your changes** and return to the Photo screen by tapping the left arrow icon in the upper-left corner and then tapping Discard in the pop-up menu.

>> **Save your changes and continue editing** by tapping the left arrow icon and then tapping Save Draft in the pop-up menu. Then Instagram takes you back to the camera screen, not your photo, so you'll have to select the photo in your library to continue editing it.

>> **Add a description** to the photo by tapping Next in the upper-right corner. The New Post screen appears, where you can add a caption and location, tag friends, and decide if you want to share the photo on other social networks (see the next section).

To follow along with the example in this chapter, tap Next.

Enriching Your Photo

After you tap Next on the Edit screen, the New Post screen appears, as shown in Figure 6-7. On this screen, you can add a caption to your photo, tag people who appear in the photo, include the photo's location, share the photo on other social media networks, and turn commenting on and off.

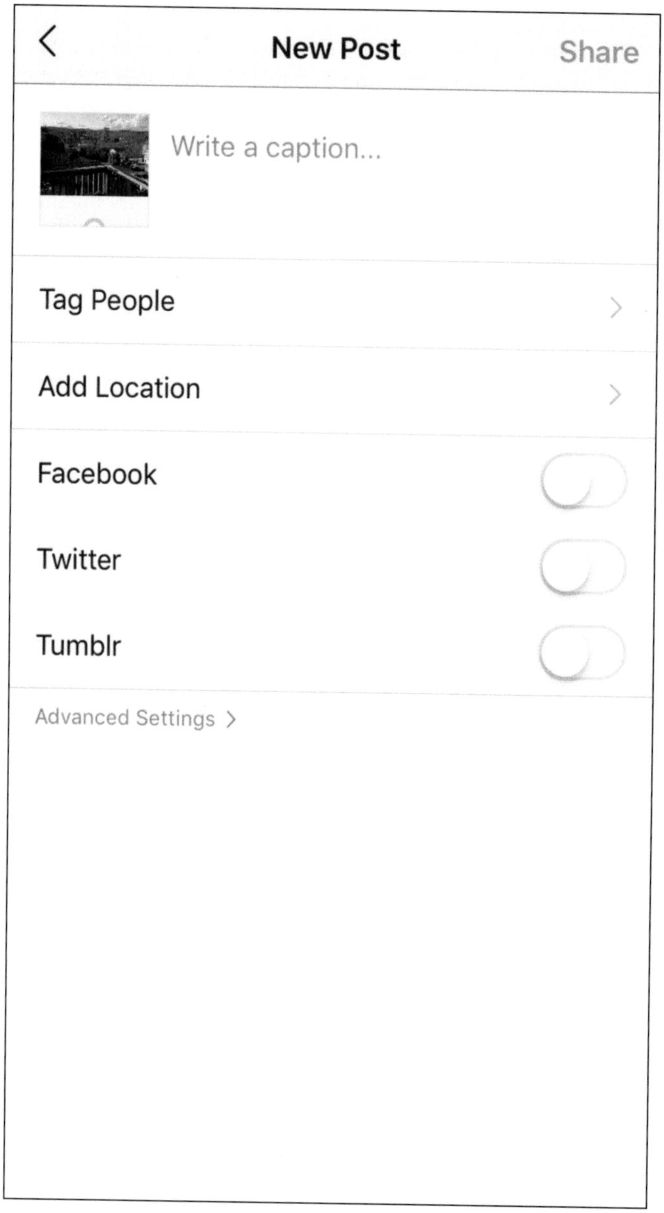

FIGURE 6-7:
Add details to your photo here.

Describing your photo

To add a description to your photo, tap in the top section where it says *Write a caption....* A keyboard appears at the bottom of the screen.

REMEMBER

Captions can't exceed 2,200 characters. You'll know you've reached the limit when you keep typing and no characters appear in the caption box.

TIP

To add a blank line between paragraphs after you type the last character of text, tap the numbers key in the lower-left corner of the keyboard and then tap the Return key. If you tap Return after a blank space after the last character, Instagram won't format your paragraph correctly when you post your photo. You can read more about formatting your caption (and the pitfalls) for the iPhone and Android smartphones at www.jennstrends.com/how-to-format-instagram-captions/.

When you've finished writing, tap OK (iOS) or Share (Android) in the upper-right corner of the screen. The text of your caption appears in the caption box.

To edit the caption, tap in the caption box and make your changes. When you're finished, tap OK.

It's good to have options

Below the caption box are five options to identify people in your photo, add a location to your photo, share your photo on other social networks, and turn commenting on and off (under the Advanced Settings link at the bottom).

Tagging people

When you *tag* people, you add their Instagram usernames to your photo so they know that you posted a photo with them in it. Instagram enables you to tag up to 20 people in a single photo. To tag a person in your photo, do the following:

1. **On the New Post screen, tap Tag People.**

   The Tag People screen appears.

2. **Tap the photo to tag.**

   The Search screen appears.

3. **In the Search for a Name box, type the username of the person you want to tag, and then tap the Search key in the keyboard.**

   A list of people appears below the box.

4. **Swipe up and down in the list until you find the person you want to tag, and then tap the person's name.**

   You can tag only people who appear in the list.

5. **Repeat this process to tag more people.**

6. When you've finished tagging people, tap Done in the upper-right corner of the screen.

Be sure that you tag only people who are in the photo. Fortunately, if you tag someone by mistake, you can tap on the tag and then click the X that appears to the right of the person's name. But if you go ahead and tag someone who isn't in the photo, the tagged person may report you to Instagram, and then you may be subject to "deleted content, disabled accounts, or other restrictions" per Instagram's Community Guidelines. However, if the photo contains a logo or product, you can tag the brand or company associated with the product or logo.

Adding your location

You can include your current location in the photo's description. Tap Add Location. Your smartphone or tablet asks if the Instagram app can use your location if it's the first time you are adding a location. Tap Allow in the pop-up window to continue.

On the Locations screen that appears, swipe up and down in the list of nearby locations. If you can't find your location, tap the Search box at the top of the screen and start typing. As you type, results that most closely match your search term(s) appear in the list. When you find the location in the list, tap the location name.

If you want to delete the location, tap the delete icon (X) to the right of the location. After you delete the location, you see Add Location again on the screen.

After you allow the Instagram app to use your location, the next time you open the New Post screen, you'll see a row of potential locations below Add Location. Swipe up in the row to view more locations. Tap the location name to select it as your location. You can still add a location by tapping Add Location and either selecting a location from the list or by typing the location in the Search box and then selecting the location in the list.

Facebook

Tap the dot to toggle the Facebook switch from left to right to log into Facebook and post your photo to your Facebook newsfeed, as well as to Instagram. If this is the first time you're posting to Facebook, you'll be asked to allow Facebook to access your Instagram account.

The post is shared only with your Facebook friends.

You have to tap the toggle dot every time you want to share on Facebook.

Twitter

If you want to tweet the same Instagram photo you're preparing, tap the dot to toggle the Twitter switch from left to right to log into your Twitter account. After you log in, you can share your photo and caption in a tweet. Remember that Twitter will cut off any caption that exceeds 280 characters. If this is the first time you're posting to Twitter from Instagram, you'll have to allow Twitter access to your account.

You have to tap the toggle dot every time you want to share on Twitter.

Tumblr

You can post your photo to your Tumblr account by tapping the Tumblr dot to toggle from left to right. Tumblr opens so you can log into your account, and then you return to Instagram. When you share your photo and related information in Instagram, you'll share it to your Tumblr feed as well.

SHARING ON FACEBOOK IS NATURAL

Consider editing your caption before you share a photo or video on Facebook (or Twitter or Tumblr, for that matter). When you remove Instagram hashtags and tweak your caption for your Facebook audience, you'll have a much better chance of reaching more people on Facebook. For example, suppose you have a photo you've posted on Instagram and you want to post it also on Facebook with the #tbt (throwback Thursday) hashtag. Simply remove the Instagram hashtags and then add the #tbt hashtag. Now when you post your Instagram photo on Facebook, people searching for posts with the #tbt hashtag can find your post.

When you share your Instagram photo or video on Facebook, it appears in your Facebook newsfeed. The post includes the caption in your Instagram photo or video, as well as the photo thumbnail or video cover frame. View a photo by tapping it. Play the video by tapping the play icon in the center of the video cover frame.

If you view your photo on the Facebook website on your computer, you can click Instagram above the caption to view the original post on the Instagram website in another browser tab. When you finish viewing the original post and want to get back to using Facebook, close the Instagram tab.

You have to tap the toggle dot every time you want to share on Tumblr.

Turning commenting on and off

Before you share your photo, you may not want to take the time to read or respond to comments. You can block your followers from leaving comments about your photo. Begin by tapping the Advanced Settings option at the bottom of the New Post screen (refer to Figure 6-7). In the Advanced Settings screen, tap the Turn Off Commenting dot to toggle from left to right. To return to the New Post screen, tap the left arrow in the upper-left corner.

Posting Your Photos: Ta Da!

Your photo or photos are now ready to share with the Instagram world, so all you have to do is tap Share in the upper-right corner of the New Post screen.

After you post a photo, the home screen appears with your photo at the top, as shown in Figure 6-8. If you've posted several photos in one post, you'll be able to swipe in your post to view them all.

Instagram automatically uploads your photo in the best resolution possible. When you take a photo with a smartphone or tablet that runs iOS or Android, resolution isn't an issue. However, if you upload a photo from your Camera Roll (on the iPhone) or Gallery (on an Android smartphone), check your image settings in a photo-editing app such as Image Size (iPhone and iPad) or Photo & Picture Resizer (Android smartphones and tablets). In the app, see that the photo has a width between 320 and 1,080 pixels with an aspect ratio between 1.91:1 and 4:5. For example, if the photo width is 1,080 pixels, the height can be between 566 pixels (1.91:1 ratio) and 1,350 pixels (4:5 ratio). If your photo height is too low or high, Instagram will automatically crop it to fit the aspect ratio. The moral of this story is to check and crop your photos before Instagram does it for you (probably to your annoyance).

FIGURE 6-8:
The 1/4 in the upper-right corner of the photo indicates that this post has several photos.

Uploading Photos from Your Camera Roll

Do you have some photos you've already shot that you'd like to share with your followers? It's easy to select one or more photos and then share them on your Instagram feed. Here's how to upload photos from your camera:

1. **Tap the plus (+) icon at the bottom of the home screen.**

   The Photo screen appears.

2. **Tap Library.**

   The Camera Roll screen appears, as shown in Figure 6-9. (Android users see the Gallery screen.) The most recent photo you saved to your smartphone appears in the viewer. Thumbnail-size photos appear below the viewer.

3. **Swipe in the thumbnail photos to view other photos. When you find one you like, tap it.**

   The selected photo appears in the viewer. Instagram automatically crops your photo to the size of the viewer.

4. **(Optional) View the photo in its original size by tapping the resize icon (labeled in Figure 6-9).**

5. **Tap Next.**

6. **(Optional) Apply filters and edit your photo as described earlier.**

7. **Tap Next.**

   The New Post screen appears.

8. **(Optional) Write a caption, tag people, add a location, change advanced settings and recipients, and share your photo on other social networks.**

   For details, bookmark this page and read the earlier section, "Enriching Your Photo."

9. **When you're ready to share your photos, tap Share.**

REMEMBER

If you have an Apple Mac (desktop or laptop) and you use the Safari web browser, there's a trick you can use to upload one or more photos from your Mac to your Instagram profile. Bookmark this page and go back to Chapter 2 to learn all about it. (Windows users, you're out of luck.)

Did you notice in Figure 6-9 the icons for the Boomerang and Layout apps? The Boomerang icon looks like an infinity symbol, and the Layout icon looks like a square divided into three sections. You use the Boomerang app to create and post mini-videos on your feed. Your camera takes a burst of photos, and Boomerang stitches them together, creating a quick video clip that plays backward and forward — like a Boomerang flies — get it? (See Chapter 13 for details on using Boomerang.) You can use the Layout app to combine multiple photos into one photo and post the combined photo on your feed without having to swipe back and forth between photos.

FIGURE 6-9:
The thumbnail of the selected photo appears dimmed.

Uploading Multiple Photos to One Post

You don't need to have one post for each photo. Instead, you can add as many as ten photos in your Camera Roll (or Gallery if you use an Android smartphone) to a single post.

Selecting multiple photos

To choose more than one photo to add to a post, do the following:

1. **In the main Instagram feed screen, tap the plus (+) icon.**

2. **Tap Library (or Gallery), in the lower-left corner of the screen.**

   The most recent photo in your Camera Roll appears in the viewer.

3. **Swipe through the thumbnail photos, and tap the first photo you want to add.**

4. **Tap the select multiple icon that contains overlapped rounded squares; the highlighted icon in blue appears above the list of thumbnail images shown in Figure 6-10.**

   The selected thumbnail appears dimmed, with a blue number 1, as shown in Figure 6-10.

5. **Tap another thumbnail.**

   The photo appears in the viewer, and a number 2 appears next to the thumbnail. That number shows you the order in which your followers will see the photos in your post.

REMEMBER

   If you select a photo but then decide that you don't want to include it, just tap the thumbnail photo. The order of your photos will change if you selected more than two photos. To deselect all photos, tap the blue select multiple icon in the lower-right corner of the viewer.

6. **Continue tapping thumbnails as needed.**

   In Figure 6-11, we've chosen three photos. The numbers reflect the order in which we selected each photo.

7. **When you've finished selecting photos, tap Next.**

   The Edit screen appears.

Edit the photos by tapping Next in the upper-right corner of the screen.

FIGURE 6-10:
The select multiple icon in the viewer appears in blue above the upper-right thumbnail image in the list.

FIGURE 6-11:
The most recently selected photo appears in the viewer.

TIP

To reorder the photos, you have to deselect them and then reselect them in the correct order. (Yes, this is something Instagram needs to work on.) For example, suppose you select five photos and want to move photos 3 and 4 to positions 4 and 5, respectively. First deselect photos 3 and 4. At this point, the former photo 5 becomes photo 3. Then select the former photo 3, which becomes photo 4, and then select the former photo 4, which becomes photo 5.

Applying filters and adding photos

After you have selected your photos and tapped Next, the Edit screen appears, as shown in Figure 6-12. The top of the screen displays the photo you're editing.

FIGURE 6-12:
The filter
name appears
above the filter
thumbnail
image.

A row of filter types appears below the photo. Swipe from right to left in the row to view all the filters. To apply a filter to all photos in the group, tap the thumbnail image under the filter name.

At the right side of the screen, you see part of the next photo in your photo group. To see the other photos, swipe left. To add another photo to your post, swipe to the end of the row, tap the plus (+) icon, and then select the photo from the Camera Roll screen, as described in the "Uploading Photos from Your Camera Roll" section earlier in this chapter.

Editing photos individually

To edit a photo, tap it in the row of photos. The selected photo appears in the center of your screen. Now you can do the following:

>> **Add a filter.** Swipe right to left in the filter row, and then tap the filter thumbnail image. Get all the details in the "Adding a filter" section.

>> **Change the exposure and brightness levels at once.** Tap the Lux icon (half-light, half-dark sun) at the top of the screen. Learn more about using the Lux tool in the "Tweaking with the editing tools" section.

>> **Perform other editing tasks.** Tap Edit, and then follow the instructions in the "Tweaking with the editing tools" section.

Tap Done in the upper-right corner when you're finished.

Adding information and sharing your photos

When your photos are the way you want them, tap Next in the upper-right corner of the Edit screen.

In the New Post screen, you can write a caption, tag people, add a location, share your photo on other social networks, and turn commenting on and off as described earlier in the "Enriching Your Photo" section.

TIP

You can't write a caption for each photo when you have multiple photos in your post. So when you write your description, the caption should describe all your photos, not just one.

When you've finished editing your photos, it's time to share them. Tap Share in the upper-right corner of the New Post screen.

Chapter **7**

Recording and Posting Great Videos

Your iPhone, iPad, and Android device all have video cameras and Instagram puts them to great use. In this chapter, we explain how to record video in the Instagram app by using a smartphone or a tablet. Sorry, Windows users: Instagram doesn't support using your webcam to take video.

After you've recorded your video, you can edit your video with Instagram's built-in editing tools. Then you can add a description of what the video is about so you don't leave your viewers wondering. Finally, we explain how to share your video with your friends and family on Instagram.

Recording Videos

Instagram gives you the flexibility to record videos that are as short as 3 seconds or as long as 60 seconds. If you find that 60 seconds is too limiting, use the video as a teaser (think of it as your own movie preview) to get people to click through to your website or to another video website such as YouTube.

Filming with a smartphone or tablet

When you're ready to start recording a video on your iPhone, iPad, Android smartphone, or Android tablet, open the Instagram app (if it's not open already) and then tap the plus (+) icon at the bottom of the home screen. In the Library or Photo screen that appears, tap Video.

REMEMBER

The Instagram apps on the iPhone, iPad, Android smartphones, and Android tablets all work the same.

The first time you open the Video screen, a pop-up window appears, as shown in Figure 7-1. Instagram wants to access the microphone on your smartphone so it can record videos with sound. Access the microphone by tapping OK.

REMEMBER

The next time you open the Video screen, you won't see this pop-up window. If you want to turn your microphone off and on in Instagram, access your smartphone's settings, open the Instagram settings, and then turn the microphone on or off.

The Video screen has the following elements, all labeled in Figure 7-2:

>> **Viewer:** Displays what your smartphone sees through its camera lens.

>> **Switch cameras icon:** Tap this icon to switch between the front and back cameras.

>> **Recording bar:** The recording bar represents how long you've been recording. The recording bar expands as you record. (If you reach the 60-second limit, the bar spans the width of the screen and Instagram stops recording.) When the recording bar is blinking, you can start recording either at the beginning of a video or after a video clip. (You find out about recording multiple video clips in the next section.)

REMEMBER

If you record for only 1 or 2 seconds, the recording bar is solid for the time you recorded. Between the recording bar and the minimum bar, you'll see a blinking recording bar. That blinking bar tells you how many more seconds you have to meet the minimum recording time to save your video.

>> **3-second recording time bar:** Indicates when the video is 3 seconds long. When the recording bar passes the 3-second spot, you can save your video.

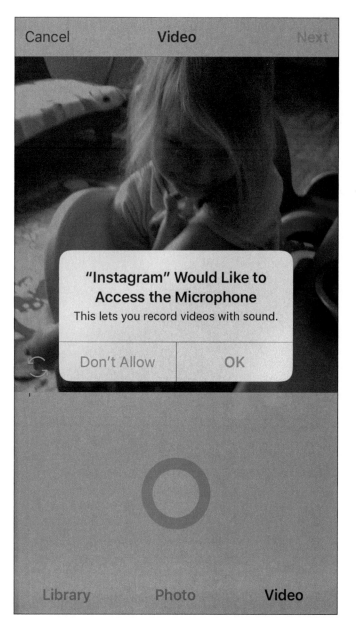

FIGURE 7-1:
If you want to
record silent
videos, tap
Don't Allow.

Switch cameras icon

Viewer

Cancel   **Video**   Next

Library   Photo   **Video**

FIGURE 7-2:
Tap Cancel if
you decide you
don't want to
record a video.

3-second recording time bar   Record button

Recording bar

» **Record button:** Tap and hold down on the Record button to start recording your video. The amount of time you've been recording appears above the Record button, as shown in Figure 7-3. When you've finished recording, release your finger from the Record button.

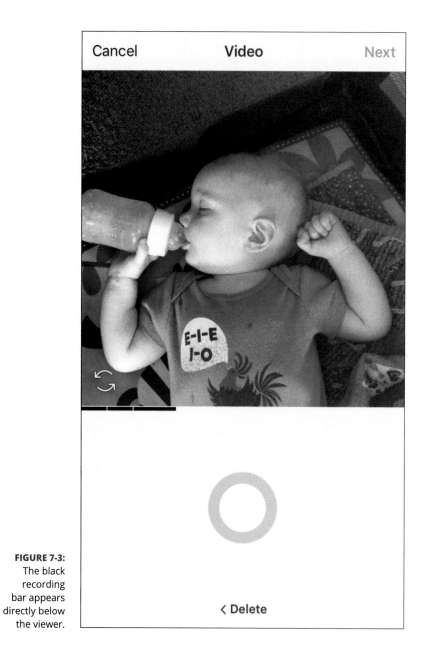

FIGURE 7-3:
The black recording bar appears directly below the viewer.

Recording multiple video clips

To save time, you can record multiple clips in one recording. For example, suppose you're recording a video of one of your favorite restaurants. After filming your favorite dish, you don't want to spend precious video time recording your move to the outside to show the exterior of the building.

After you record your first clip, release your finger. When you're ready to start recording again, tap and hold down on the Record button again. You may repeat this process as many times as you want within the 60-second limit for a video. The timer above the Record button continues from the time you paused the recording.

The recording bar places a white line between each clip. In this way, you can see how many clips you have. Figure 7-3, for example, has three clips of varying times.

Deleting video clips

If you decide that you want to delete the last video clip you recorded, tap Delete at the bottom of the screen (refer to Figure 7-3). The color of the Delete button and the recording bar changes to red. Then tap Delete again. The Delete option disappears and the blinking recording bar appears so you can record a new video clip.

If you want to delete more clips, just repeat this process. Easy like Sunday morning.

Checking out your video

After you record your video, you'll want to review it before posting. From the Video screen, tap Next. You see the Filter screen, which you learn about in the next section.

WARNING

If you haven't recorded for the minimum 3 seconds, you'll see a pop-up above the minimum bar when you tap Next. This pop-up points to the minimum bar and tells you to record at least to that point. After a few seconds, the pop-up disappears and you can record another clip.

The video starts playing in the viewer. To stop playing the video, tap anywhere in the viewer. To resume, tap the Play button, in the middle of the viewer, as shown in Figure 7-4.

TIP

You can toggle video sound on or off by tapping the speaker icon at the top of the page. If you've stopped your video, the video will start playing after you turn the video sound on or off.

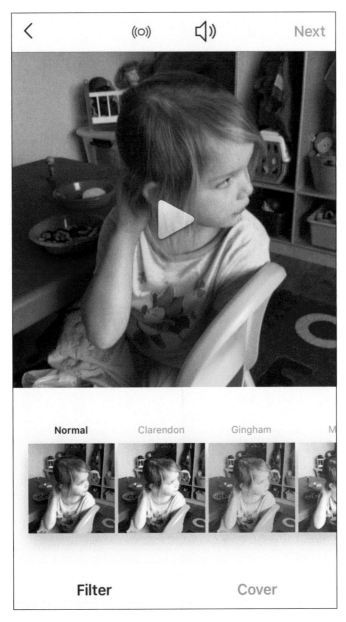

FIGURE 7-4:
Begin playing the video by tapping the Play button.

Improving Your Video

You can improve your video in several ways: by adding a filter, changing the cover frame, and trimming the video. In this section, you start by applying a filter to your video in the Filter screen.

Applying a filter

Below the viewer is a row of filters. (The Normal, Clarendon, and Gingham filters are shown in Figure 7-4.) The thumbnail image below each filter shows you the filter's effect on your video.

Swipe in the row of thumbnails to view all 23 filters. (Normal is the default, so it isn't considered a filter.) Tap a filter's thumbnail, and the video with the applied filter plays in the viewer.

You can change the intensity of any filter by tapping the filter's thumbnail, and then moving the slider to the left or right. (The default intensity is 100.) As you move the slider, the video reflects the change. When you've finished selecting an intensity, tap Done.

The video continues to play when you apply a new filter or change the intensity of a filter. If you want to return the video to its original state, tap the Normal thumbnail.

Changing the cover frame

Instagram uses the first frame from your video to produce a *cover frame,* which is the frame that appears at the start of your video. You can change the cover frame as follows:

1. **On the Filter screen, tap Cover.**

    The default cover frame appears in the viewer and also below the viewer in a white focus box. The other frames appear next to the focus box and are dimmed, as shown in Figure 7-5.

2. **Tap and hold down on the frame in the focus box, and then drag the frame within the row.**

    As you drag, the focus box moves to another frame in your video and you see this new cover frame in the viewer.

3. **When you find a cover frame you like, release your finger.**

4. **Tap Next.**

The cover frame will appear in your Instagram feed, so be sure that the frame you select isn't blurry.

FIGURE 7-5:
Frames that aren't selected appear dimmed.

Adding details

In the screen that displays your video (refer to Figure 7-4), tap Next. The New Post screen appears, as shown in Figure 7-6.

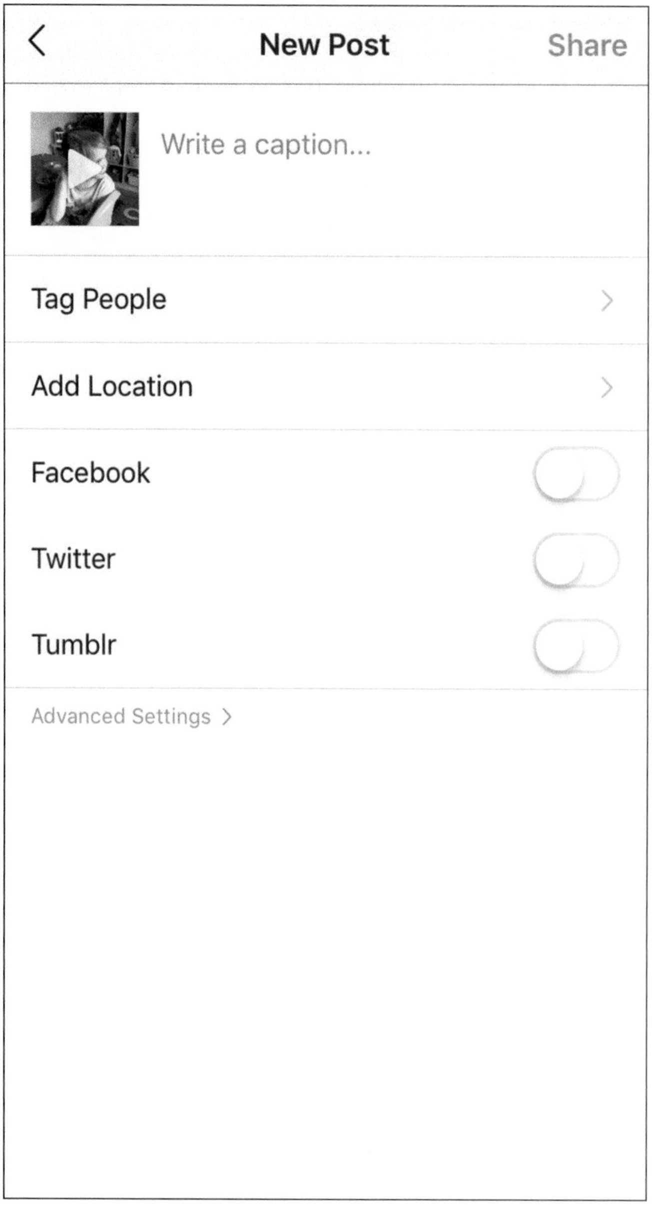

‹	**New Post**	Share

Write a caption...

Tag People ›

Add Location ›

Facebook

Twitter

Tumblr

Advanced Settings ›

FIGURE 7-6:
Your video
frame appears
as a thumbnail
in the upper-
left corner.

On this screen, you can add a caption, include a location where the video was recorded, share the video on other social media networks, and turn commenting on and off. The process for adding all this good stuff is described in Chapter 6. (Note, however, that you can't tag people in videos, so you can skip the instructions about tagging in Chapter 6.)

Posting your video

When you're ready to post your video, tap Share in the upper-right corner of the New Post screen (refer to Figure 7-6). After a few seconds, your video appears on the Instagram home screen, as shown in Figure 7-7.

FIGURE 7-7:
The video plays
on the home
screen.

The video starts playing as soon as you view it and will play continuously every time you view the post. The video plays without sound, but you can turn on the sound by tapping the video icon in the lower-left corner of the video.

Uploading a Stored Video

It's easy to upload a video that you've already recorded and stored on your iPhone, iPad, or Android smartphone or tablet. Simply follow these steps:

1. **Tap the plus (+) icon at the bottom of the Instagram feed screen.**

2. **If the Library screen is not displayed, tap Library.**

3. **Select the video you want to upload by tapping its thumbnail image in the Camera Roll or Gallery screen, as shown in Figure 7-8.**

   The video plays continuously in the viewer. Stop playback by tapping anywhere in the viewer.

   TIP

   Instagram automatically crops your video to the size of the viewer, but you can resize the video to its original size by tapping the resize icon (labeled in Figure 7-8).

4. **(Optional) Apply a filter, change the cover frame, and trim your video.**

   These tasks are described in the "Improving Your Video" section, earlier in this chapter.

5. **Tap Next.**

6. **(Optional) Add a caption and a location, specify other social networks where you want to share your video, and turn commenting on or off.**

   These tasks are the same for photos and videos. For details, see the section on enriching photos in Chapter 6.

Resize icon

FIGURE 7-8:
The selected
video
thumbnail
image is faded
so you know
it's the video
playing in the
viewer.

Cancel   All Photos ⌄   Next

0:03   0:06   0:03

0:04   0:20   0:36   0:14

Library   Photo   Video

Uploading Multiple Videos from an iPhone or iPad

If you've already taken videos with your iPhone or iPad and saved them to your Camera Roll, you can upload them to a single Instagram video and share it with your followers. Sorry, Android users; this feature isn't available on Android smartphones yet.

Follow these steps to upload multiple clips into one Instagram video:

1. **Tap the plus (+) icon on the Instagram feed screen.**

2. **If the Library screen isn't displayed, tap Library.**

3. **Select the first video you want to upload by tapping its thumbnail image in the Camera Roll screen. Then tap Next.**

    The Filter screen appears.

4. **Tap Trim, at the bottom of the screen.**

    The Trim screen appears, and your selected video plays in the viewer, as shown in Figure 7-9.

5. **Tap the plus (+) icon, and then tap the thumbnail for the video that you want to add to the first video.**

    The selected video now sports a 2, which tells you that this is the second clip that will appear in the video. This second clip plays continuously in the viewer; to stop playing, tap anywhere in the viewer.

6. **Repeat Step 5 until you've added all the video clips you want.**

    As you add each clip, Instagram assigns it a number indicating its order in the video.

7. **Tap Done.**

    The Trim screen appears, with thumbnails of your video clips in the order in which they will appear in the video. You can add more clips at this point, if you want. (Tap the plus [+] icon, tap the clip's thumbnail, and then tap Done.)

    The viewer displays all the clips playing continuously so you can see how they'll appear to your followers. To stop video playback, tap anywhere in the viewer.

WARNING

If you add a clip that puts your video over the 60-second limit, Instagram will automatically trim the last clip so that your entire video lasts for exactly 60 seconds.

FIGURE 7-9:
The plus (+)
icon appears
to the right
of the video
thumbnail
image.

8. **(Optional) To remove a clip from your video:**

   a. *Tap and hold down on the clip's thumbnail.* The viewer is replaced by
   an X inside a box.

   b. *Drag the thumbnail to the X.*

9. **(Optional) Apply a filter or change the cover or both.**

These tasks are described in the "Improving Your Video" section, earlier in the chapter.

10. **Tap Next.**

The New Post screen appears.

11. **(Optional) Type a caption, add a location, share your photo on other social networks, and turn commenting on or off.**

For more information, read the section on enriching photos in Chapter 6. All the information there applies also not only to photos but also to videos, with the exception of tagging people. (You can't tag people in a video.)

REMEMBER

When you upload a video with multiple clips, you can't change the orientation of the clips to landscape or portrait. Each clip appears in its original orientation, so keep that in mind when you want to create a video with multiple clips.

Chapter **8**

Personalizing Your Post

Earlier in this book, we show you how to add content to Instagram in the form of both photos and videos. In this chapter, we show you how to use the captions and additional tagging features to boost that content for even better exposure and engagement.

This chapter helps you craft captions that people are more likely to read and respond to, while also showing you how to tag people, places, and add hashtags for more exposure and growth.

Determining How Long Your Captions Should Be

A caption adds context to your post and lets people know what they're seeing. If you don't add a caption, your viewers may be confused, and that reflects poorly on your content. For example, if you post a selfie, but you don't tell viewers why you posted it or what the backstory is to that image, they may think you're just self-ish and posting photos of yourself. Or, if you just a post a photo of a flower with no context, they may think it's pretty, but it won't generate a lot of dialog. When you leave out a caption, the viewer doesn't know what you're doing and may not engage with your post, and you'll be left wondering why you're not getting any attention.

After you create a post and edit your photo or videos, you add the caption in the New Post screen. Begin typing in the section where it says "Write a caption" (see Figure 8-1).

FIGURE 8-1:
You can add the caption to your post on the New Post screen after uploading and editing a post, but before you publish it.

TIP

How much text should be in your caption? It's generally a good idea to communicate too much rather than too little, so consider writing one to three short paragraphs. Simple one liners can work for some people on Instagram if they're very clever and creative.

Due to the formatting and layout on Instagram, a paragraph may actually be a single sentence — and that's okay! It's better to have your content well spaced and easy to read than trying to read one very long paragraph. Your three short paragraphs may only be a handful of sentences, or they may be longer, descriptive paragraphs.

We should also point out that you are not limited to just three paragraphs! You can actually write a significant amount of content on your Instagram captions. Instagram allows you 2,200 characters for a caption. When you hit that limit, you aren't able to write any more content.

Some accounts choose to use Instagram as a micro-blog, writing longer captions to add more value and information for their audiences. Figure 8-2 shows an example of both a short caption and a long caption. Use whatever works for you!

FIGURE 8-2: An example of a short caption and a long caption that capture the attention of the audience in both cases.

Formatting Your Caption

A caption without formatting becomes one very long, run-on paragraph that can be hard to read. To avoid this, use spacing, emojis, and formatting tricks to break up the content for more visual appeal. Figure 8-3 shows an example from @tanya.plummer.health with spacing and emojis to make it easier to read and follow.

FIGURE 8-3: Good formatting on Instagram allows your content to be easily read and stands out as visually appealing.

Getting spacing to work on Instagram can be incredibly frustrating if you don't know this trick! Make sure that when you end your paragraph, there is no space after the last character. Most keyboards default a space after a word or punctuation mark, but that simple space will remove the formatting to drop a line and create a new paragraph. Backspace right up to the last character to avoid this issue.

Additionally, you can only have one special character as your last character. So, you can have a period or a question mark at the end of a paragraph, but you can't have a question mark and an exclamation point together, or the formatting won't work. The same thing applies to emojis. Unfortunately, you can't have an emoji as the last character on the paragraph or the formatting won't work.

Android users seem to have an easier time formatting their captions directly within the Instagram app and retaining the spacing. For iPhone users, it's often recommended that you write your captions in the Notes app on the device and then copy and paste that caption into the Instagram post for better formatting options.

Instagram truncates all captions after two or three lines of text. If there's more text to read, a "more" button appears at the end of the truncated text. To read the entire caption, you have to tap the "more" button.

Make sure that the first few lines are enticing enough that your viewer will want to tap or click the "more" button to read your entire caption. This first sentence of your caption should be captivating like a great title, or bold with emojis or capital letters. It should make a statement or ask a question. You want to entice the viewer to read more!

Including Calls to Action in Your Caption

Instagram is a visual platform, and you can't leave a clickable link in a post description, so if you want your audience to take action, you have to give them a clear call to action (CTA) in the post caption.

In Chapter 3, we show you how to set up your profile and decide if you want to include a URL in that section. If you want to review that information again, bookmark this page and turn back to Chapter 3.

In order to make CTAs effective on Instagram, you want to keep them as simple as possible. They should be one-step actions. The most commonly used one is "Click the link in my bio." But you could also use actions like: "Tag a friend in the comments below" or "Send me an email for more information."

The key is to keep the CTA simple to follow. It should be designed to reward the viewer by providing him some sort of value. He may learn something by reading an article you linked to on a website, or get a free product if he clicks the link, or be able to enter a contest by posting a photo and tagging you.

Calls to action are most commonly reserved for business accounts that want their audiences to follow through on an action for a reward. However, personal accounts may still use them if they want to drive traffic to a website. Maybe you want people to go to your YouTube channel or Flickr account and you have that link in your bio. A CTA would direct viewers to watch the full video by clicking the link in your bio.

Tagging People in Your Posts

After you've written your caption, you can still add more components to your post by adding tags to the post.

For example, you can tag another person's Instagram account. From the New Post screen where you type your caption, you see a Tag People option. Tap that and follow these steps to tag someone in the post (see Figure 8-4):

1. **After you tap Tag People, the next screen allows you to tap anywhere on the image to select a person.**

   In most instances, you want to tap the actual person or area of the image where that person or brand appears in the image.

2. **In the Search bar at the top of the screen, type the name or username of the account you want to tag.**

3. **Select the account from the list of options.**

4. **Add more accounts if appropriate.**

5. **Tap the check mark or Done button when you're finished tagging.**

When you're all done, you'll see the username of the person tagged listed in the section for "Tag People." If you've tagged multiple people, it will say "[number] people."

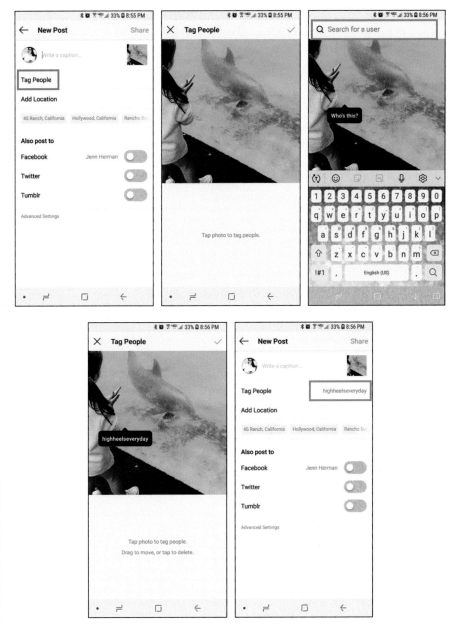

FIGURE 8-4:
To tag someone in your Instagram post, tap Tag People and follow the steps to search for and add that account to your post.

WARNING

You should only tag people or accounts that are actually in the image. For example, if your friend is in the photo, you can tag her. If, in the photo, you're holding a coffee cup from Starbucks, you can tag @Starbucks in your post. But don't tag @ Starbucks if the photo was taken in your backyard and you're not holding a Starbucks cup — that's just considered spam.

Adding Locations to Your Posts

Similar to tagging other accounts in your Instagram post, you can also tag a location. In the New Post screen, below where you tag people, there is the option to Add Location (see Figure 8-5). You usually see locations directly related to where you are at the time of upload listed there as well.

Why would you want to add a location? Sometimes you just want to tell people where you were, and adding the location will provide that information. Adding a location can also help your content get exposed to more people as well. If your account is public, and you add a location, your post may show up in search results for that location.

If you added a local restaurant to your post, and someone else is looking for information on Instagram about that restaurant, she might see your post in that list of results.

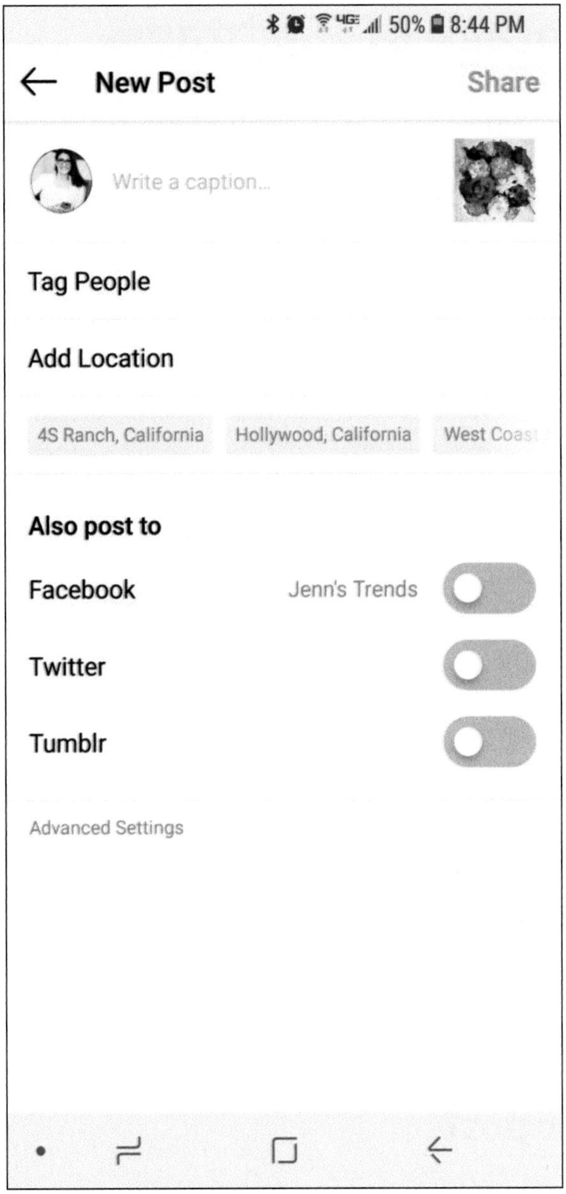

FIGURE 8-5:
Use the Add Location option during the upload process to add more exposure to your posts.

You can also tag broader locations like a city name if you don't want to be super-specific about your location.

If the location you're looking for isn't in the list of prepopulated options, simply tap in the Add Location field and begin typing the name of the location. A list of available options will appear for you to choose from.

Taking Advantage of Hashtags

Hashtags are the single best way to achieve growth and exposure on the platform. Hashtags always start with the # sign (found on the bottom right of your mobile phone keyboard when typing, or by pressing Shift+3 on a desktop computer keyboard) followed by a word, a phrase, a number, or an emoji with no spaces, such as #sundayvibes or #instamood.

TECHNICAL STUFF

On an iPhone, the # sign is on the lower right of the mobile keyboard *only* when using the Instagram app (and some other social media apps like Twitter). If you're writing your captions in the Notes app on your phone, you'll need to tap 123 on your keyboard and then #+= to access the # sign in the special characters keyboard.

After you add a hashtag to your caption or comment, the hashtag becomes a searchable link that takes you to a page of all the posts using that hashtag (a hashtag hub) when tapped.

Figure 8-6 shows the hashtag hub for #bicyclebuiltfortwo.

Hashtags are added to a hashtag hub chronologically, based on when the photo was posted, not when the hashtag posts. Going back days later and adding hashtags to a post will not bump your post back up in the hashtag hub.

People search hashtags to find content for a variety of reasons, such as to find a product, to learn how to do something, to follow a brand, or even to watch videos of a certain theme.

WARNING

If you have a private account, only users who are your approved followers will see your posts, even with a hashtag. If you're trying to get a wider audience, set your account to public so anyone can search for your content via hashtags.

Knowing where to place hashtags in your post

Hashtags can be added to the caption itself before you upload the post to Instagram. Or you can upload your post and add the hashtags to a comment on the post.

There is no functional difference between placing your hashtags in the caption or in the comments. The method you should use is a matter of personal preference. Both options allow your content to appear in hashtag hubs.

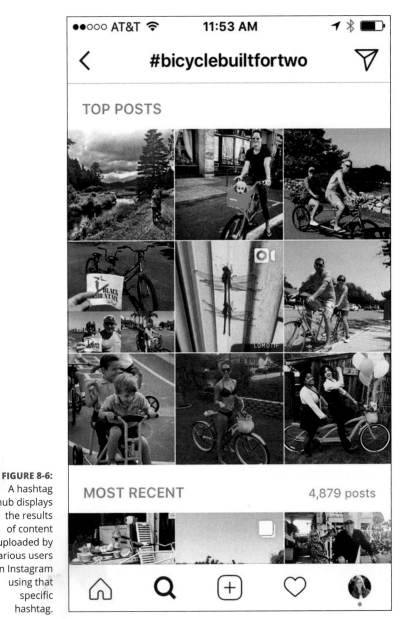

FIGURE 8-6:
A hashtag
hub displays
the results
of content
uploaded by
various users
on Instagram
using that
specific
hashtag.

All hashtag results pages on Instagram are algorithmically sorted. This means that not everyone will see the same results when they look at a hashtag gallery or hub. One user may see slightly different results and you may not even see your own post in a hashtag hub that you used on your post. This doesn't mean others won't see your content! But it's not a guarantee that everyone looking at that gallery will see your post.

Identifying how many hashtags is ideal

If you're familiar with using hashtags on Facebook or Twitter, you're probably used to putting a couple of hashtags directly in your post. On Instagram, however, you can use up to 30 hashtags in a caption or in a comment.

You can use up to 30 hashtags for viable search. But you can use more than that in your content — they simply won't be searchable after the 30th hashtag. For example, you may post 25 hashtags in your post caption and one of your friends may come and post 7 hashtags in a comment on your post. Your post would appear in your 25 listed hashtags and the first 5 of your friend's, but not in the remaining 2 hashtags your friend posted in your comment.

REMEMBER

Hashtags are a use-them-or-lose-them mentality. If you don't use them, there's no way you'll appear in those searches. If you do use them, you have a good chance of appearing in those searches. If you're looking to expand your reach and have more people find your content, then you'll want to use as many hashtags as possible, up to that limit of 30.

Finding the right hashtags for you

There are endless hashtags available to use or create! So, how do you know which ones are right for you? It's important that you find the right ones for you and the ones that are relevant to your content.

If you have a theme or style for your content, you can use hashtags related to that. For example, if you're a stay-at-home mom, you may want to use hashtags related to #MomLife and #MomSoHard.

You can also use hashtags related to your content itself. For example, if the image is of a pool at the hotel you're staying at, you can use hashtags like #Pool or #SummerVacation or #Poolside or #HotelLiving.

Additionally, when it comes to picking your hashtags, just like students in high school, some hashtags can be popular and some not so popular. You can view any hashtag by searching it in Instagram to see how many posts are associated with it. Follow these steps:

1. **Tap the Search menu (the magnifying glass icon at the bottom navigation bar).**

2. **Tap on the Search bar.**

3. **Tap the Tags tab.**

4. **Start typing the hashtag topic.**

5. **Select the topic to review the results.**

   You're taken to the hashtag hub (see Figure 8-7).

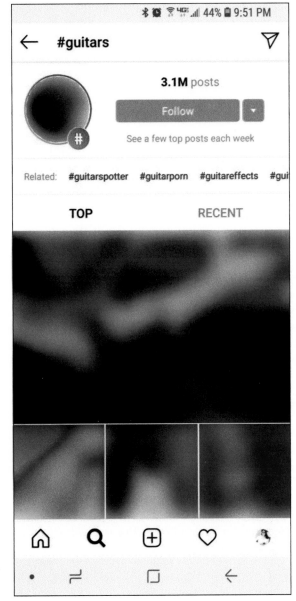

FIGURE 8-7: A hashtag hub displays the results of content uploaded by various users on Instagram using that specific hashtag.

In addition to the hashtag you searched for, Instagram will show you a list of other hashtags related to that one you chose. You can tap through to any of those to see that content. And you can use these recommendations to find new hashtags to use, related to the content you're sharing.

The hashtag results are divided into two tabs — one for top posts and one for recent posts. The top posts are sorted algorithmically for your preference, whereas the recent posts are sorted chronologically with the most recent post at the top of the feed. Even though this content is chronological, there is still some algorithmic determination of what will appear in this hub.

Using really popular hashtags — those with over a million posts associated with them — can be perceived as great exposure, but in reality they don't usually yield quality results. This content gets replaced incredibly fast by millions of other posts being uploaded as well. You may see some additional likes on your post by using these hashtags, but they aren't often your ideal audience, and they're often automated tools that are scouring that hashtag, rather than real people looking to connect with your content.

WARNING

You should also be wary of some "blocked" or "banned" hashtags. Any hashtags that reference sexual activity or body parts are generally blocked and don't normally belong on a post anyway. Using hashtags like this may get your account flagged for inappropriate activity.

However, you may also come across generic hashtags like #iphone that don't produce any results. And during heavy peak post times like #July4th, you often won't see any content on those hashtags either. Instagram will put a block on these hashtags simply because they're too popular and they have too much content associated with them. Using these hashtags won't get you flagged or punished. Your content just won't appear in those searches — nor will anyone else's!

Saving hashtags for repeated use

When you've figured out which hashtags you want to use on your content, you may find that there are some you'll want to use on more posts in the future. Typing those same hashtags over and over again can get cumbersome!

TIP

Android users can take advantage of predictive text, which recalls the series of hashtags you used if you previously listed a number of hashtags. As you begin typing one hashtag, the Android predictive text will show you the next one you commonly use (see Figure 8-8).

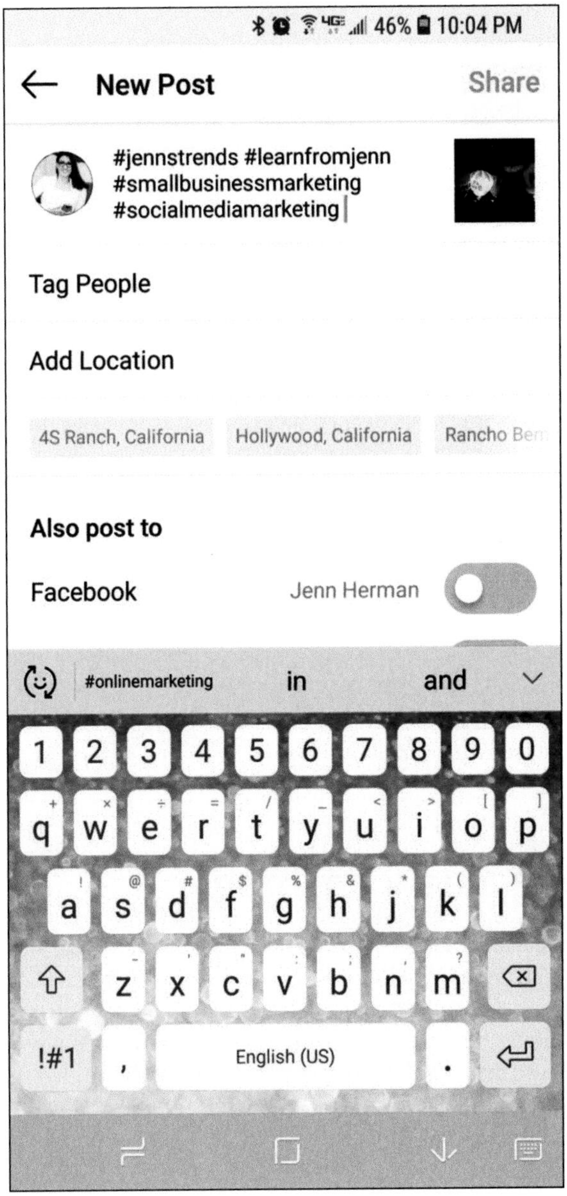

FIGURE 8-8: Android devices utilize predictive text to easily select common hashtags.

If you don't want to rely on predictive text, or if you use an Apple device, there are a few other options you can utilize to easily store and access your common hashtags:

>> **Notes:** The Notes app is preloaded on iPhones, and similar apps like ColorNote or Evernote are available for download on Android phones. Create a new note for different categories or themes, and then list up to

30 hashtags, as shown in Figure 8-9 (left). Before you tap Share on your post, go over to your note and copy the desired hashtags. Tap Share and open a comment to paste the hashtags.

» **Email:** Another easy solution is to email yourself lists of hashtags. Simply open a new email, use the hashtag category in the Subject line, and then type up to 30 hashtags, as shown in Figure 8-9 (middle). Create several emails with different hashtag lists, and then store them in a special email folder to retrieve and cut and paste quickly and easily.

» **Tailwind:** A complete all-in-one solution, the Tailwind app, shown in Figure 8-9 (right), offers hashtag saving, plus content management for Instagram and Pinterest. You can upload your content, schedule it, get hashtag suggestions, save hashtag lists for later, and measure analytics. Unlike the Notes app or email, Tailwind is not free and you'll have to pay a monthly fee for the service.

FIGURE 8-9:
Store hashtags
in a notes
app (left), an
email message
(middle), or the
Tailwind app
(right).

	A	B	C	D
1	**Competitor Hashtags**			
2	**Competitor**	**Category**	**Hashtags**	**High Likes**
3	Bob's Grocery	Vegetables	#summersbest #locallygrown #organic #organicveggies #pesticidefree #tomatoes #broccoli #lettuce	Y
4				
5				

Creating a new hashtag

Anyone can use any hashtag! No one owns any one hashtag, and anyone can create any hashtag phrase they want.

You'll commonly see popular hashtags like #VacationMode or #tbt (throwback Thursday) or #Love or #TheStruggleIsReal. But you may also see a brand or a person use a hashtag like #IWouldntDoItIfIDidntWantTo. This is just a phrase that they would normally use in a sentence, but they turn it into a hashtag.

Similarly, you can create any hashtag you want! You can have one for your wedding guests to use, incorporating your names or the date of the wedding. You can create a hashtag related to your company name or nickname from college. Simply string those words together, and — boom! — you've got a hashtag.

REMEMBER

You don't own the hashtags you create, so if you're creating a hashtag for, say, your wedding, you may want to start by searching for the hashtag you have in mind to see if anyone else is using it already. Instead of #JoniLovesChachi, you might want to go with something more specific like #JoniChachiWedding2020. Does that mean someone won't come along and use your more specific hashtag? Nope. But it will reduce the chances.

If your hashtag is something really long, you may want to consider an acronym. For example, instead of #OutfitOfTheDay, you'll often see #ootd on fashion posts.

And, finally, be careful to see how your hashtag reads as one long run on phrase. Just because you know what it's supposed to say, doesn't mean others will know what it says. Take this one for example: It should read Susan Album Party, but as a hashtag #susanalbumparty, you may read "Su's anal bum party" — and yes, this is a REAL example that happened to Susan Boyle from *Britain's Got Talent.* So, be careful when you're creating new hashtags!

3

Connecting with a Community on Instagram

IN THIS PART . . .

Figure out who you should connect with and follow.

Uncover the etiquette of interacting with others on Instagram.

Dive into Instagram Direct to connect personally with other people.

Chapter **9**

Finding People to Follow

G rowing your Instagram following is one of the hottest topics on Instagram. If you've spent any time there, surely you've encountered sales pitches to buy followers or purchase a crazy software program to increase likes and follows. Don't do it. Yes, it's impressive having a big following, especially when starting your account. However, any followers you buy are likely fake accounts or people who would never interact with you.

In this chapter, you discover how to find followers the right way. First, you learn how Instagram can access the contact list on your phone to find more followers. Next, you discover ways to explore and search for followers in the Instagram app. After you start getting followers, find out who is worth following back and when it's best not to bother. Finally, learn how to develop a tribe — an online family that helps and supports you along the way as you grow your account.

Where Are My Peeps?

If you're new to Instagram, you may be wondering where to start. Instagram is happy to help you make connections. You can find people in a few different ways, as you discover in this section.

Syncing your contact list

Instagram can connect you with the contacts stored on your phone or tablet. After you activate this feature, your contacts are periodically synced with Instagram's servers. Instagram does not follow anyone on your behalf, and you can disconnect your contacts at any time so that Instagram can't access them.

WARNING

This feature may be best as a one-and-done in the beginning versus a constant connection for privacy purposes.

To connect your contacts, follow these steps:

1. **Go to your Instagram profile page by tapping your photo at the bottom right of your phone's screen.**

2. **Tap the three lines (and possibly a red number) at the top right.**

3. **Tap the Settings link.**

   The next screen offers you a variety of account settings to choose from.

4. **Tap Account.**

5. **To proceed, scroll down and tap Contacts Syncing.**

   The next screen offers you the ability to have Instagram periodically sync and store your contacts on Instagram's servers. Instagram will not auto-follow them for you; you can pick which contacts to follow.

6. **Slide the tab at the top right so it turns blue to allow syncing.**

7. **Tap the back arrow at the top left of the screen twice to get back to the main Settings menu.**

8. **Tap Follow and Invite Friends and then tap Follow Contacts.**

9. **Tap Follow next to the names of the people you would like to follow, as shown in Figure 9-1.**

If you change your mind at some point and want to disallow Instagram's access to your contacts, tap the three lines on your profile page, tap Settings, tap Accounts, and then tap Contacts Syncing. Tap the Connect Contacts tab to return it to white, which terminates Instagram's access.

TIP

Some of your friends may have set their accounts to private. In this case, you see Requested after you tap Follow. They need to approve you before you can view their profile and posts.

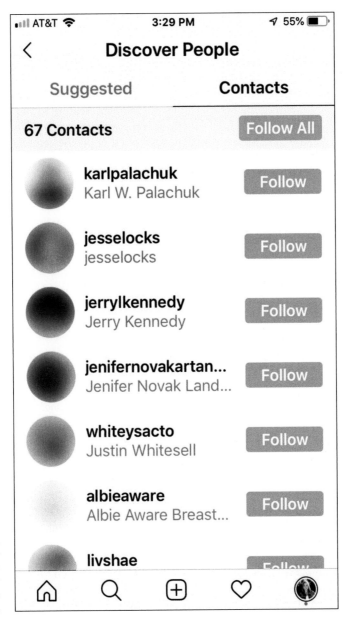

Finding New Friends

Now that you've found your phone contacts on Instagram, it's time to follow the
people who you might have a genuine interest in based on the content they provide. Instagram offers several options for exploring, searching, and suggesting
new followers to you.

Exploring the Explore function

Instagram loves growth. The more people you engage with, the more users they get. And to keep those people, Instagram offers many ways to engage with them. One way is through the Explore page. The Explore page offers photo, graphic, and video posts that Instagram thinks might be interesting to you. No one knows the exact algorithm, but they usually present a variety of posts that have received at least 1,000 likes mixed in with posts that other people you follow have liked.

Here's how to use the Explore page:

1. **Tap the magnifying glass at the bottom of any screen.**

   Several photos, videos, and stories are presented, as shown in Figure 9-2.

   If you're trying to get your posts displayed on the Explore page, note that the Instagram algorithm rarely selects graphics such as charts or infographs. It tends to favor photos or videos.

2. **Tap any photo or video that interests you.**

   Now you can scroll down to see that post and other similar posts.

3. **Tap the Instagram username at the top of any post that interests you.**

4. **Look around the page. If you like what you see:**

   a. *Like one or more photos: Double-tap each individual photo or tap the heart icon.*

   b. *Leave a comment: Tap the photo, and then tap the comment bubble below the photo. Enter your text, and tap the blue Post link.*

   c. *To follow a user: Tap the blue Follow button at the top of the user's profile page.*

   After you follow this page, Instagram offers several other accounts that it thinks you'd enjoy following. We detail this method of finding accounts to follow in the "Checking out who Instagram suggests for you" section, later in this chapter.

This method of finding followers is time consuming. Also, popular accounts may not be looking to follow many new people, so there's no guarantee that you'll get a reciprocal follow. However, it's always worth a shot and is a nice addition to your follower strategy.

FIGURE 9-2:
The Explore page displays stories, videos, and posts you might like.

Searching the Search feature

Another great way to find new accounts to follow is through searching Instagram. Instagram offers four ways to search: Top, Accounts, Tags, and Places.

To try out the Search feature, tap the magnifying glass on any page. The Explore page appears, as described in the preceding section. Tap the Search field at the top of the page; you see Top, Accounts, Tags, and Places are now available for your choosing, as shown in Figure 9-3. (Android users will see icons under the Search bar.)

The *Top feature* shows you accounts that you interact with often, followed by accounts you most recently interacted with. To find new followers, search for a topic or a keyword that interests you. For instance, typing **healthy eating** presents several accounts that have *healthy* and *eating* in their usernames or in their profile titles. Scroll through those that are interesting, and follow those you like!

The *Accounts feature* can be used in a similar manner to the Top feature, but you may also choose to search by someone's name. If you have a list, try searching for people by name. For those that pop up, scroll through to their accounts and follow them if they seem to be active. Personal accounts are more likely to be private, so you'll need to request access.

The *Tags feature* allows you to search by hashtag. Start simply by choosing your interest and see what appears. For example, if you're a dog trainer, start with #dogtraining. If you get too many results to be useful, add your city or state, such as #dogtrainingsacramento. Scroll through the accounts and tap the ones that call out to you. Then follow the ones that seem active and engaging.

The *Places feature* enables you to search by location. If you'd like to find people or businesses near you, the easiest way to start is to tap Near Current Location. Several nearby locations pop up for your choosing. Tap a location near you, and all the posts that marked that location on their post pop up. Tap some posts that catch your eye, and follow the ones you like.

REMEMBER

On all the accounts you follow, make sure to like several posts and leave a meaningful comment or two (not just an emoji). This technique greatly increases the odds that the account will follow you back.

Letting Instagram suggest users to you

Instagram is on a mission to grow. Therefore, its main goal is making its users happy by making their accounts grow. When you follow someone, an algorithm kicks in and displays other similar accounts that you may like following. In Figure 9-4, we decide to follow @elevateitnow, a marketing and creative agency. Instagram then presents many other social-media-marketing business accounts, and we can decide whether to follow them.

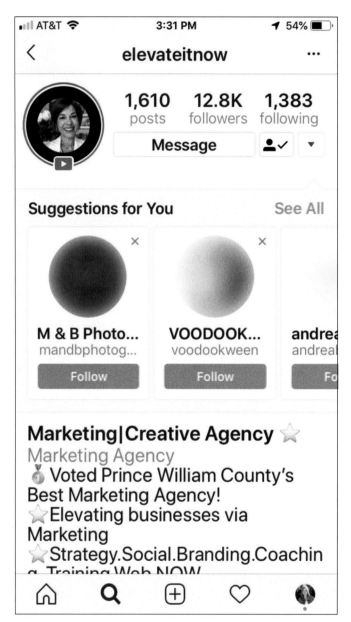

FIGURE 9-4:
After you follow an account, Instagram presents similar accounts you might like.

Deciding Whom to Follow Back

After you've employed the techniques described previously in this chapter, you'll begin to get more followers. It's a great feeling to see that number go up on your profile page. Your next decision is whether to follow those accounts back if you weren't already following them. In this section, you discover how to view your followers and decide who is best to follow back.

Viewing and following your followers

So, you're starting to see more followers on your account. Now it's time to learn a simple method to follow them back. You're not required or even expected to follow someone back, but searching through your followers often yields some great finds! New followers appear in your notifications, but if you don't check your notifications often, it's worth checking out your follower list every few days to see whom you might want to follow back.

Checking your follower list is easy:

1. **Go to your profile page and click the number above *followers*.**

   All of your followers appear, with the most recent followers at the top. As shown in Figure 9-5, followers you haven't followed back have a blue Follow button to the right that you can tap to follow. If you're already following them, it says Following.

2. **Unless you recognize the username, click that name to view the user's profile page.**

3. **If you think that the user is someone you'd like to follow, click the blue Follow button on his or her profile page. Otherwise, use the arrow on the top left of the page to go back to your follower list and try again.**

4. **Like a few posts and leave a meaningful comment.**

   In this way, the follower is more likely to engage with you in the future.

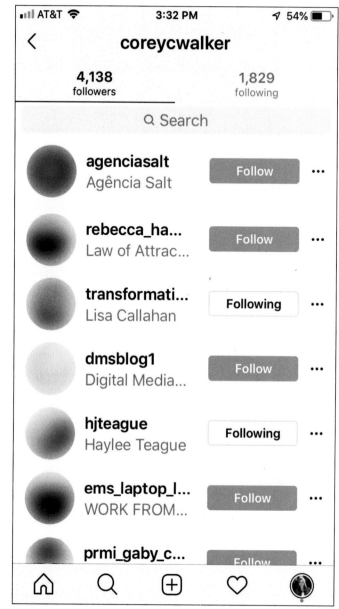

FIGURE 9-5:
Followers you haven't followed back have a blue Follow button to the right.

Reciprocating a follow or not

Now that you know a simple method for following back, the question is whether the account is worthy of following back. Some accounts have a habit of following accounts but then unfollowing them if they didn't follow back. You might see your numbers rise by 25, just to fall back by 22 the next day. It's a frustrating game that you should avoid.

Do follow back the following:

>> Accounts of friends, local businesses, and other people you know and like in real life (or as the kids say, "IRL").

>> Accounts of businesses you do business with or other related associates.

>> Accounts that provide content inspiration.

>> Accounts of people you have met on other networks, such as Facebook, Twitter, or LinkedIn.

>> Accounts that you find personally interesting and satisfying to view and interact with.

Don't follow back:

>> Everyone who follows you because you feel some sort of obligation.

>> Spammy accounts whose profile probably lists only a few posts and who often sell follower services.

>> Accounts that use bots to leave automated comments. (Nothing is worse than having someone write "Love it!" when you post that your dog just died.)

>> Accounts that contain content you have no interest in personally or professionally.

>> Accounts that follow you for a few days, then unfollow you, and then follow you again a week later. They often use the #follow4follow hashtag. Stay away!

TIP

You may discover your own rules for following accounts. Keep in mind that it's okay to unfollow people, too. Maybe they stopped posting, or their content no longer interests you. Clean up your feed every so often to ensure that you're viewing the best content for you.

Finding Your Tribe

If you compare all the popular social networks — Facebook, Twitter, LinkedIn, Snapchat, and Instagram — the one that takes the cake on community engagement is Instagram. This section explains how to use hashtags influencers, interaction, and Instagram pods to find your ultimate Insta-tribe!

Finding or creating a community you vibe with

If you've been on Instagram for a while, you've probably seen posts talking about community and finding your tribe. But what does that mean? A *community,* or *tribe,* is a supportive group of people talking about and interacting with you on Instagram. They offer advice, give a heads up about changes on Instagram, provide support, and leave comments that can help boost your posts.

Your first step is finding a community that fits with your interests. An easy way to do this is through hashtags. If you like cats, for example, searching #cats yields several other relevant hashtags such as #catsofinstagram, #catstagram, #catscatscats, #catsagram, #catsoftheday, and #fluffycat.

All of these hashtags are large, so by selecting one and creating a new search (as shown in Figure 9-6), you can find more specific hashtags, such as #blueeyedcats, #tabbycat, and #sweetcat. Follow these niche accounts and share your mutual interest of whatever you like most by commenting and liking their posts.

While you're commenting on their posts, you'll probably start seeing other people showing up frequently on the same accounts. Follow, like, and comment on those accounts, too, and before you know it, your tribe is developing!

To further solidify your relationship, send them quick direct messages (DMs) to introduce yourself. (DMs are covered in Chapter 11.) Let the relationship flow naturally, and tell them how much you enjoy the conversations you've had.

You may also find your tribe completely away from Instagram. For example, Facebook groups catering to niche markets often have Instagram tribes that coincide with the group. They may have their own unique hashtags to easily identify them on Instagram. You may also discover them by following the admin of the group and seeing the same people interacting on Instagram.

Not finding the tribe you're seeking? Start your own! Run a contest or campaign asking people to submit a photo that goes with your hashtag. For example, if you're a graphic designer, you could start a challenge using #graphicdesignotd, where designers post what they worked on that day. People love challenges like this because it provides post inspiration and an excuse to show off their work! Keep checking the hashtag for submissions, and thank everyone for participating. Then follow them, and keep coming back regularly, commenting and liking their posts. All of a sudden, a tribe is forming!

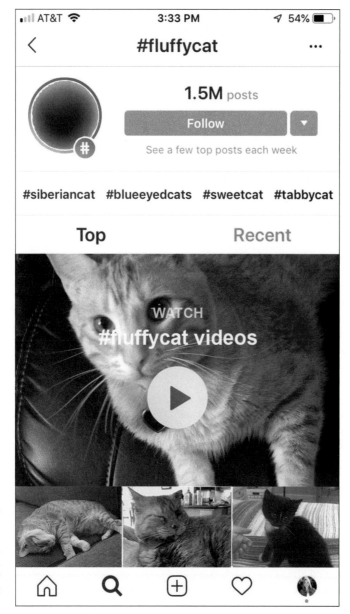

FIGURE 9-6:
Search
hashtags to
see Instagram's
suggestions
of other
more specific
hashtags.

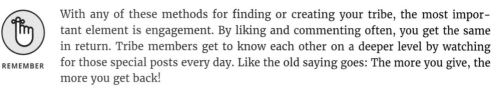

REMEMBER

With any of these methods for finding or creating your tribe, the most important element is engagement. By liking and commenting often, you get the same in return. Tribe members get to know each other on a deeper level by watching for those special posts every day. Like the old saying goes: The more you give, the more you get back!

Deciding whether Instagram pods are beneficial

An Instagram *pod* is a group of 10 to 20 accounts that usually have something in common. Maybe they're all photographers, or DIY crafters, or mommy bloggers. They all have the main goal of getting more engagement.

This is how a pod works:

>> Instagrammers recruit several other accounts via Instagram DM or a Facebook group. (See Chapter 11 for details on direct messaging.)

>> The people in the pod post their content on Instagram, and then share that post via a group DM set up for the pod members, as shown in Figure 9-7.

>> Pod members then click through to the person's Instagram account, liking and commenting on the post as soon as possible to help boost the post in Instagram's algorithm. Likes and comments within the first hour of a post do the most work to get a post shown more often in Instagram feeds.

>> Pod members have a responsibility to engage as often and as quickly as possible on other pod members' posts to boost engagement. Some people find the responsibility overwhelming, particularly if members of the pod post several times a day.

Does it work? Is it worth the time? The data isn't clear. If you have an active group, the comments should help your engagement and likes somewhat. However, participating in a pod can be a huge time commitment and can leave you feeling tethered to your phone waiting for the next post.

Often people join a pod, use it for a while, form a few good friendships, and then break up at some point due to the time commitment. You may find your Insta-tribe during this process and still interact with the same accounts from your pod after the breakup but without the pressure of commenting on demand.

TIP

If you'd like to try a pod, start small, with no more than 15 accounts. If you like the results and can keep up, try a larger one. However, your pod should never detract from your larger follower group. If you find that you have time to comment on only the same few accounts in your pod, it's best to let the pod go and get back to interacting with your followers as a whole.

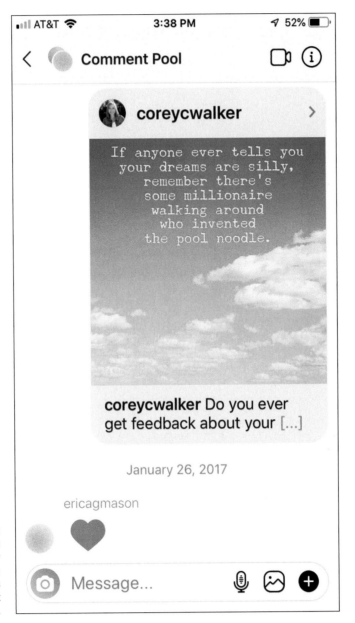

FIGURE 9-7:
Pod members share their posts with other members via direct message.

Chapter **10**

Interacting with Other Instagrammers

Half the fun of Instagram is in interacting with the people who connect with you and your posts. In this chapter, we explain how to interact with other content by liking and commenting on other people's posts. We also explain how to respond to people's comments on your own posts and how to report less-than-honorable comments.

Interacting with the Posts in Your Feed

Your home feed is what you see when you tap the house icon from the bottom navigation bar. This feed is full of the content from all the people you follow on Instagram.

TECHNICAL STUFF

Instagram employs an algorithm that sorts through all the content created by each person you follow. This content is then re-sorted in your feed, displaying the content you're most likely to engage with near the top of your feed. There are multiple components that impact the algorithm, including how often you interact with an account's content, the type of content you typically interact with, the time you spend on Instagram, and how popular a piece of content is with other users.

Below each photo or video on Instagram are three icons: the heart, the speech bubble, and the paper airplane (see Figure 10-1). Here's what each of those icons is for:

>> **Heart:** Tap the heart icon to like a post. After you've liked a post, the heart turns red.

A shortcut for liking a post is to double-tap the photo or video. If the post is a carousel (in which multiple photos or videos are in one post), double-tapping any image or video will assign the "like" to the entire post, not the individual image on which you tapped.

>> **Speech bubble:** Tap the speech bubble to leave a comment on the post. The comment screen opens; here, you can read the original caption and see all other comments on the post. You see your cursor flashing in the comment box where it says, "Add a comment." Type your comment in this area and tap Post when you're done.

You don't have any formatting options on comments so everything will be one long paragraph. You also can't add images, GIFs, or other items to comments. You can use emojis, however.

>> **Paper airplane:** Tap the paper airplane to share the post with someone else. You can type a message to be included with the post you share. Then select the person you want to send it to from the list of names. If you follow a lot of people, you can use the Search bar to find the specific person you want to send it to. That person will receive the message as a direct message where he or she can then view the original post.

If someone has her account set to private, the photo can only be shared to other people that follow her. If you share it to someone who is not following her, that person won't be able to see the post.

Additional sharing methods allow you to share a link from anyone's Instagram post. Tap the three-dot button at the top of a post on Instagram and select Copy Link to save the link to your clipboard. You can then post this link anywhere — in an email, in a direct message, or on social media elsewhere.

Tapping Share Link offers a similar method for sharing the post, but instead of copying the link to your clipboard, you get a list of apps you can select to share the link to.

FIGURE 10-1:
You can use
the three icons
below the
post to like,
comment on,
or share
the post.

Replying to Comments on Your Own Posts

On Instagram, it's considered good etiquette to reply to people who leave comments on your posts. Not every comment warrants a response, but Instagram makes it easy to respond if you want to.

Responding to comments from the Notifications tab

Whenever someone comments on your post, you receive a notification in the Notifications tab, which you can access by tapping the Heart icon in the lower navigation bar on Instagram.

To quickly acknowledge the comment, you can tap the heart below the comment. The heart will turn red and the person who wrote the comment will receive a notification that you "liked" the comment.

You can also quick reply to the comment simply by tapping the Reply button below the comment (see Figure 10-2). This opens the comment response box and keyboard. Type your response and tap Post to send your reply.

TECHNICAL STUFF

Some users may see the comment box as Comment as [username]," as shown in Figure 10-2. Other users may see the comment box as Add a Comment. Different operating systems and different devices sometimes have slightly different features.

In some situations, there may be multiple replies to a thread, or you may be mentioned in someone else's comment. In this case, when you tap the Reply option in your notifications feed, you'll notice that the username of the person you're replying to is listed at the beginning of the comment box. This is to ensure they're mentioned in the reply and they'll get the notification that you replied to their comment.

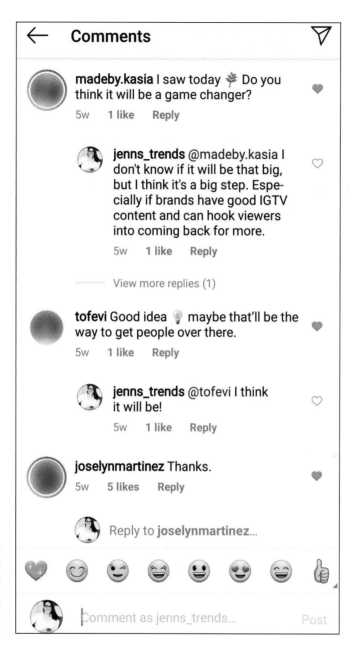

FIGURE 10-2:
Replying to
comments
on your
posts creates
meaningful
conversations.

Responding to comments from the post itself

You can always go to any one of your Instagram posts and tap the comment bubble below the image or video to access all the comments on that post.

Similar to the Notifications tab, you can tap the heart next to the comment to acknowledge the comment with a "like" and the heart will turn red while also sending a notification to the person who posted it. You can tap the Reply option to reply directly to any comment left on your post.

Any replies to the original comment are indented and nested beneath the original comment. This keeps the dialog connected to the original comment so anyone can see that thread of conversation.

TECHNICAL STUFF

If you want to reference someone in a comment, type the at (@) symbol followed directly by the person's username. For example, you would type @jenns_trends to mention author Jenn Herman in an Instagram comment. This ensures she's notified of the reference so she can see and view that comment or conversation.

When you add the @ symbol, a list of names from those you commonly interact with will appear. As you start typing the letters of the person's name or username, more suggestions will appear. You don't need to type the full person's name. When you see them in the suggested list, you can tap on the person's name to select it.

Deciding to delete a comment

You may want to delete a comment from your post. In this section, we show you how to do that.

iPhone and iPad users

If you're using an iPhone or an iPad and you want to delete a comment, find the comment on the post. The swipe the comment to the left to open the comment options. Tap the red trash can option on the right to delete the comment (see Figure 10-3).

WARNING

After you delete a comment, a red bar appears at the top of the comments screen so you can undo the deletion. If you don't tap the bar within five seconds, the comment is deleted permanently.

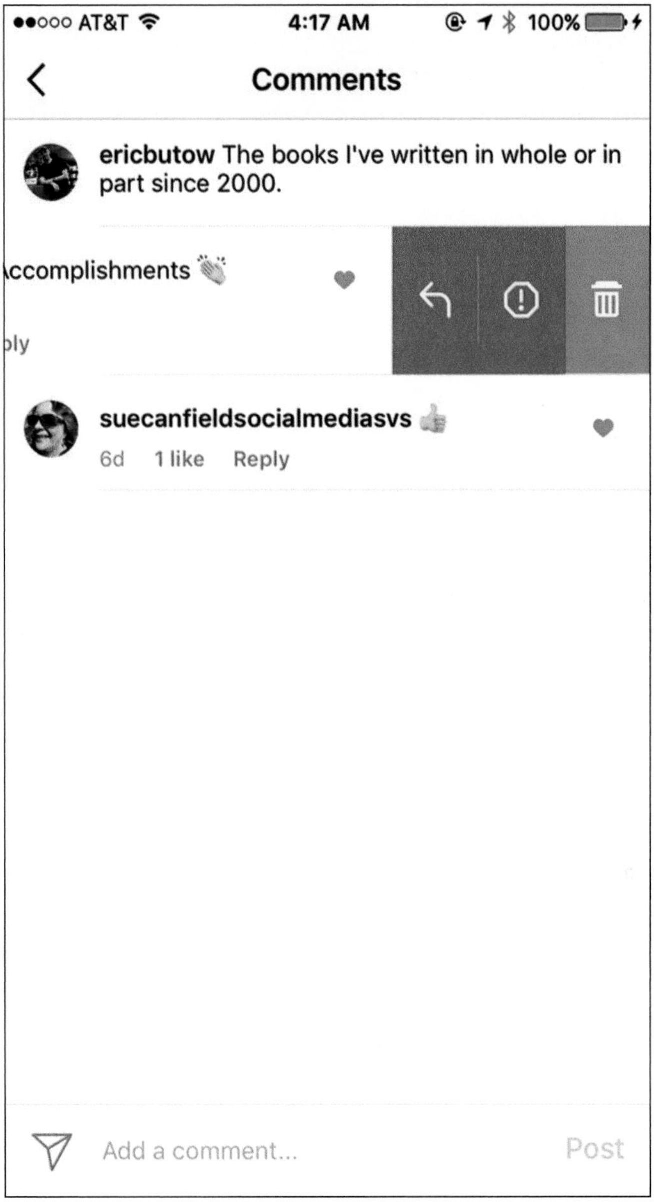

FIGURE 10-3: Deleting a comment on iPhone and iPad.

Android smartphone and tablet users

To delete a comment on an Android device, tap the comment on the post. A blue bar at the top of the screen appears with the exclamation point icon and the trash can icon. Tap the trash can icon to delete the selected comment (see Figure 10-4).

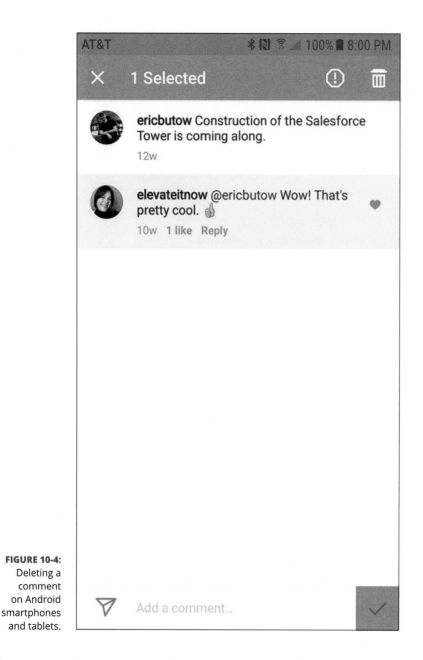

FIGURE 10-4:
Deleting a
comment
on Android
smartphones
and tablets.

If you want to delete more than one comment, you can scroll through the comments and select multiple comments by tapping each one and then tapping the trash can icon to delete all the selected comments.

WARNING

After you delete a comment, a red bar appears at the top of the comments screen so you can undo the deletion. If you don't tap the bar within 5 seconds, the comment is deleted permanently.

Website users

If you're using the website version of Instagram, you can also delete comments from any of your posts. Here's how to delete a comment:

1. Click or tap the profile icon in the upper-right corner of the web page.

2. Scroll or swipe until you see the thumbnail image of the post that contains the comment.

3. Click or tap the thumbnail image.

4. Hover over the comment.

You see a three-dot button appear in the upper-right corner of the comment.

5. Tap the three-dot button.

Keeping Instagram Healthy by Reporting the Bad Eggs

Instagram asks that you resolve disputes between you and another person who posts a photo, video, or comment that you think may violate Instagram's Community Guidelines. For example, if someone's comment contains inaccurate information about you, you can post a comment or send a direct message and ask the commenter to remove the comment.

If the commenter won't cooperate or if the comment is clearly a violation of the Community Guidelines (such as a threat of violence), Instagram strongly recommends that you don't escalate the situation yourself. Instead, report the user to Instagram and have Instagram staffers review the situation.

WARNING

If you refuse to heed Instagram's warning and decide to attack the commenter with nasty comments of your own, you may find yourself in trouble if the commenter reports you for harassment.

Reporting a commenter

Before you report a commenter, review the latest Community Guidelines at `https://help.instagram.com/477434105621119`. If you still believe the commenter must be reported to Instagram for further action, you can use Instagram's built-in reporting tools.

You can report a user from your iPhone, iPad, or Android smartphone or tablet. The following sections offer more details on how to report someone using these devices.

From the website version of Instagram, you can report a user by hovering over the person's comment to reveal the three-dot button. Tap the three-dot button, and select Report from the pop-up menu.

Reporting from an iOS device

If you're reading comments on your iOS device and you come across a comment that violates the Community Guidelines, tap and hold down on the comment in the list and then swipe to the left.

The gray report button appears to the right of the comment between the reply and delete buttons. Tap the button to open the menu at the bottom of the screen, and then select the Spam or Scam option or the Abusive Comment option.

If you select Spam or Scam, the menu closes and the comment disappears from the Comments screen so you can continue to read comments. If you select Abusive Content, the Report Comment screen opens. You can decide how to report the comment and take any additional steps to get more information. For example, if you choose "I don't like the comment," the Blocking People page appears so you can proceed to block the commenter.

Reporting from an Android device

When you see a comment on your Android device that you think violates the Community Guidelines, tap the comment in the list. The comment gets highlighted in a light blue background, and a blue bar appears at the top of the screen. In that top blue bar is an exclamation point. Tap the exclamation point to open the menu, and then tap one of the reporting options: Spam or Scam or Abusive Content.

When you tap Spam or Scam, the menu closes and the comment disappears. Now you can get back to reading other comments. When you tap Abusive Comment, the Report Comment screen opens so you can decide how to report the comment and take any additional steps or get more information.

Blocking a commenter

If a commenter is obnoxious, that alone isn't a reason to report the commenter to Instagram, but you can block the commenter from your content. That user will no longer be able to see your content or leave any comments on your posts. Instagram doesn't tell users that they've been blocked.

Here's how to block a user:

1. **In the comments below the photo or from the comments screen, tap the username of the commenter.**

   The username is the first text you see in the comment and is in bold text.

2. **In the commenter's profile page, tap the three-dot button in the upper-right corner of the screen.**

3. **Tap Block from the pop-up menu.**

4. **Follow the prompts from the remaining screens to confirm the person is blocked.**

5. **Tap the < icon to return to the Comments screen.**

   The blocked user's comments no longer appear on the screen.

To unblock someone, follow the same steps, except tap Unblock in Step 3.

To block someone from the desktop, the steps are similar. Click on the person's username, and click the three-dot button from the person's profile. Select Block the User from the pop-up menu, and follow the prompts to block that person.

> » Sending photos or videos privately

> » Sharing a GIF via direct message

> » Recording and sending a voice message

> » Messaging with a group

> » Responding to direct messages

> » Chatting live with other Instagram users

> » Managing the direct messages in your inbox

> » Getting rid of messages you don't want to see

Chapter **11**

Direct Messaging with Others

Posting photos and videos to your profile is just one of many ways to share your content. You can also use the Instagram Direct service to send a private message to a single follower or a group of 2 to 32 followers.

This chapter tells you all about how to share a direct message with your friends and fans. Because anyone can follow you (unless your account is private), direct messaging is Instagram's way of letting you connect with one person or a group of people in a private setting.

In this chapter, we start by showing you how to send a simple text message via Instagram Direct. Then we get more advanced with sending photos, videos, GIFs, and voice messages, and show you how to reply to the direct messages you receive. Next, you discover how to use the live chat feature within Instagram Direct. Finally, we show you how to navigate (delete and mute) through the messages you've sent and received so your inbox doesn't get overwhelmed with messages.

Starting a New Direct Message

If you want to start your conversation with a text message, Instagram makes it easy for you. Follow these steps:

1. **If the Direct screen isn't open, tap or click the Instagram Direct icon (it looks like a paper airplane) in the upper-right corner of your home screen (see Figure 11-1).**

   This is also where you receive new messages. A red circle with the number of messages waiting for you is shown on top of the Direct icon. Your new messages are revealed when you tap the number.

2. **Tap or click the pencil in a square icon as shown in Figure 11-2.**

   The New Message screen appears.

3. **Search for a name in the Search box or scroll in the Suggested list to find the recipients, and then tap or click their usernames (see Figure 11-3).**

   A blue check mark appears to the right of each recipient name after you tap or click it. You can also search for one or more recipients as described in the preceding section.

4. **On iPhone, tap or click Next. On Android, the message box appears at the bottom of the screen after you select one or more recipients.**

5. **Start typing in the message box at the bottom of the page, and tap Send when you have completed your message (see Figure 11-4).**

6. **Return to the Direct screen by tapping or clicking the < icon.**

   The message you just sent appears at the top of the list. Each message entry in the list shows you the recipient's or group's name, followed by whether the recipient is active now, or when they were last active.

   View your message on the screen by tapping the message entry.

7. **Return to the Instagram home screen by tapping or clicking the < icon.**

TIP

You can unsend a message by holding down on the message. Then tap Unsend (iPhone) or Unsend Message (Android) to unsend it. The message has now been erased from the conversation (but it may have been seen if the contact is quick to read messages!).

FIGURE 11-1:
The Instagram Direct icon is located at the top right of your home screen.

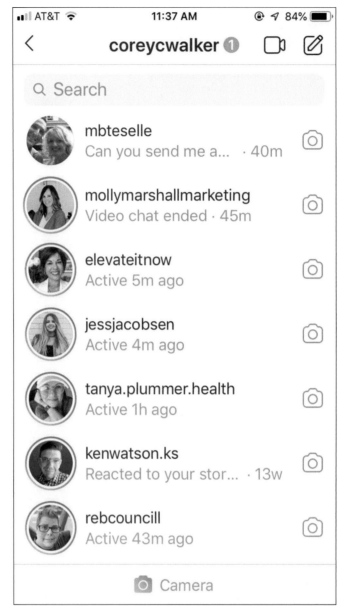

FIGURE 11-2:
Create a new message by tapping the + at the upper right of your screen.

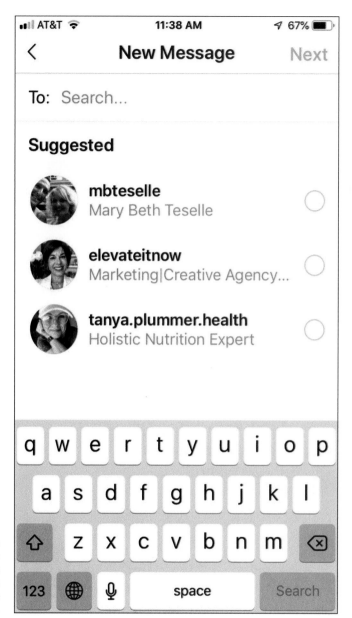

FIGURE 11-3:
The New Message page allows you to select message recipients.

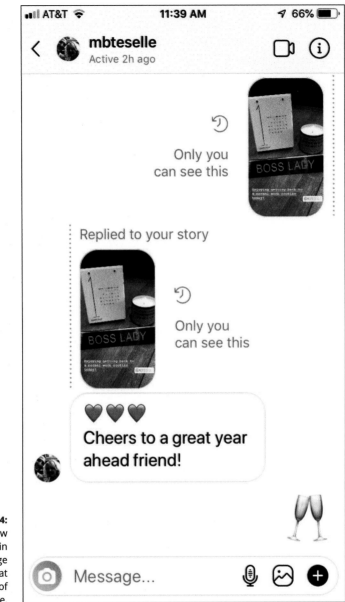

FIGURE 11-4:
Type a new message in the Message screen at the bottom of the page.

Sharing Photos and Videos via Direct Message

If sending a text message is too boring for you, you can take a photo or video (or use one from your camera roll) and send it to the other person. You can even customize the photo with text, filters, GIFs, and more.

1. **In the main Direct screen, tap or click the blue Camera link as shown in Figure 11-5.**

    If you need to get to the Direct screen, first tap or click the Direct icon from the Instagram home screen or window.

2. **Take a photo by tapping or clicking the white button (as shown in Figure 11-6) or hold the white button down to film a video. Alternatively, you can choose a photo or video from your camera roll by tapping the small square at the lower left of the camera screen and choosing the photo/video by tapping it.**

    The switch cameras icon appears to the right of the white button so you can switch between the front and rear cameras, if necessary. If you're unhappy with what you shot, tap the X to delete the photo or video and try again.

3. **If you want to layer text on top of your photo or video, tap or click the text (Aa) icon. Type your message (as shown in Figure 11-7), and then tap Done.**

    Photos and videos here have all the same custom capabilities as they do in Instagram stories. For more information about how to add filters, GIFs, polls and more, refer to Chapter 14.

4. **Tap Send To > at the lower right.**

5. **Select your recipients by scrolling through the recipient list and then tapping Send next to one or more usernames.**

    The photo is sent right away and a blue bar that says Done appears at the bottom of the screen. You can also send your photo to be shown on your Instagram story or to your Close Friends Only list, as shown in Figure 11-8.

    You can search for a recipient by tapping the Search box above the list and typing your search terms. As you type, the usernames that most closely match your terms appear in the results list. When you find the name of the recipients you're looking for, tap or click their names in the list.

    TIP

6. **Tap Done.**

    The Direct screen appears and contains the message you sent to the recipient at the top of the conversation list.

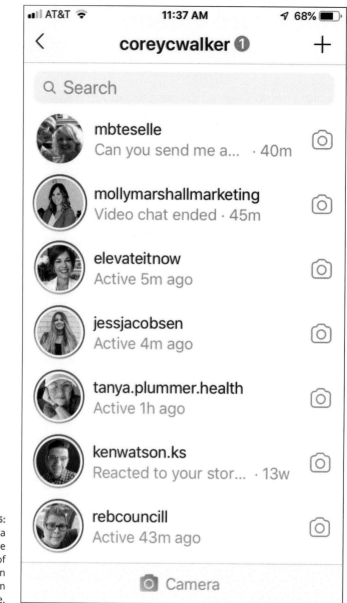

FIGURE 11-5:
The Camera link is at the bottom of the main Instagram Direct page.

FIGURE 11-6:
Tap (for photos) or hold (for videos) the white button to take a photo or video.

FIGURE 11-7:
Add text to
your photo by
tapping the Aa.

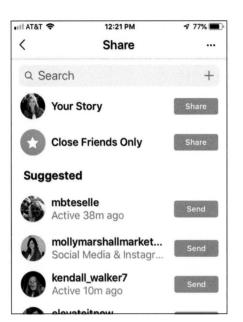

WARNING

Direct messages are private, and Instagram means it — you can't do several things with a direct message that you can do with a public message:

>> You can't share photos or videos sent with Instagram Direct to other social networking websites.

>> Any hashtags or locations you add to your private message aren't searchable in Instagram.

>> Your messages won't appear in the feed screen or in your profile. You can, however, send a photo or video filmed within Instagram Direct to your Instagram story.

Do photos and videos last forever or do they disappear? The answer is: It depends. If you send a photo or video using the method outlined earlier, the photo or video remains viewable in the recipient's message indefinitely. However, if you would like to send a disappearing photo or video, follow these instructions:

1. **Tap or click the Instagram Direct icon, which appears in the upper-right corner of your home screen.**

2. **Type in the Search feature to locate the contact you want and tap their name once you find the correct person, or scroll through your existing messages to find the person.**

   If you had a previous conversation with the contact, the old message thread appears. Otherwise, you'll see a blank screen with the contact's name at the top and a message bar at the bottom.

3. **Tap the blue camera icon at the bottom of the screen to go to the camera.**

4. **Take a photo by tapping or clicking the white button, or hold the white button down to film a video (refer to Figure 11-6 for an example).**

   The switch cameras icon appears to the right of the white button so you can switch between the front and rear cameras, if necessary. If you're unhappy with what you shot, tap the X to delete the photo or video and try again.

TIP

   If you'd rather use a photo or video you took previously, you can choose one from your camera roll by tapping the small square at the lower left of the camera screen and choosing the photo/video by tapping it, as shown in Figure 11-9. You can also choose multiple photos/videos at once by tapping Select Multiple, tapping each thumbnail you want, and tapping Next at the bottom of the screen.

5. **If you want to layer text on top of your photo or video, tap or click the text (Aa) icon. Type your message, and then tap Done.**

   Photos and videos here have all the same custom capabilities as they do in Instagram stories. For more information about how to add filters, GIFs, polls, and more, refer to Chapter 14.

6. **After any customizing is complete, you can decide how you want the photo to be viewed by scrolling left or right directly over the words to choose View Once, Allow Replay, or Keep in Chat, as shown in Figure 11-10.**

   View Once allows one view and then it disappears. Allow Replay allows one view and one replay, then it disappears. Keep In Chat keeps the photo or video in the message thread indefinitely.

7. **After a method of viewing is selected, tap the Send button.**

   You can also choose the Send to Others button if you want to send to your Instagram story, close friends only, or other contacts.

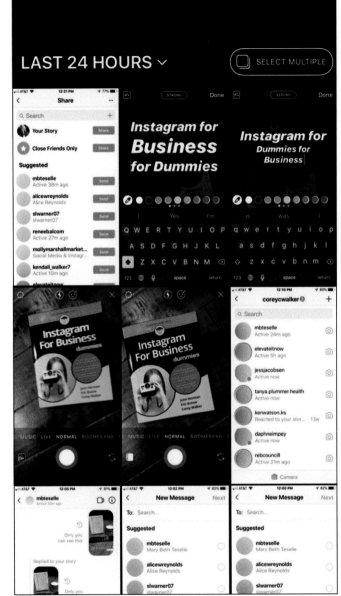

FIGURE 11-9:
Choose photos or videos you've taken previously by tapping the small square at the lower left of the Camera screen.

FIGURE 11-10:
Choose how you would like your message to be viewed.

Sharing GIFs

Sometimes all you need to communicate a message is a fun GIF. Instagram imports hundreds of available GIFs via Giphy for you to use in Instagram Direct.

To send a GIF in a message, follow these steps:

1. **Tap or click the Instagram Direct icon.**

2. **Type in the Search feature (or scroll through your recent messages list) to locate the contact you want and tap their name to reveal the message screen.**

3. **Tap the black + button located in the right corner of the Message bar at the bottom of the screen.**

   A GIF button appears, as shown in Figure 11-11.

4. **Tap the GIF button to see suggested GIFs, as shown in Figure 11-12.**

   You can also use the Search Giphy bar to search for specific GIFs.

5. **Tap the GIF you like best.**

   It automatically sends the GIF, so be careful what you tap!

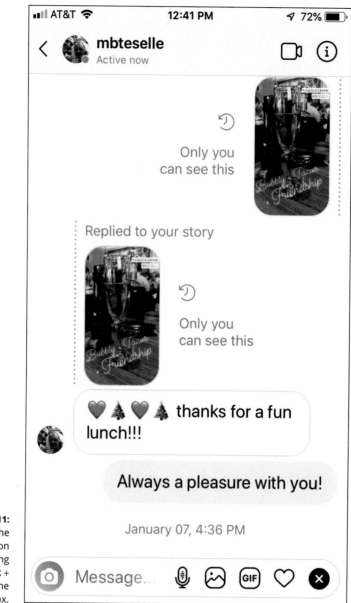

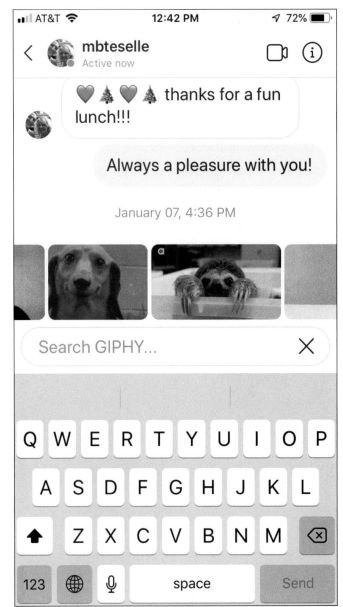

FIGURE 11-12:
You can
select from
suggested
GIFs, or you
can search for
other GIFs.

Using Voice Messages

Tired of typing, or have a lot to say, and prefer to leave a quick voice message? Instagram has a solution for that!

To send a voice message, follow these steps:

1. Tap or click the Instagram Direct icon.

2. Type in the Search feature (or scroll through your recent messages list) to locate the contact you want and tap their name to reveal the message screen.

3. Press and hold the microphone icon located in the right corner of the Message bar (as shown in Figure 11-13) while recording a message of up to one minute.

WARNING

When recording a voice message, the message will automatically send when you release the microphone button. If you want to delete the message and re-record it, slide your finger to the trash can on the left; then hold down the microphone again to re-record.

FIGURE 11-13:
Press and hold
the microphone
icon while
recording your
voice message.

Creating a New Group Message

If you'd like to send a private message to two or more people at once, you can create a group conversation. To create a new group conversation:

1. **Tap or click the Instagram Direct icon.**

2. **Tap the + icon at the upper right of the screen.**

3. **Type names in the Search feature (or scroll through the Suggested list) to locate the contacts you want and tap their names.**

   The names appear in blue at the top of the screen, and can be deleted by tapping them again.

4. **Tap Next.**

   The next screen appears and allows you to enter a name for the group.

5. **Enter the name of the group, as shown in Figure 11-14.**

   This group is saved after you name it. You can send other messages to the same group later by looking for it in the Search box, or scrolling through your sent messages.

TIP

   You can rename your group name later by tapping the group name and entering a new name. The members of the group are able to see this name, so choose wisely!

6. **Type a message, take a photo or video, or send a GIF or a voice message to the group.**

   Instructions for sending each of these message types are outlined earlier in the chapter and are the same for a single message or a group message.

Adding new group members to the conversation

If you need to include more group members later, there's an easy way to do that! Simply tap the group name, tap Add People, search and select the contacts you'd like to add, and tap Next (iPhone) or Done (Android). The new group members are now added to your thread and can see the entire previous conversation except for any disappearing photos or videos.

FIGURE 11-14:
Enter the name of the group to save it for future messages.

Replying to a Direct Message

If you've had a previous conversation with one or more recipients, you can tap the individual or group name in the Direct screen to view your past conversation(s) and write a new message to start a new conversation. The Message screen appears and you see all the text, photos, and videos you sent previously to that recipient or that group.

Swipe or scroll to view your entire conversation. You can also type a new message, as described earlier in this chapter.

If you're already having a private message conversation in Instagram Direct, you can respond by sending a photo to one or more of your followers. Here's how:

1. **Tap or click the Instagram Direct icon.**

   The Direct screen appears with the most recent direct message conversations appearing at the top.

2. **Tap or click the camera icon to the right of the user name in the list.**

   The Camera screen appears with the front camera active. In the Windows app, your webcam becomes active so you can take a photo of yourself. You may be prompted to enable access to your camera or microphone or both.

3. **Take a photo by tapping or clicking the white shutter button at the bottom of the screen or window, or hold it down to take a video.**

   You can switch between the front and back camera on your iPhone, iPad, Android smartphone, or Android tablet by tapping the switch icon.

4. **Tap Send.**

Using Live Chat in Direct Messages

Sometimes it's nice to carry on a conversation face-to-face, even if it's not in person. You can now live chat with up to six people using Instagram Direct.

To use video chat on Instagram:

1. **Tap or click the Instagram Direct icon.**

2. **Type in the Search feature (or scroll through your recent messages list) to locate the contact or group you want and tap their name to reveal the message screen.**

3. **Tap the movie camera icon at the top right of the screen, as shown in Figure 11-15.**

   The contact or group is notified that you're requesting a live chat and can choose to answer or dismiss the call as shown in Figure 11-16.

FIGURE 11-15:
Live Chat is
accessed by
tapping the
movie camera
icon at the top
of the message
screen.

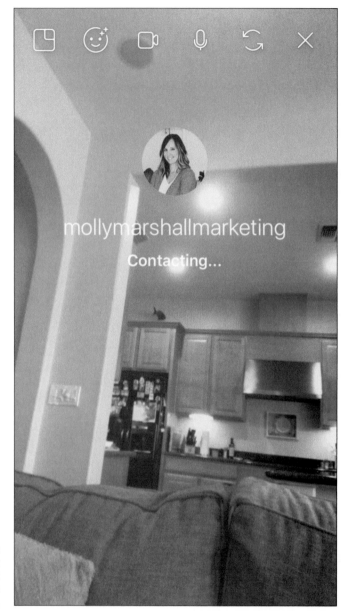

FIGURE 11-16:
Your contact
is notified that
you'd like to
live chat.

WARNING

Anyone you've direct messaged with previously can request a live chat. If you don't want them to have this capability, on iPhone you can Mute Video Chat by scrolling to their name, swiping left, and then tapping Mute; then tap Mute Video Chat. On Android, you hold down on the person's name and choose Mute Video Chats from the pop-up list of options.

If you've already started a chat with one or more people, you can add more people (up to six people total on the chat) to an ongoing conversation.

To add more people to your video chat, follow these steps:

1. **While still in your video chat, simply swipe up to add another contact.**

   Your list of recently messaged contacts are shown, or you can use Search to find other contacts.

2. **When you've located your contact, tap Add next to their user name.**

   The contact receives a notification that you'd like to video chat, and they can pick up the chat, ignore it, or choose to decline it.

Navigating Your Inbox

If you've been following the instructions within this chapter, you likely have several message threads piling up in your inbox that you need to manage. You may have even discovered some contacts you'd rather not hear from anymore.

New messages are indicated by a red circle with the number of messages waiting next to the Direct icon at the top of your home screen, as shown in Figure 11-17. By tapping the Direct icon, you are taken to the Messages screen where you can tap on the new message to view it.

When you're done viewing the message, you have choices to make:

» Let it sit in your inbox indefinitely.

» Reply to the message with text, photo, video, a GIF, or a heart (as described earlier).

» Delete the message (see instructions in Figure 11-18).

» Mute the conversation so they can no longer contact you on Instagram Direct (see instructions in Figure 11-18).

» *iPhone only:* Flag the message to remember to view it later by swiping left and tapping Flag.

» *iPhone only:* Mark the message as Unread so it's highlighted in bold again by swiping left and tapping Unread.

FIGURE 11-17:
You are
notified about
new direct
messages by a
red circle with
the number
of messages
on top of the
Instagram
Direct icon
on the home
screen.

That's really all there is to it! The Instagram Direct inbox is fairly simple to navigate with limited options for handling your messages after it's viewed.

Instagram Direct's message search capabilities are slim. At this point, you can only search for messages based on the contact or group's name. Unlike an email inbox, you can't filter a search by subject, keywords, or date.

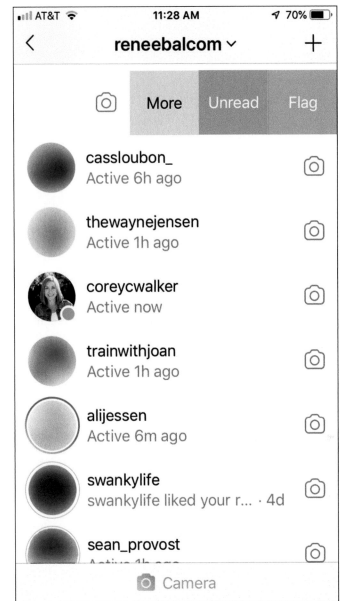

FIGURE 11-18:
To delete a message on iPhone, swipe left and tap More. From there, you can tap Delete or Mute. On Android, hold down over the account name and choose Delete from the pop-up menu.

To search for a conversation by username or group name, follow these steps:

1. **Tap or click the Instagram Direct icon.**

2. **Type in the Search feature (or scroll through your recent messages list) to locate the contact or group you want and tap their name.**

   Once the name is tapped, you see your previous conversation and can choose to reply if you'd like.

Getting Rid of Unwanted Messages

Instagram is a huge platform with millions of users. This can result in messages from a variety of sources, and there's a good chance you'll receive a message from someone that you'd rather not hear from.

Initially, if the user isn't someone you're following or you've messaged with previously, Instagram funnels them into a different section. You see their initial request to speak with you with a blue link that indicates the number of requests waiting. When you tap that blue link, a new page appears revealing the usernames of the people who would like to contact you. You now have choices to make (as shown in Figure 11-19):

>> Swipe left and tap Allow to allow a communication between you, or tap Decline to end any communication.

>> If there are several messages from users waiting that you don't want to communicate with, Instagram makes it easy with a Decline All link at the bottom. Tap that link to decline any future messages from those usernames.

You may have started a conversation with someone, only to find out later that they're sending inappropriate messages. If you feel they should be reported for their actions, it's simple to do. To report an inappropriate message, follow these steps:

1. **Inside the conversation thread, tap and hold the individual comment that was inappropriate.**

   A Report button appears above the message.

2. **Tap the Report button and follow the instructions.**

   The message and username is sent to Instagram and the user is reported. The user is not notified that you're the person who reported them.

FIGURE 11-19:
A page showing your message requests appears and lets you choose whether to allow them to message you or decline their messages.

4

Telling Tales with Instagram Stories

IN THIS PART . . .

Learn the basics of Instagram stories.

Plan a story from beginning to end.

Experiment with different tools to personalize your stories.

Determine how to share stories in different ways.

Use Story Highlights to keep your stories forever.

Find the excitement in going live on Instagram.

» Navigating and replying to Instagram stories

» Finding out about size limitations for images and video

» Using the built-in camera for stories

Chapter **12**

Exploring Instagram Stories

nstagram stories were introduced in the latter half of 2016 in an attempt to get more users to post content. The lure was that the content disappears within 24 hours, allowing those who had been meticulously curating their semiper-manent Instagram feeds to hang loose a bit. Users now have a place on Instagram where they can be more spontaneous, by, say, taking a quick behind-the-scenes photo or shooting a 15-second video showing something they did that day.

In this chapter, you learn all about watching and interacting with Instagram sto-ries. You also learn about the size limitations for photos, graphics, and videos. In the next chapter, you find out about enhancements you can add to your stories.

Instagram stories are a great complement to your regular Instagram feed, so don't skip out on this chapter!

Finding Stories to Watch

Instagram stories are located in a bar at the top of your newsfeed and are represented by a multicolored ring around the profile picture of the story's creator, as shown in Figure 12-1. Tap the profile picture, and the story opens full-screen for you to watch.

FIGURE 12-1:
View stories by tapping a profile picture at the top of your newsfeed.

New stories (personalized for you) are shown first. By scrolling left, you can see all stories that the people you follow have published in the last 24 hours. The story vanishes 24 hours after it was posted.

WARNING

When you view a person's story, he can see that you've watched it, as shown in Figure 12-2. There is currently no way to block this feature. So, be aware if you're looking at an old boyfriend's story. He knows!

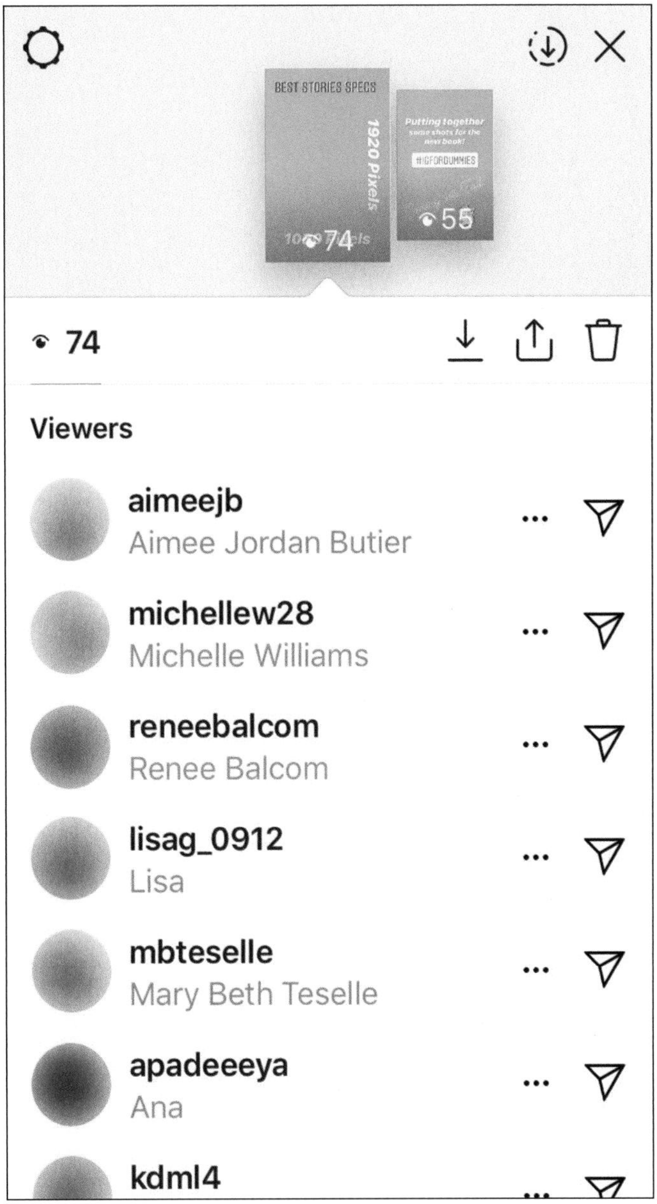

FIGURE 12-2:
You can see who saw your story by tapping on the Seen By link at the bottom left of the screen.

Instagram stories are also accessible from the top left of a person's profile page. If the person has an active story, his profile picture has a multicolored ring around it, as shown in Figure 12-3. You don't need to be following the person to see his stories, as long as his account isn't private. Tap the profile picture, and the story opens full-screen for you to watch. After that person's stories have finished, the stories page closes and you're returned to his profile page.

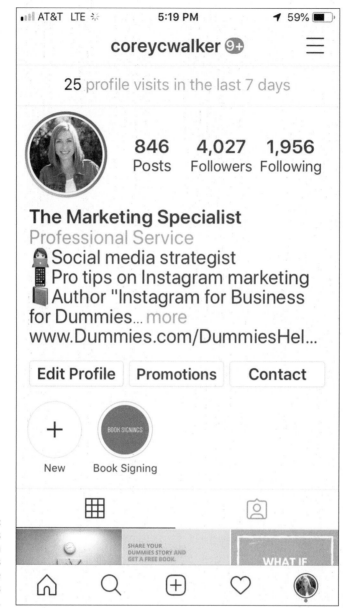

If you want to watch a continuing sequence of stories from people you follow, you must access the stories from the top of your Home feed. Instagram always takes you to the content you haven't seen in that person's story. For instance, if you watched two out of five stories by someone, Instagram would play the third story in the sequence when you came back within the 24-hour window of the post. Each person's story has white dashes at the top that indicate the number of stories for that person that day. Stories continue to play through each person's entire sequence, and then go directly to the next person you're following who has a current story until you tap the X to exit (iPhone) or swipe down (Android) from Instagram stories, as shown in Figure 12-4. (You'll see some ads interspersed with stories from the people you follow.)

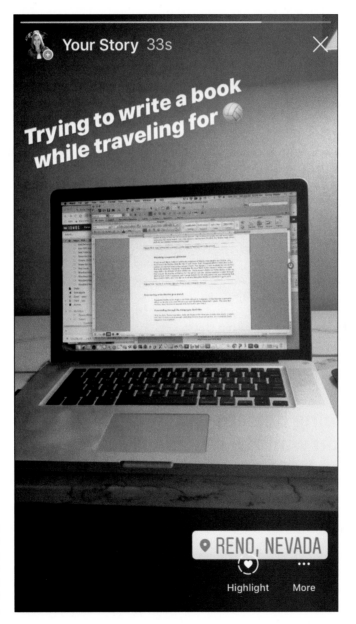

FIGURE 12-4: On iPhone, tap the X at the top right of a story to exit. On Android, swipe down.

Interacting with Stories You Watch

The next few sections describe how to interact with the stories you watch. You can find out how to skip the stories you're not interested in, how to rewatch things you want to see again, how to pause a story, and how to react to a story.

Forwarding through the things you don't like

With so many stories out there, there are bound to be some you'd rather not watch. Lucky for you, it's easy to skip through individual stories from one person, or a complete story sequence from a person.

To forward through one story within a person's full story sequence, simply tap on the right side of the screen. You'll skip to that person's next story, unless it's her last or only story; in that case, you'll be taken to the next person's story.

To forward through a person's entire sequence of stories, swipe left from the right side of the screen. You'll skip that person's full set of stories and move on to the next person's stories.

TIP

If you're searching for a particular person's story, it may be easier to go directly to her profile and watch, or you can scroll through the profile circles at the top of your Home page to find the person whose story you want to watch. Tap that person's circle to see her story.

When you're finished watching, tap the X at the top right of the screen or swipe down to be returned to your Home screen.

Going back to the things you want to see again

The process of going back to see a story is the opposite of forwarding through a story (makes sense, right?). If you've already watched a few stories from one person, and you want to rewatch one or more stories from her, tap the left side of the screen until you reach the story you're seeking.

To go back to a different person's sequence of stories, swipe right from the left side of the screen until you get back to that person's story.

Similar to forwarding, if you're seeking a certain person's story, it's easier to go directly to her profile to watch, or scroll through the circles at the top of your Home screen to find that person.

When you're finished watching, tap the X at the top right of the screen or swipe down to be returned to your Home screen.

Pausing a story to see more

Stories tend to whip by pretty fast, and sometimes people add lots of text, or talk really fast to squeeze a lot of info in before getting cut off. Lucky for you, there is a way to pause a story so you can take it all in. To pause a story, just tap and hold anywhere on the screen, and the story remains frozen until you let go.

Reacting to a story

Reactions to stories are more limited than posts in the regular Instagram feed. You can't "like" a story; you can only send a direct message or send a photo or video message back.

To send a direct message in response to a story, follow these steps:

1. **Tap the Send Message area at the bottom of the screen.**

Quick Reactions (emojis) and a keyboard appears, as shown in Figure 12-5.

2. **Type a message or use one of the Quick Reaction emojis above the keyboard.**

3. **When your message is complete, tap Send to send your message.**

To send a photo or video message in response to a story, follow these steps:

1. **Tap the camera icon at the lower-left side of the screen.**

The photo/video screen appears with all the capabilities to add text, emojis, GIFs, and so on.

2. **To take a photo, tap the white circle. To take a video, tap and hold the white button for up to 15 seconds.**

You can turn the camera for selfie mode by tapping the circle arrows at the bottom right.

TIP

3. **Add any text, emojis, or GIFs you'd like to add to your photo or video.**

We go into more details about adding style to your stories in Chapter 14.

4. Use the slider at the bottom of the screen to allow the person to View Once or Allow Replay, as shown in Figure 12-6.

5. Tap the profile picture above Send to send your message.

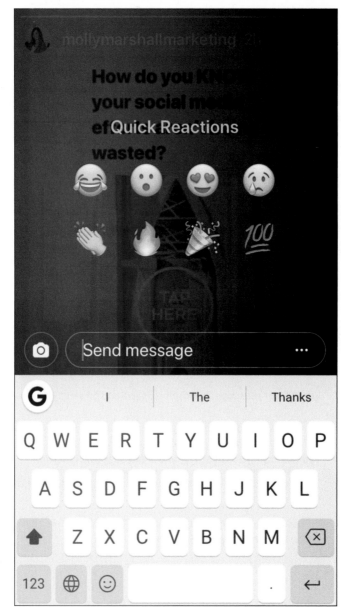

FIGURE 12-5:
Send a
message by
tapping in the
Send Message
box and typing.

FIGURE 12-6:
Use the slider
at the bottom
to choose
your viewing
method and
tap the profile
picture to
Send.

Understanding Story Limitations

If you've watched a few Instagram Stories by now, you've probably noticed that they're all in vertical or portrait mode, and videos are in short sequences. This section gives you the exact criteria for your photos, videos, and graphics in stories.

Upload criteria limitations

All photos, graphics, and videos are best in the following formats:

>> **Image ratio:** 4:5 (vertical only) or 9:16 for photos

>> **Image size minimum:** 600 x 1,067 pixels

>> **Image size maximum:** 1,080 x 1,920 pixels (see Figure 12-7)

>> **File type:** PNG or JPG for photos/graphics or MP4 or MOV for videos

>> **File size max:** 30MB for photos, 4GB for videos

TIP

If you take a photo or video within Instagram stories in portrait mode (described in detail in the next chapter), you won't have to worry about these size ranges — it will automatically fit. If you import photos, graphics or videos from other sources, you need to pay closer attention to sizing.

WARNING

You can upload photos, graphics, and videos that are not in these image size ranges, but the Stories editor will likely either cut off part of your image or zoom in to wherever it likes, causing poor image quality.

Playing-time limitations

Currently, you can only record or upload in 15-second increments. If you're filming within the app, the camera will stop recording at the 15-second mark, and longer videos will not load from your camera if they're over 15 seconds. This can be very challenging if you're trying to explain something or tell a story.

TIP

If you need to record for longer amounts of time, there are several apps available to help you. Try CutStory, Continual, StoryCutter, or Storeo. They all work in a similar manner, allowing you to record a single longer video on your smartphone outside of Instagram, and then splitting it up into 15-second segments that are placed on your camera roll so you can upload them one-by-one. The app also makes the transition between stories more seamless than when you film them within the Instagram app.

FIGURE 12-7:
The best size for a story image is 1,080 x 1,920 pixels.

Accessing the Story Camera

Accessing the story camera is easy but not always obvious. There are a few methods for accessing the camera as shown in Figures 12-8 and 12-9:

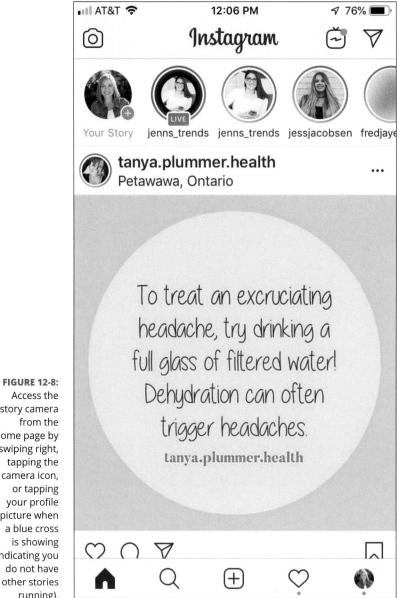

FIGURE 12-8: Access the story camera from the Home page by swiping right, tapping the camera icon, or tapping your profile picture when a blue cross is showing (indicating you do not have other stories running).

>> From the Home page, swipe right.

>> From the Home page, tap the camera icon at the top left of the screen.

>> If you do not have any stories running currently, tap on your profile picture on the Home page or your personal profile. If there is a blue plus (+) sign next to your profile picture, you'll be able to access the camera to create a new story.

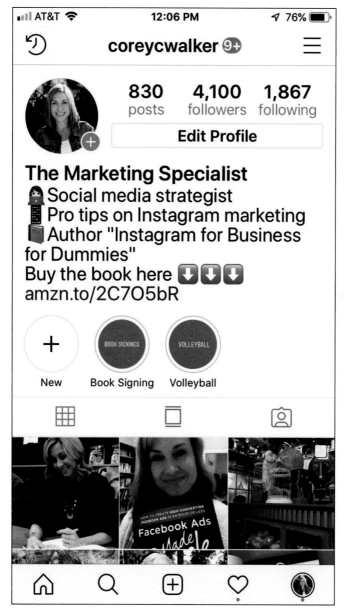

FIGURE 12-9:
Access the story camera from your profile page by tapping your profile picture when a blue cross is showing.

When you're on the story creation page, the camera is available for taking photos or videos via the white button. Tap for photos, hold for videos for up to 15 seconds. We provide details on what to share and how to add bells and whistles to your photos or videos in Chapters 13 and 14.

Editing your settings

Instagram stories have several behind-the-scenes settings you can control to decide who sees your stories, who responds to them, and who shares them. You can also choose to save your stories to your camera roll or to an archive, or share your story directly to Facebook Stories.

To access your settings, follow these steps:

1. **Access the camera as detailed in the last section.**

2. **Tap the gear icon at the top left of the page, shown in Figure 12-10.**

   You will then see the Story Controls page, shown in Figure 12-11.

From the Story Controls page, you can change the following settings:

>> **Hide Story From:** Allows you to select people who cannot watch your Stories and live videos. Maybe you don't want your mom (or your kids!) to see what you've been up to.

>> **Allow Message Replies:** You can allow replies from everyone, from the people you follow, or from no one.

>> **Saving:** You can save all your stories to your Camera Roll or save them to the Archive. The Archive lives within your Instagram account and can be accessed at any time to view old stories.

>> **Allow Sharing:** You can allow people to share your post on their story, or share your story as a message to other users. You can also set your stories to automatically post to your Facebook story.

After you make all your selections, tap Done to save them and return to the story camera.

FIGURE 12-10:
Tap the gear icon at the top of the camera page to access Settings.

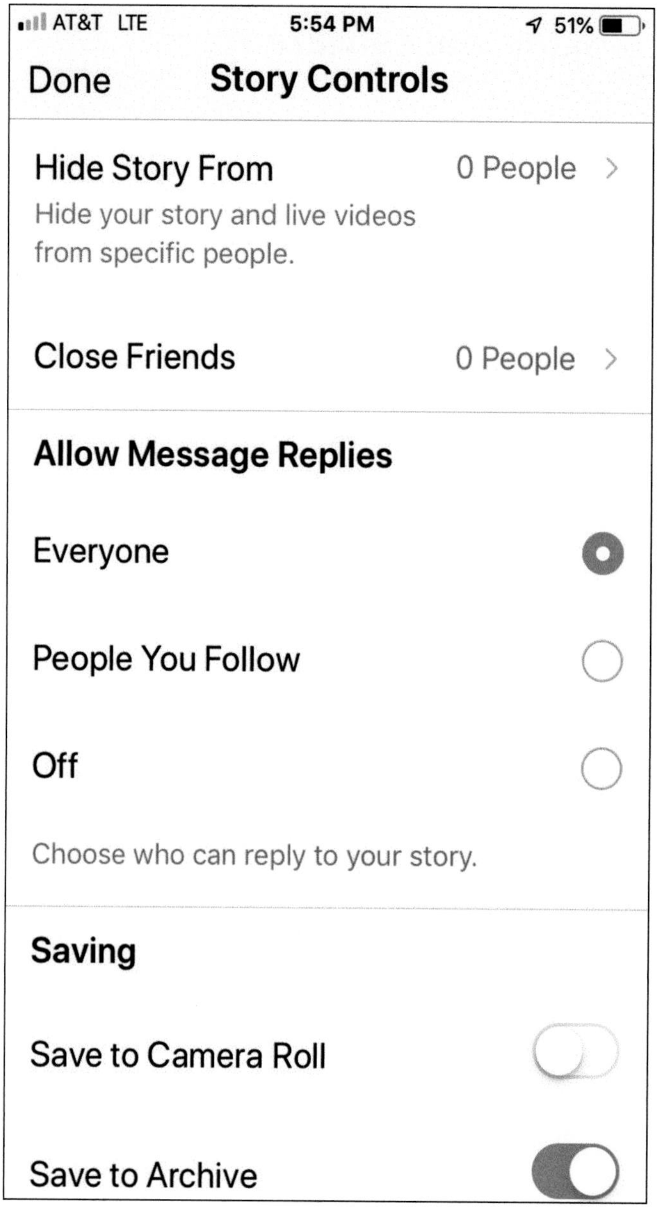

▪ll AT&T LTE   **5:54 PM**   **◥ 51% ▪**

Done   **Story Controls**

Hide Story From   0 People ›
Hide your story and live videos from specific people.

Close Friends   0 People ›

Allow Message Replies

Everyone   ⦿

People You Follow   ○

Off   ○

Choose who can reply to your story.

Saving

Save to Camera Roll

Save to Archive

FIGURE 12-11:
The Story Controls page offers a variety of settings for allowing people to view, message, share, and save your stories.

Changing the camera from regular to selfie mode

REMEMBER

The camera in the Stories creation page is automatically set to take a regular front-facing photo or video. However, if you want to take a photo or video of yourself, simply tap the double arrows to the right of the camera or double-tap anywhere on the screen to change the camera, and the view will flip to selfie mode.

Chapter **13**
Creating Instagram Stories

I n the last chapter, we explain the history of Instagram stories, where to watch them, how to watch them, and their specifications for images and videos. In this chapter, we go into more detail about how you can plan out the Stories you share (if you intend on planning), deciding what to share, and exactly how to upload photos, videos, and images to your stories. We also discuss camera effects, and how to save and access your stories after you've archived them.

Planning a Story from Start to Finish

If you're using Instagram stories strictly for personal use, you may choose not to plan your stories at all, and publish things on the fly as they happen. However, many businesses, brands, and influencers use stories in a much more strategic way to truly, well, tell a story.

TECHNICAL
STUFF

An *influencer* is an individual with the ability to influence potential buyers of a product or service by promoting or recommending the items on social media.

TIP

If you want your followers to stand up and take notice of your stories, here are some planning tips to make them "next level":

>> Use a planning tool such as Later or Planoly to "lay out" and schedule your stories so you can view them as you would a storyboard. You can find these tools in the app store for your device or find them online on your desktop if you like to load graphics and videos from your computer.

>> Use consistent colors and fonts throughout the story so your story looks cohesive.

>> Use a template to make your stories all look identifiable to you.

>> Think about which tags, hashtags, or locations you want to add to your story.

Deciding What to Share

Instagram stories were designed to be a looser, less perfect part of Instagram. Many Instagrammers agonize over choosing the right photo or caption for their profile page so their aesthetic is flawless. Instagram stories allow those users to offer a less polished version of themselves, and offer a glimpse into their everyday lives that automatically goes away in 24 hours. In this section, we detail some of the common ways people use Instagram stories.

Sharing your less-than-perfect stuff

You may want to share

>> **Behind the scenes photos and videos:** Because many Instagrammers are involved in launches, events, conferences, podcasts, and other exciting activities, behind-the-scenes stories are a great way to let your audience in on how the magic really happens. Whether it's showing the types of equipment used (see Figure 13-1), hanging decorations for an exclusive party, or interviewing speakers backstage before a conference starts, followers love to get to know more about you through behind-the-scenes stories.

>> **Travel photos:** You may have that one gorgeous meticulously edited shot of your trip for your profile page, but you have *so* many more that you're dying to share right away! Stories are the perfect opportunity to load lots of photos that may not make the cut on your profile (like that funny one of Aunt Ethel wearing a sombrero and drinking tequila).

FIGURE 13-1:
@isocialfanz
shows his
followers the
equipment he
uses to record
his stories.

Showcasing your personality and lifestyle

To showcase who you really are, you might try the following:

>> **Talking to the camera:** The popularity of video has surged in the last several years, so what better way to grab your followers' attention than talking to

them via Instagram stories (see Figure 13-2)? Talking directly to your followers gives them a familiarity with you that can't be matched through still images.

» **Candid shots or videos:** Kids doing something silly around the house? Dog chasing a squirrel up a tree? These are perfect moments to share with your followers in a story to show the day-to-day happenings around you.

FIGURE 13-2: @MartinHolsinger talks directly to his followers regularly using stories.

>> **Before and afters and series:** Before and afters and series of photos are an exceptional way to tell a story. Maybe you recently remodeled your kitchen and want to show the differences, or you want to show the progression of a project that took you weeks to complete. Stories are a unique way to display the results along with how far you've come (see Figure 13-3).

FIGURE 13-3: @eggleston designs shows how she made over a messy room using before and after Stories.

Adding a Story Photo

To get started creating a photo story, follow these steps:

1. **From your newsfeed (home screen), swipe right or tap the camera icon at the top left of the screen.**

   You can also tap your profile picture with the blue plus sign in the row of stories at the top of your screen.

   Make sure the setting at the bottom of the screen is Normal, as shown in Figure 13-4.

FIGURE 13-4:
Tap the white circle in Normal mode to take a basic photo with the stories camera.

2. **Take a photo.**

To take a photo, hold the phone up vertically and tap the white circle (refer to Figure 13-4).

If you want the phone in selfie mode (camera facing you versus away from you), tap the two arrows located to the right of the white circle before you tap the white circle. You can also double tap anywhere on the screen to switch the camera back and forth between the front- and rear-facing cameras.

3. **To retake the photo or video, tap the X at the top left of the screen, and repeat Step 2.**

4. **Share your Story by tapping Your Story; save it by tapping the arrow; or send it as a DM by tapping Next, selecting the recipients, and tapping Send.**

A face filter is an app that applies a filter over your face using the camera, making you look, for example, like a dog, a rock star, or just bathed in a warm glow. Here's how to take a photo with a face filter:

1. **Open Instagram stories by swiping right or using the camera icon at the top of the newsfeed.**

2. **Put the camera in selfie mode by tapping the arrows to the right of the white circle.**

Some filters can be used in rear-facing mode to add a filter, color or lighting element.

3. **Tap the smiling face at the top of the screen.**

Filters appear at the bottom of the screen. Scroll to the left to see all available filters. Instagram often adds new filters seasonally or when there are big events like the Super Bowl or the Grammys.

4. **To apply a filter to your face, as shown in Figure 13-5, tap the filter.**

To change filters, simply tap a different one.

5. **Take a photo by tapping the white button, or record a video by holding down the white button.**

REMEMBER

You can use filters in the following camera settings: Live, Normal, Boomerang, Rewind, Hands-Free, or Music.

6. **To try again, tap the X at the top left of the screen and go back to Step 4.**
   If you want to try the photo without a filter, simply tap the smiling face to exit.

7. **Share your story by tapping Your Story; save it by tapping the arrow; or send it as a DM by tapping Next, selecting the recipients, and tapping Send.**

FIGURE 13-5:
Face filters allow you to take on a whole new persona in your story!

You may prefer to upload a photo stored on your camera roll instead of capturing it in the Instagram app.

TIP

In the past, Instagram stories would load only photos or videos taken in the last 24 hours. Luckily, that has changed, and you can now access your entire camera roll. When you swipe up or tap the small photo icon to load a photo or video, you see photos from the last 24 hours first. If you keep scrolling up, you'll see your entire camera roll, and you can load older items by tapping them.

Follow these steps to upload an existing photo to Instagram your story:

1. **Swipe right from the newsfeed or tap the camera icon at the top of the newsfeed to access your Instagram story.**

2. **Swipe up from the bottom of the screen or tap the box with a small photo thumbnail at the bottom left.**

   Thumbnails of all available photos and videos are displayed at the bottom of the screen, as shown in Figure 13-6.

TIP

   This section shows photos or video taken in the last 24 hours first, but if you keep scrolling, you see your older content. You can also tap where it says last 24 hours on iPhone or Gallery on Android to select a specific folder from your gallery, like videos and screen shots.

3. **Tap the photo you'd like to post, or tap Select Multiple to choose up to ten photos.**

   Be sure to select them in the order you'd like them to appear in your story.

4. **To add a photo filter (not a face filter) to your photo, swipe right until you reach the filter option you want.**

5. **Tap Your Story to post your Story, Close Friends, or Send To to send it as a direct message to an individual or group.**

FIGURE 13-6:
Swipe up from the bottom of the Instagram stories screen to see available photos to post.

Adding a Story Video

As video grows in popularity, so do the number of Instagram story videos! Video can definitely enhance your story, and it's always fun to include. A standard story video is only 15 seconds long, but in this section we show you a new way to film up to a minute.

Filming with the stories camera

Filming a video within stories is very similar to taking a photo within stories. The main difference is holding down the button for video versus tapping it for a photo. Here are complete instructions for filming a video within stories:

1. **From your newsfeed (home screen), swipe right or tap the camera icon at the upper left of the screen.**

   You can also tap your profile picture with the blue plus sign in the row of stories at the top of your screen.

   Make sure the setting at the bottom of the screen is Normal, as shown earlier in this chapter (refer to Figure 13-4).

2. **Take a video.**

   To take a video, hold the phone up vertically and hold the white circle down. On the iPhone, you see a red line form around the circle letting you know how much time you have left within your available 15 seconds. On Android, you'll see a purple line that shifts to orange and yellow.

   If you want the phone in selfie mode (with the camera facing you instead of away from you), tap the two arrows located to the right of the white circle before you tap the white circle.

3. **To retake the video, tap the X at the upper left of the screen, and repeat Step 2.**

4. **Share your story by tapping Your Story; save it by tapping the arrow; or send it as a DM by tapping Next, selecting the recipients, and tapping Send.**

As mentioned earlier, a standard Instagram story is only 15 seconds long, which is rather short, especially if you're trying to convey important information or tell a complete story verbally. However, after several apps came along to "stitch" together longer videos, Instagram rolled out a way to do that directly in the app to allow for up to one minute of "seamless" video.

Here's how:

1. **From your newsfeed (home screen), swipe right or tap the camera icon at the upper left of the screen.**

   You can also tap your profile picture with the blue plus sign in the row of stories at the top of your screen.

   Make sure the setting at the bottom of the screen is Normal, as shown earlier in this chapter (refer to Figure 13-4).

2. **Hold down the white circle, but instead of releasing it when the red line moves all the way around the circle, keep holding it down.**

   The camera saves the first 15 seconds in a thumbnail that shows directly above the white circle. It may allow you to film over 1 minute, but it will only allow you to *post* the four 15-second segments to total 1 minute.

3. **When you're done filming, release the white circle.**

   The video thumbnails move down to the lower left of the screen, as shown in Figure 13-7.

4. **To upload all segments of the video, tap Next.**

5. **The Share screen appears, allowing you to post Your Story by tapping Share and then Done.**

WARNING

If you want to delete a longer video, you must delete each segment of the video. It doesn't delete the entire video at once, even though it has been stitched together.

Experimenting with all the camera options

Instagram stories packed a lot in to their little piece of the Insta-world. Their camera has many added features to add fun and drama to your stories. In this section, we offer an overview of the different camera options.

FIGURE 13-7:
Each
15-second
segment will
move down to
the bottom left
of the screen.

Using SuperZoom for drama

SuperZoom is already loaded automatically within stories and allows you to add ten different dramatic effects to your photos. The stories camera zooms in on whatever you're filming and then adds music and/or graphics to enhance the drama. Follow these steps to create a SuperZoom story:

1. **Open Instagram stories by swiping right or using the camera icon at the top of the newsfeed.**

2. **Slide the Normal setting to the left, changing it to SuperZoom, as shown in Figure 13-8.**

3. **Slide through the ten available effects above the SuperZoom title until you find the one you like.**

   To switch from forward-facing video mode to selfie video mode and back, tap the arrows to the right of the white circle.

4. **Tap the white circle with the SuperZoom logo (circle inside other circles).**

   You don't need to hold down the white button as you would for video. The app zooms in on its own and adds the effect for you.

5. **If you're not satisfied with your SuperZoom and you want to try again, tap X at the upper left and repeat, starting at Step 4, or Step 3 if you want to try a different effect.**

6. **Share the SuperZoom Story by tapping Your Story or Close Friends; save it by tapping the down arrow; or send it as a DM by tapping Send To, selecting the recipients, and tapping Send.**

Using Boomerang and Rewind for fun

Boomerang is an app that takes a burst of photos and creates a looping backward and forward video clip from them. An action such as twirling a pencil or blowing a bubble becomes more exciting when played in a loop!

Follow these steps to use Boomerang:

1. **Open Instagram Stories by swiping right or using the camera icon at the top of the newsfeed.**

2. **Slide the Normal setting to the left, changing it to Boomerang, as shown in Figure 13-9.**

3. **To switch from forward-facing video mode to selfie video mode and back, tap the arrows to the right of the white circle.**

   You can also use Boomerang with one of the face filters, as described earlier in this chapter.

FIGURE 13-8:
Find the
SuperZoom
setting by
sliding left
from the
Normal
camera setting.

4. **Tap the white circle with the Boomerang logo (infinity symbol).**

   You don't need to hold down the white button as you would for video. The app is actually taking several pictures in a rapid burst.

5. **If you're not satisfied with your Boomerang and you want to try again, tap X at the upper left and repeat, starting at Step 4.**

6. Share the Boomerang Story by tapping Your Story or Close Friends; **save it by tapping the down arrow; or send it as a DM by tapping Send To, selecting the recipients, and tapping Send.**

FIGURE 13-9:
Find the Boomerang setting by sliding left from the Normal camera setting.

Rewind stories often appear to look similar to Boomerang stories, but instead of taking a photo burst, it's taking video. Your video replays over and over in a loop. The directions for Rewind are the same as Boomerang (although you must scroll a little farther left from the Normal camera setting to get to it), but instead of tapping the white button, you hold it down for the length of your video.

TIP

Rewind videos are 15 seconds, but you can also hold longer to piece together up to four segments to make a 1-minute video. Instructions for filming longer video are detailed earlier in this chapter.

Using Focus for great portraits

The Focus feature is a nice way to take photos or videos of yourself or others, enhancing their faces, but slightly blurring the background. Here's how to create a Focus Story:

1. **Open Instagram Stories by swiping right or using the camera icon at the top of the newsfeed.**

2. **Slide the Normal setting to the left, changing it to Focus, as shown in Figure 13-10.**

3. **To switch from forward-facing video mode to selfie video mode and back, tap the arrows to the right of the white circle.**

4. **Tap (for a photo) or hold (for a video) the white circle with the Focus logo (human avatar symbol).**

5. **If you're not satisfied with your Focus Story and you want to try again, tap X at the upper left and repeat, starting at Step 4.**

6. **Share the Focus Story by tapping Your Story or Close Friends; save it by tapping the down arrow; or send it as a DM by tapping Send To, selecting the recipients, and tapping Send.**

Using Hands-Free to make life easier

To film a video without the hassle of holding down the button the entire time, use the Hands-Free setting. Swipe left from the Normal setting until you reach Hands-Free. You can then record video by tapping the white circle with the colorful box inside. Tap the circle again to stop. If you don't tap it again, Hands-Free will keep filming a longer video, but it will only allow four 15-second segments to post as a "stitched together" video.

FIGURE 13-10:
Find the Focus
setting by
sliding left
from the
Normal
camera setting.

Uploading a video from your camera roll

Have a great video on your camera roll already? It's easy to upload to stories. Here's how:

1. **Swipe right from the newsfeed or tap the camera icon at the top of the newsfeed to access Instagram Stories.**

2. **Swipe up from the bottom of the screen or tap the box with a small photo thumbnail at the bottom left.**

Thumbnails of all available photos and videos are displayed at the bottom of the screen, as shown in Figure 13-11.

FIGURE 13-11:
Available photo and video thumbnails are shown and can be selected by tapping on them.

3. **Tap the video you'd like to post, or tap Select Multiple to choose up to ten videos (can be combined with photos).**

   Be sure to select them in the order you'd like them to appear on your Story.

4. **To add a photo filter (not a face filter) to your video, swipe right until you reach the filter option you want.**

5. **Tap Your Story to post your Story, Close Friends, or Send To to send it as a direct message to an individual or group.**

Adding a Text Post

When Instagram Stories first released, only photos or videos were available to use as a backdrop for text. After several clever Instagrammers came up with work-arounds for a solid colored background to create a text post, Instagram finally built that functionality into the app. Now you can easily select a color background, and type a text message overlay to your followers. Here's how:

1. **Swipe right from the newsfeed or tap the camera icon at the top of the newsfeed to access Instagram stories.**

2. **Slide the Normal setting to the right, changing it to Create, as shown in Figure 13-12.**

3. **For a text-only post, make sure the white circle says Type underneath it.**

4. **Tap the screen where it says, "Tap to type."**

5. **Enter your text.**

6. **Change your text's color by tapping any of the colors below your text.**

TIP

   You can scroll left for more text colors, or use the eye dropper to sample a specific color. You can also change the background color of the screen by tapping the same-colored circle at the bottom of the screen on the iPhone or top of the screen on Android, and you can change the justification from left, center, or right by tapping the four lines at the upper left of the screen (only available on certain fonts).

7. **Tap the bar marked Modern at the top of the screen to choose another font, or leave it in Modern mode.**

8. **Tap Done.**

9. **Tap Your Story to post your Story, Close Friends, or Send To to send it as a direct message to an individual or group.**

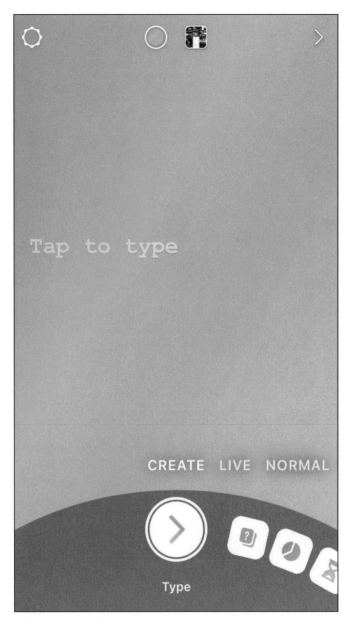

FIGURE 13-12:
Use the Create function to create a text-only post, or slide the icons to the left to reveal more features.

Other features in the Create setting

The Create setting also offers some other cool add-ons by scrolling past the Type option (refer to Figure 13-12):

>> **Questions:** Ask your followers one of the preformatted questions, or tap the white question box to write your own question.

>> **Poll:** Ask your own question with two replies, and Instagram will tally your responses.

>> **Countdown:** Countdown to a big occasion like your birthday by editing the event title and countdown clock.

Saving Your Story

Sometimes stories are so good, you can't bear the thought of them disappearing forever. Well, you're in luck. You can save them to enjoy later and to repost on other social media networks in the following three ways.

Saving before publishing

After you create or upload a photo or video, tap the down arrow at the top of the screen and it will save it to your camera roll (see Figure 13-13). You must do this before you tap Your Story, Close Friends, or Send To.

Saving after publishing (within the 24-hour active window)

Go to the newsfeed or your profile page and tap your profile picture. If you have an active story, it will appear. Tap the right side of the screen until you see the story you want to save. Tap the three small dots at the lower right of the screen, and then tap Save (see Figure 13-14).

Automatically saving all your stories

Tap the gear icon (Settings) at the top left of the stories page. On the Story Settings screen, you can choose to Save to Camera Roll (saving all stories to your phone) or Save to Archive (saving all stories to an accessible archive on Instagram). You can also choose neither of these options, or both! Sliding the slider to blue means that functionality is on. After you've made your selections, tap Done, as shown in Figure 13-15.

FIGURE 13-13: Tap the down arrow at the top of your screen to Save a Story before sharing it.

FIGURE 13-14:
Tap the three dots at the bottom of your screen and then tap Save to save an active story.

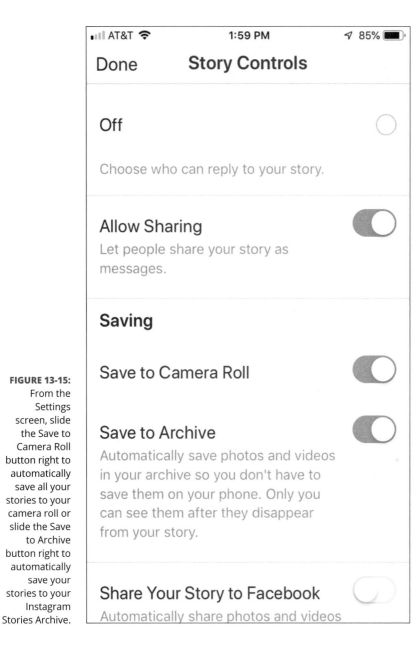

FIGURE 13-15:
From the
Settings
screen, slide
the Save to
Camera Roll
button right to
automatically
save all your
stories to your
camera roll or
slide the Save
to Archive
button right to
automatically
save your
stories to your
Instagram
Stories Archive.

Accessing your archives

In the previous section, we explain how to save your stories to Instagram's archives (saving precious space on your camera roll). Here, we show you how to access them.

From your Profile page, tap the three lines at the upper right of the screen, then tap Archive, as shown in Figure 13-16. All the stories that you've posted since enabling the archive are available for you to view or reshare (see Figure 13-17). Instagram also suggests memories of photos taken on that day in years past to view or reshare with your followers.

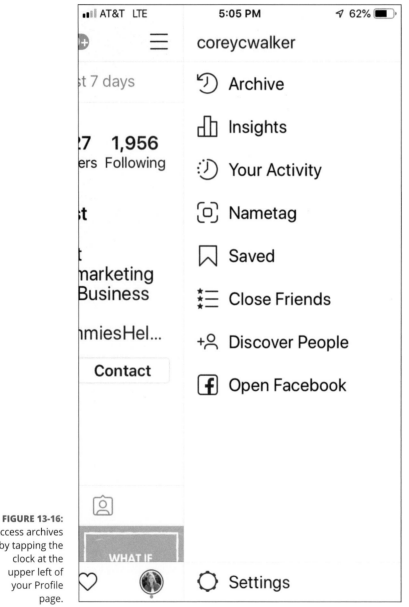

FIGURE 13-16:
Access archives by tapping the clock at the upper left of your Profile page.

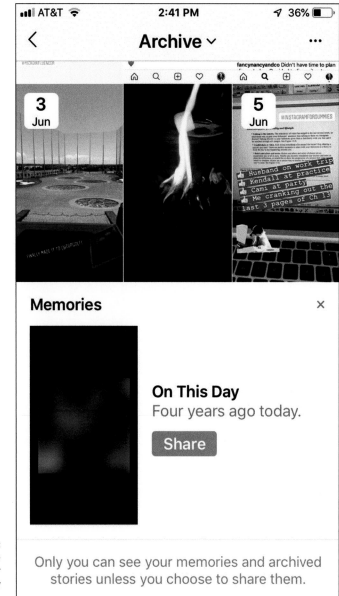

Chapter **14**

Adding Style to Your Stories

In this chapter, we explain how take your Stories to another level by adding personalized style and content, including various stickers, animations, doodles, and text. These features can be combined in a variety of ways to create your own unique style and message.

Jazzing Up Your Story Post Using Stickers

There are so many fun stickers to choose from on Instagram. And they keep adding more, so there are always fun new ways to augment your content. In this section, we look at some of the more common stickers available and explain how you can use them in your content.

Stickers are available by tapping the square smiley face icon in the story screen after you've uploaded or taken a photo or video. Tapping the sticker icon will open a screen (or tray) with various options of stickers and emojis (see Figure 14-1).

FIGURE 14-1:
Access story
stickers by
tapping the
sticker icon
that looks like
a smiley face.

Location, mention, and hashtag stickers for search and notifications

Just as you can @ mention someone on an Instagram post, or tag a location in a post, or use hashtags for search, you can do much the same with your Instagram stories.

Using these three stickers can help you appear in more searches, enable new people to find you, and let others know you're talking about them.

Location stickers

Adding a location sticker to your post lets your followers know where you are. It also allows you to show up in search results (if you're a public profile) for that location and others nearby.

When people look for locations in Instagram search, they see posts associated with that location. These search results combine both feed posts and stories in the results. When you add a location sticker, you may appear in those search results.

TIP

For more exposure, use a location tag for the smallest location possible. Don't tag a city; instead, tag a physical location or smaller area. When you tag a specific location, you increase your chances of appearing in more location results in surrounding areas, or in larger location results. For example, if you use a location sticker for a specific restaurant, the map system in Instagram knows exactly where that restaurant is located. You may show up in search results for that restaurant, for a park nearby, for that local neighborhood, and maybe even for that city as a whole (see Figure 14-2).

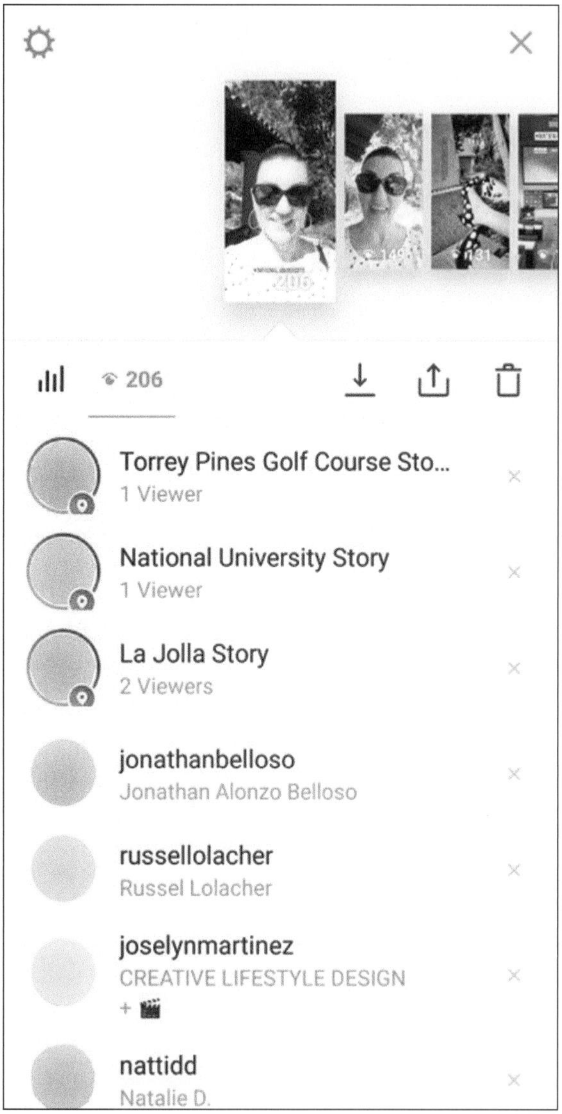

FIGURE 14-2:
Tagging a small location — in this case, National University — allowed this post to appear in multiple other search results for surrounding areas.

When you tap the Location sticker to select it, a new screen appears with a list of nearby locations. You can scroll through this list and tap to select the location you want to add. If your location isn't listed, or the location isn't near you when you're adding the story, you can type in the search bar for the name of the location you want to tag. A list of related locations will appear, and you can select the correct one by tapping on it (see Figure 14-3).

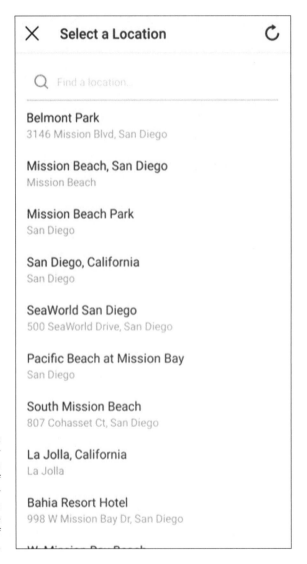

FIGURE 14-3:
Select your
location from
the list of
locations or
use the search
bar to find the
location of
your choice.

After you select the location, the sticker will appear on your story. You can pinch to zoom to make it smaller or larger. You can drag it around the screen or turn it on an angle to place it where you want.

You can also tap the location sticker to change the background. There are typically three color options available that you can tap through (see Figure 14-4).

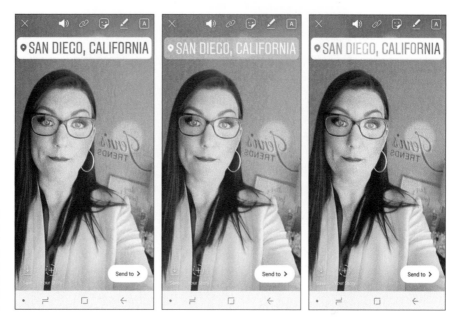

Mention stickers

If you want to tag someone in your Instagram story, you simply have to tap the @ Mention sticker.

Begin typing the name of the person or their username to find them. Relevant users who match that name will appear along the screen (see Figure 14-5). Keep typing until you find the person you're looking for; then tap their profile photo to select their username and add the sticker to your story. As with Location stickers, you can drag the sticker around, pinch to enlarge or shrink, and tap to change the background and color options.

You can @ mention multiple people in your story. Simply add another @Mention sticker for each person you want to tag.

TIP

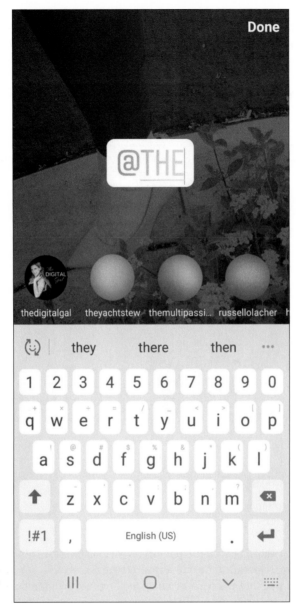

FIGURE 14-5:
Type the name or username of a person you want to @ mention with a sticker and select the user from the list of options.

REMEMBER

The person or people who are tagged in your story will be notified via a direct message that you tagged them, and they'll be able to see your story.

Hashtag stickers

You can use up to 30 hashtags on a feed post on Instagram, but you're limited in terms of the number of hashtags you can use in a story post. If you use the hashtag sticker, you can only add one hashtag to each individual post.

To add your hashtag sticker, choose the Hashtag option from the sticker screen and start typing your hashtag (you don't need to include the #). When you're done, tap Done in the upper-right corner. You'll see the sticker added to your story. Just as you did with the Location sticker, you can tap through to change color options, move the sticker around, and resize it.

TIP

You can add more hashtags to a story post by using the text box and manually typing in a list of hashtags. You should be aware, however, that Instagram will only recognize the three hashtags in a text box, so don't use any more than that.

GIFs, sliders, emojis, and more

The previous three stickers are incredibly functional and help with search and exposure. But they don't do much for the fun factor or to drive engagement. Fortunately, there are plenty of other sticker options to up the fun factor!

GIF stickers

A cultural norm with social media is the use of GIFs (short animated pieces) to convey a thought, emotion, or response. Instagram is partnered with Giphy so that you can add GIFs to your stories, too.

Select the GIF sticker option from the sticker screen. A list of popular and trending GIFs will appear for you to choose from. You can also search for a keyword or topic related to the GIF you want to use (see Figure 14-6).

You can add multiple GIFs to a story post to add the style and context you want. This is also a creative way to take a simple photo and make it animated and engaging.

Slider stickers

The Slider sticker is designed to boost engagement and interaction with your story. Viewers can physically drag the sticker to indicate their level of participation. There are plenty of creative ways you can find to utilize this sticker!

To add the sticker, select the Slider sticker (with the heart eyes emoji) from the sticker screen. Then select the emoji to include as the slider mechanism. Note that there are multiple options and you can scroll left and right on the emojis to see more options. Then type in your question and tap Done when complete. You can drag and resize the sticker to place it anywhere on the image (see Figure 14-7).

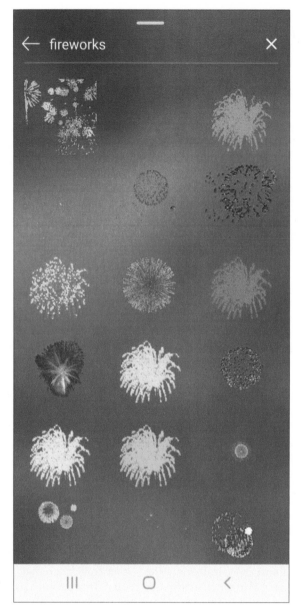

FIGURE 14-6:
Use the search bar in the GIF sticker screen to find animations related to any topic of your choice.

Emojis

You have the whole emoji keyboard to utilize and add as stickers to your stories. Tap the sticker icon and scroll up on the sticker screen to reveal trendy stickers, emojis, and more.

FIGURE 14-7:
In this
example,
dragging the
smiley face will
indicate how
much wine
a viewer
might want.

Questions, polls, quizzes, chats, and more

Do you want to learn more about your followers? Or maybe share more about you? The variety of questions, polls, quizzes, and chat stickers will allow you to do that and really draw participation from your followers.

Questions sticker

The Questions sticker allows you to pose a question to your audience and have them submit responses. Your question can be on any topic you choose! Responses will appear in the story insights for that post and are only visible to you.

Select the Questions sticker from the sticker screen, type in a question of your choice, and post the sticker to the story. Your followers will have the option to type in a response in the sticker itself. And you'll be able to see those responses by tapping the viewers in the lower-left corner of your own story to navigate to the post insights (see Figure 14-8).

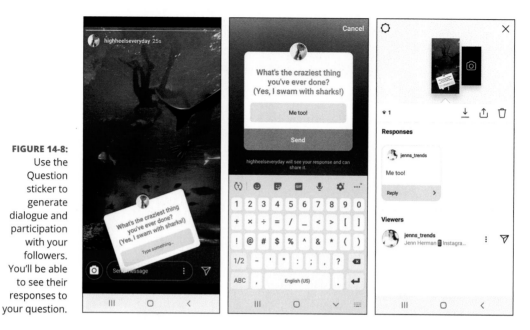

FIGURE 14-8:
Use the
Question
sticker to
generate
dialogue and
participation
with your
followers.
You'll be able
to see their
responses to
your question.

Poll and Quiz stickers

Both the Poll and Quiz stickers work much the same as the Questions sticker. You can create a question and provide answer options for your audience to choose from. The polls results will appear after the viewer has selected a response.

For the Quiz sticker, type in the question and then add answers. It defaults to two, but you can add more options. Tap the option that is the correct response to highlight it (see Figure 14-9).

As with all stickers, pinch, drag, and move them where you want them in your story.

Chat sticker

Again focused on interactions with your followers, the Chat sticker allows you to create a unique direct message thread exclusively for those who reply to the Chat sticker on your story.

When you add the sticker, followers can tap it to request to join the chat. When you approve them, this adds them to the direct message thread along with anyone else you approve into the chat. You can stop the chat thread at any time by turning it off, and no one will be able to continue chatting in that conversation.

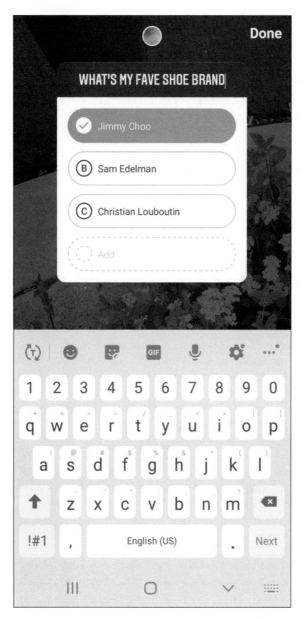

FIGURE 14-9:
The Quiz sticker allows you to test your followers. Add multiple options for responses and select the correct one before adding it to your story.

TIP

These chats are great for making weekend plans or coordinating a meetup with a group of people.

Countdown and Music stickers to intrigue your followers

One of the best ways to keep your followers on top of what you have going on is to use the Countdown sticker. This allows you to set a date and time for an upcoming event. People can subscribe to the sticker to be notified when it expires.

If you're hosting a party, or going live on Instagram, or leaving on vacation, or doing any other type of event, you can use the Countdown sticker to let people know when that event is going to happen.

The Music sticker may be one of the most sought-after stickers for most Instagram users. It's widely available, but not everyone always has access to it. But it does allow you to add a music overlay to any Story post.

You can choose from Instagram's music library (not your own) and add up to 15 seconds of music to an individual post. Select the Music sticker, navigate through the music options or search for a song or artist of your preference. Select the song by tapping it. Tap the number to the left of the slider to choose how long the music will play for (between 5 and 15 seconds). Drag the slider to the clip of the song you want to use (see Figure 14-10).

Lyrics for the song will appear on the screen. Slide through the Aa icons to choose the font option for the lyrics or choose one of the last options to display the song name or cover image instead of the lyrics.

Picture in picture for the fun of it

To make things even crazier with your stories, you can take a photo with the selfie (front-facing) camera to add to your story. Select the camera icon sticker from the sticker screen.

A small window will appear in your story showing the camera is on (see Figure 14-11). Position yourself or the object in the view of the lens and tap the white shutter button below the window to take the picture. Then you can drag the photo around the screen and pinch to change the size. You can also tap on the photo to change the frame of the photo.

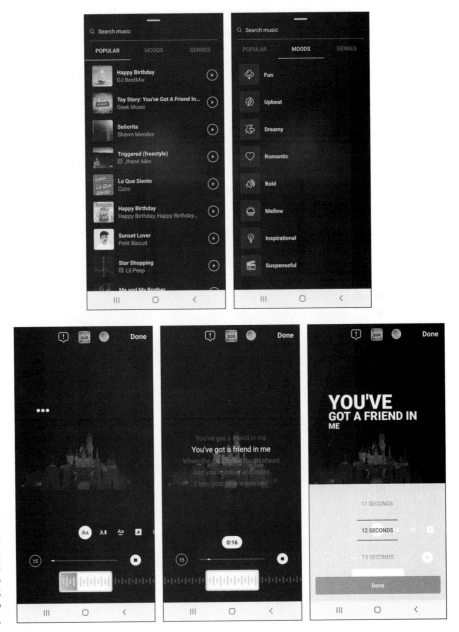

FIGURE 14-10:
The Music sticker allows you to add a music clip of 5 to 15 seconds onto a story post.

Deleting stickers that don't work

It's easy to add stickers, and it's just as easy to remove them if you don't like them (before you post the story). After you've added the sticker to your story, you can tap and hold the sticker. You'll see the garbage can appear at the bottom of the story screen (see Figure 14-12). Simply drag the sticker to the garbage can and it'll be removed.

FIGURE 14-12:
Tap and hold
any sticker in
a story to drag
it down to the
trash can to
remove it from
your post.

Personalizing Stories with Doodles

Instagram stories have a variety of drawing tools that allow you to add freehand doodles and scribbles of your own. To access the drawing tools, tap the pencil icon at the top of the story screen (see Figure 14-13).

FIGURE 14-13:
Select the
pencil icon
from the
story toolbar
to access the
drawing tools.

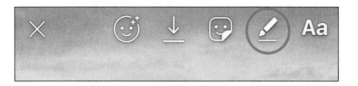

You'll notice a variety of pen and drawing tools along the top of the screen. Each pen offers a different effect, from a simple pen/pencil to a highlighter, an eraser, and more.

On the left side of the screen, you'll notice a sizing tool. You can drag the dot up and down to make the drawing tool thicker or thinner. Along the bottom of the screen are color options. You can scroll left and right along the color option bar to access more color selections (see Figure 14-14).

TIP

You can also get really creative and choose any color of the rainbow, not just the color options listed. If you tap and hold any color circle on the row of colors, the whole spectrum of colors will appear and you can drag your finger to find the perfect shade.

If you want to match something specific, you can tap the eyedropper tool next to the color palettes and then tap the specific color you want to match on your image. That color will become your pen color.

TIP

If you want to fill the screen with a certain color, choose the standard pen tool, pick the color of your choice, and then tap and hold the screen. The color you chose will fill the entire screen, creating a blank canvas to work from.

You can even layer various aspects to get really creative with your drawing tools. For example, upload an image to your story. Then select the pen tool and color. Tap and hold the screen to fill the screen with that color, laying it on top of the image you uploaded. Then select the Eraser tool from the drawing tools and erase the color fill to reveal the image behind it (see Figure 14-15).

When you're done with any doodle, tap the check mark to save it to your story.

TIP

While you're adding doodles, you'll notice a backward-facing curved arrow at the top of the screen. Tap that arrow to undo the last doodle you created. You can keep undoing all the way back to the first one you added. However, when you tap the check mark to apply the doodles, you can't undo them.

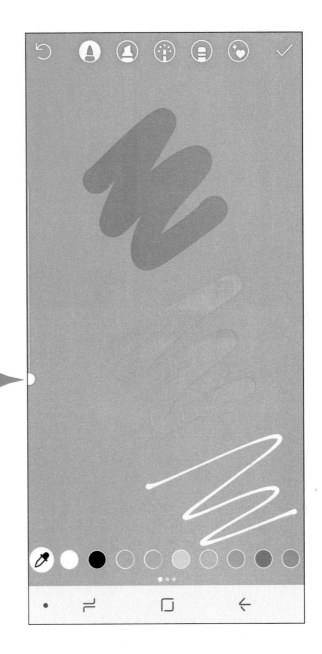

FIGURE 14-14:
Doodle tools offer different pen options, different thickness options, and different color options.

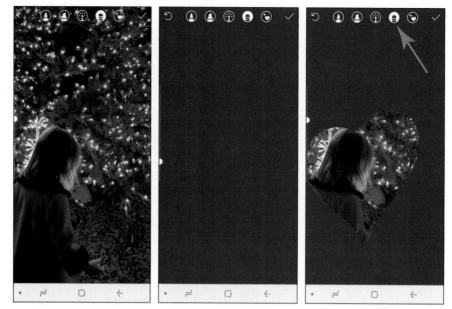

Saying More with Text

For all the fun you've had this far creating doodles and adding stickers, there's still another way to personalize your stories! You can add text boxes to your stories, too.

To access the Text option, tap the Aa icon in the top toolbar when creating your story or simply tap anywhere on the screen to open the text tool.

You can add multiple text boxes to your story and place them wherever you choose. They can be pinched to change the size and rotated as you please.

Changing your font option

The font option will default to Classic. You can change this easily to one of the other font options by simply tapping the name of the font at the top of the screen. You'll navigate through the available options (see Figure 14-16).

Figure 14-17 shows you some examples of what the different fonts look like in stories. Choose the font that best represents your style or the purpose of that story.

FIGURE 14-16:
Instagram
stories offer a
variety of font
options for you
to personalize
your posts.

In addition to font choices, you can choose different colors for your fonts.

Some font options will allow you to change the justification from left to center to right justified by tapping the alignment icon in the upper-left corner of the screen. This option is only available for certain fonts; if the alignment icon isn't available, it's not available for that font choice.

Certain fonts will also allow you to add background colors or to fill the text box with a color. If you see the "A**" icon, that lets you know that option is available. Tapping the "A**" icon will fill the text box with the selected color, which you can also change by tapping a color palette of the options.

Removing your text boxes

Similar to stickers, text boxes can be easily removed if you decide you don't want them. Simply tap and hold to reveal the trash can icon and drag the text box onto the trash can to remove it.

REMEMBER

FIGURE 14-17: Instagram stories offer a variety of font options to choose from.

IN THIS CHAPTER

» **Sharing other people's stories to your own**

» **Limiting who you share stories with**

» **Exploring the ability to share regular feed posts to your stories**

» **Adapting your story post to a regular feed post**

Chapter **15**

Sneaky Story Sharing

Sometimes you want to use content that someone else created or you want to repurpose your own content for your stories. In this chapter, we show you how to repost Instagram stories, how to reuse existing content, and how to be selective in who you share your stories with.

Sharing Another Story to Your Own Story

You may come across a cool Instagram story that you want to share to your own stories. Unfortunately, you can't directly share just any story to your own. There isn't an existing tool within Instagram that allows this. There are, however, two workarounds:

» **If you're tagged in someone's story, you can share that story to your own.** If a friend of yours posts a story and includes your username tag in the post, you'll receive a notification in your direct messages. Included with the notification that you were mentioned in their story will be an option to Add This to Your Story (see Figure 15-1).

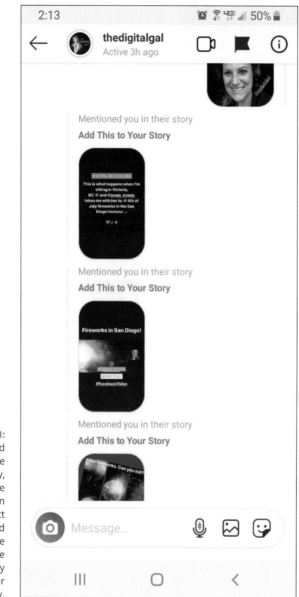

FIGURE 15-1:
When tagged
in someone
else's story,
you'll receive
a notification
in your direct
message, and
you have the
option to share
that story
post to your
own story.

When you tap that option, you initiate a story post where their post appears in the screen. You can shrink or enlarge it, reposition it, and add your own content to it using stickers, doodles, and more.

» **You can take a screen shot of their story, saving it as an image.** It should be pretty obvious that this only works well with photos, not videos. When you have the screen shot of their story, you can upload that image as your own story.

WARNING

Taking a screen shot and reposting it does put you in the area of copyright infringement, and you never want to use someone's post without their permission. Always ask them first if you have their permission to repost it. You can send them a direct message or reply to their story to ask for that permission.

Sharing Some Stories to Select People

For all the fun you can have creating Instagram stories, you may not want every post to be available to every one of your followers or to anyone publicly. Fortunately, Instagram has provided a few solutions to allow you to send stories privately or to select groups of people.

Sharing via a direct message

If you want to share a story post to one or a number of individuals via a direct message, you can easily do so. Create your story as you normally would, adding all your personalized components.

At the bottom of the screen, tap the Send To button instead of the Your Story button. A new screen opens with a list of people you commonly send messages to (see Figure 15-2).

If the person you want to send it to is listed there, simply tap the Send button next to her name and she'll receive the story in her direct messages. You can repeat this process to send the same story to more than one person using this method.

TIP

If the person you want to send it to is not listed, use the Search bar to type in his name and select him to send the story to him.

FIGURE 15-2:
Tap the Send
To button on
a story to send
it to only a
select group.

Sharing to your Close Friends list

You may have noticed that there is also an option to send stories to your Close Friends list. This feature is a messaging tool that allows you to select a number of the people you follow on Instagram and put them into a group, called Close Friends.

To set up your list of close friends, go to your Instagram profile and tap the three-line button in the upper-right corner. The Menu page appears, where you can tap Close Friends to select and set up your list (see Figure 15-3).

In the Close Friends screen, you'll see a list of recommended friends, based on those you most normally interact with. You can add any of them by tapping the Add button next to their names. If the person or people you want to add are not listed in the suggestions, you can use the search bar to type the name of the person you follow and add him to your list.

FIGURE 15-3:
Navigate to
the menu tab
on your profile
to access the
Close Friends
tab to set up a
list of friends.

You can add multiple people to this list, but you can only have one list. You may want to use this list for family, friends, or colleagues.

If you add someone by accident or you later want to remove someone from the list, navigate back to this Close Friends list, tap the tab for Your List and tap the Remove button next to his name (see Figure 15-4).

FIGURE 15-4:
Remove
anyone from
your Close
Friends list
by navigating
to Your List
and tapping
Remove next
to the person
you want you
delete from
the list.

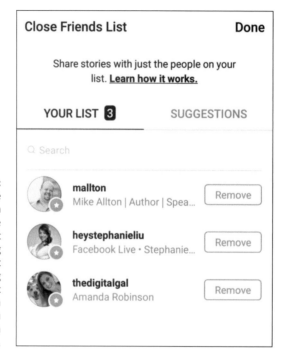

Now that you have your Close Friends list set up, you can share stories specifically with them!

When you're in your story creation screen (see Figure 15-5), you can tap the Close Friends icon at the bottom of the screen to share it with the list, or you can tap the Send To button and choose the Close Friends list from the next screen.

FIGURE 15-5:
Easily share a story to your Close Friends list by tapping the Close Friends icon or the Send To button when creating a story.

Sharing Regular Instagram Posts to Your Stories

As creative and unique as Instagram stories are, you may want to share regular Instagram posts to a story. A good educational piece, a post about news or something trendy, or even just good entertainment can be worthy of sharing with your followers.

Instagram has provided a simple sharing tool that you can use to share a feed post to your Story. Under any post (your own or someone else's), you'll see a paper airplane icon (see Figure 15-6). This is the share icon.

Tap the share icon to open a screen that allows you to choose how you want to share that post. To share it to your story, simply tap the Add Post to Your Story option.

This will open your story creation screen with the image of that post added to the story. If you tap the image of the original post, you can toggle between two display options, one (shown in Figure 15-7) with just the original image and the account's username, or a screenshot of the original post, including the first couple of lines of the caption.

You can edit the story, moving the post image or adding text, doodles, and stickers. When the story is published, the post image is a hyperlink back to the original post so others can view it.

WARNING

This share to Story feature is widely available, but not everyone has access to it. You should have the share icon but you may only see the options to share to individuals, not to add it to your story.

TIP

Some of your followers may only watch your stories and not regularly see your feed posts. If you have a great piece of content you uploaded to your Instagram account, but you want to make sure people who watch your stories see it too, you can share your own post to your story. Go to the post on your own profile that you want to share, and follow the instructions earlier to share the post to your story.

FIGURE 15-6:
The paper airplane icon is the share button to share a post on Instagram.

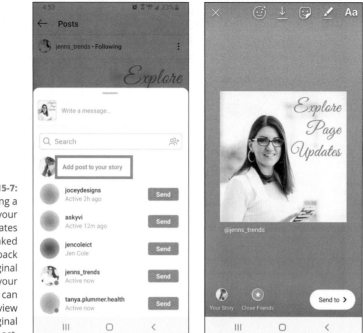

FIGURE 15-7:
Sharing a
post to your
story creates
a hyperlinked
image back
to the original
post that your
followers can
tap on to view
the original
post.

Changing Your Story into a Regular Instagram Post

In the reverse of sharing posts to stories, you might create an incredible Instagram story and want to share that to your regular feed. And, yes, you can do that, too!

Open any story, current or archived, and tap on the three-dots More button in the lower-left corner of the Story post. A screen appears with a variety of options, including Share as Post. Tap that option and the post will open in a regular Instagram feed upload screen (see Figure 15-8).

If your story post was a static image, it will transfer to the feed post as an image. Any stickers, text, or doodles, will remain on the image. If your story post was a video or included animated stickers like GIFs, the post will upload to your feed as a video, retaining those features.

Any interactive components like polls, sliders, and chat stickers will not retain their functionality in the feed post. They'll simply appear as static stickers.

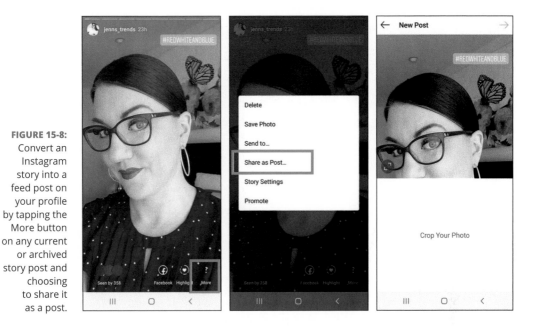

FIGURE 15-8:
Convert an Instagram story into a feed post on your profile by tapping the More button on any current or archived story post and choosing to share it as a post.

Because stories are uploaded at a 9:16 dimension, you'll have to edit the image orientation and sizing of the feed post to select the area of the story you want to showcase. You won't be able to display the full 9:16 original post. An Instagram feed post has a maximum ratio of 4:5.

TECHNICAL STUFF

After uploading the story post and arranging it for the right orientation, continue editing the post, adding a caption, and adding any other components as you would to upload any other Instagram post.

Chapter **16**

Using Instagram Highlights to Keep Your Content Alive

When you start using Instagram stories, you can keep those stories alive longer! Stories disappear after 24 hours, so it can be frustrating to know that the content you created is lost. Fortunately, however, highlights allow you to select certain stories to stay active on your profile in specific galleries you set up.

In this chapter, we explain how to set up highlights and how to add content to them. We also talk about some of the reasons why you may want to use highlights and give you some creative ideas for highlight topics.

Getting Acquainted with Highlights

Story Highlights are the series of circles directly beneath a person's bio on his Instagram profile (see Figure 16-1). A person may only have a few of these galleries, or he may have a number of them that you can scroll through.

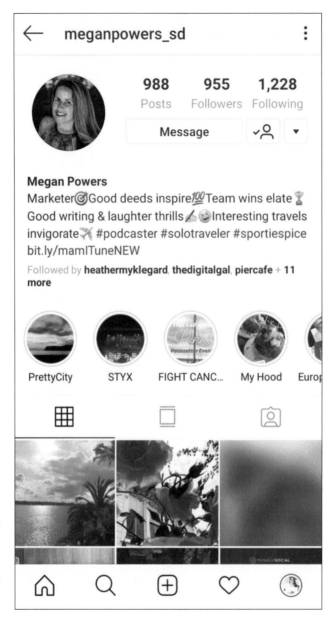

FIGURE 16-1:
Story
Highlights are
the series of
circles beneath
the bio and
are a place to
collect stories
to live more
than 24 hours.

The highlight galleries are each a collection of stories from that account. There may be only one story post or a series of multiple story posts from various times uploaded to each highlight.

A story disappears from the account after 24 hours, but highlights are an opportunity to keep that content on your profile for as long as you want it there.

You can customize all the highlights for your own profile with whatever topics and titles you would like!

Creating a New Highlight Gallery

Story Highlights are available to all users. You do have to have active or archived stories on your profile, though, in order to have access to adding a highlight gallery. If you've never shared a story before, go ahead and create one! That will open up the option to add highlights to your profile.

If you do have access to the highlights, you'll notice the Story Highlights section beneath the bio information on your profile. If you haven't yet created any highlights, the circles will be gray and you'll see a circle with a plus sign (+) to create a new highlight easily.

Adding a highlight from your profile

To create a new highlight from your profile, tap the plus sign (+) in the circle below your bio. A list of your archived stories will appear (see Figure 16-2). Scroll through the list of posts and select one or more you want to add to that highlight.

Tap Next after you've selected your posts and move on to the following instructions for naming and customizing your highlight.

Adding a highlight from an active story

If you have an active story on your profile and you want to use that one to create a new highlight, you can easily do that by opening the story post from your profile or feed.

At the bottom of your story post is a variety of buttons, including the Highlight button, which is a circle with a heart in the center (see Figure 16-3). Tap that icon, and then select New from the Add to Highlights screen. Proceed with the following instructions for naming and customizing your highlight.

FIGURE 16-2:
When starting a new Story Highlights gallery, you'll be able to choose from your archived stories which post(s) to add to the highlight.

FIGURE 16-3:
When you access your active stories, you'll see the Highlight icon (the circle with the heart in the center), which will allow you to add that active story to a highlight gallery.

Naming and customizing your highlight

Now that you've started a highlight, you need to give it a name! Here are some things to be aware of:

>> Highlight titles can be up to 16 characters in length.

>> The titles get cut off after a handful of characters (there's no set limit).

>> Keep the titles as short as possible and keep the important title info at the start of the title.

Type in your highlight title and tap Add to create the new Highlight on your profile.

Setting a cover image for your highlight

When you're done naming the highlight, you need to assign it a cover image. By default, the cover image will be the first image you uploaded into the highlight. Because stories are vertical 9:16 images, and the cover image is a circle, chances are, the image won't crop the way you want it to.

To improve the look of your cover image, tap Edit Cover and then drag or zoom (by pinching) to reposition your cover image (see Figure 16-4).

At any point after creating your highlight, you can edit the cover image to be a crop of any image in that highlight gallery. Simply tap that highlight from your profile to open the gallery. In the lower-right corner, tap the three-dots button and select Edit Highlight from the list. Then tap Edit Cover and follow the same steps to select a new image and position it for the cover image.

Creating a custom cover image

You may notice that people have specific images or logos set up for their highlights (see Figure 16-5). In this situation, they've uploaded a custom-designed image to their stories and then added it to their highlight.

FIGURE 16-4:
The cover image for your highlight isn't likely to crop to a nice section of the first photo in your highlight. Reposition the placement for a more favorable alignment.

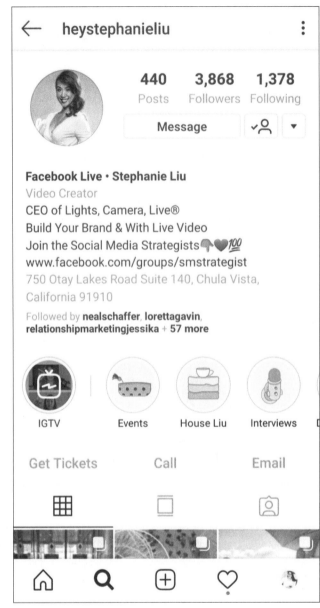

FIGURE 16-5:
Custom covers
for highlights
offer a creative
and appealing
way to
showcase the
topics of each
highlight.

Tools like Canva offer templates for creating these types of covers, but you could also create them in Photoshop or other design tools. Simply create the background color or design you want and place your cartoon, graphic, or logo in the center of the image. Edit your highlight following the steps earlier to select a cover image and set this as your cover image for each individual highlight.

Adding Content to a Highlight

Now that you've got your highlights set up, you'll want to keep adding content to them. Here, we walk you through the steps to add and delete content from a highlight.

Sharing a current story

If you have an active story on your profile that you want to add to an existing highlight, you simply have to access that story from your profile and tap the Highlight icon (the circle with the heart in the middle) just as you would when creating a new highlight.

Scroll through the list of highlights and select the one you want to add the story to. Tap that highlight cover image, and your story will be added to the highlight.

Finding an archived story

To add more content to an existing highlight, you can also select from older, archived stories.

The first option is to tap the highlight on your profile. When you're in the highlight, tap the three-dots button and tap Edit Highlight. You can then select the Add tab (on Android devices) or the "Archive" tab (on iOS devices) to scroll through archived stories and select as many as you want to add to that highlight (see Figure 16-6).

Alternatively, you can go into your archived stories by tapping the three-line button on your profile screen, and selecting the Archive tab from the menu page to view all your old stories in that feed. Select any story from the list and tap the Highlight icon at the bottom of the story to add it to a highlight (see Figure 16-7).

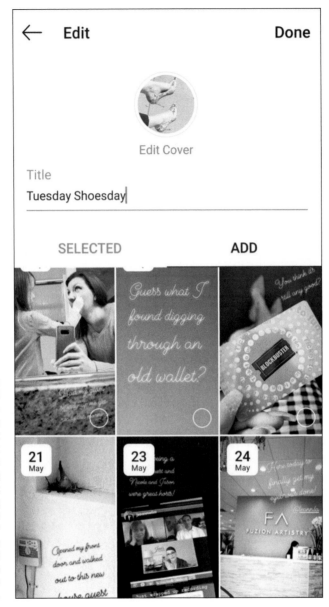

FIGURE 16-6:
Add archived stories to a highlight from the Edit Highlight option on any existing highlight by tapping the Add tab (Android) or the Archive tab (iOS) and selecting the story posts to include.

Deleting a story from a highlight

If, at some point, you decide you no longer want a particular story to appear in your highlight gallery, you can easily remove it.

Select the highlight from your profile and advance through the story posts in the highlight until you arrive at the one you want to remove. Tap the three-dots button in the lower right. Tap Remove from Highlight from the pop-up screen (see Figure 16-8), and confirm that you want to remove that item from the highlight.

If you want to delete a bulk number of story posts, you can go to Edit Highlight from the three-dot button and uncheck all the story posts from the list. Tapping Done will save the changes, removing those stories from the highlight.

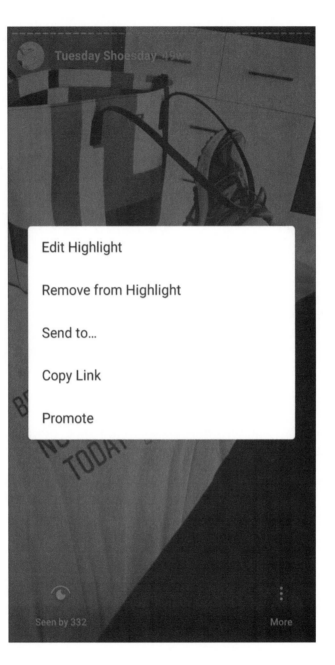

Coming Up with Fun Ideas for Highlights

You can use highlights for any topic that you create with your stories! It's best to group your stories into specific topics for your highlights, though.

For example, you may have a lot of stories of your family. But you could create one highlight for family vacations, another one for holiday celebrations, and another one for just your pets.

TIP

You can have plenty of different highlights so feel free to use them as best suited for you. Just realize that only the four most recently used highlights appear on the profile. After that, users will have to scroll to see your other highlight galleries.

IN THIS CHAPTER

» Understanding how Instagram Live works

» Determining when to go live

» Discovering how to interact on live videos

» Learning how to save and share live videos

Chapter 17
Going Live on Instagram

Quickly after they launched, Instagram stories dramatically changed the way people used Instagram. Some users even abandoned the newsfeed and went all in on Instagram stories.

With the popularity of stories and the growth of Facebook LIVE, including a live video option in Instagram stories seemed like a natural next step.

In this chapter, you learn all about how to go live, and get tips for making your live broadcast more successful before, during, and after filming.

Getting Started with Live Videos

So, you're ready to go live, but how do you even get to it? How do you use it? Its location is not exactly obvious. Follow these steps:

1. **Open Instagram stories by swiping right or using the camera icon at the top of the newsfeed.**
2. **At the bottom of the screen, swipe Normal to the right so you're on Live.**

   Figure 17-1 (upper left) shows the Instagram Live screen.
3. **If you want only certain people to view your live broadcast, tap the gear icon (Settings) at the upper left, tap Hide Story From, and select the followers you want to omit.**

4. **When you're ready to start, tap Go Live.**

   Instagram checks your connection, and then the timer counts down 3, 2, 1, and you're on! You'll begin seeing *Username* Has Joined and the number of people who have joined.

5. **Wait a minute or two before diving into your topic so that people have time to join.**

   Greet as many people as possible. Say hi, calling them by their name or username. Make them feel welcome.

6. **Now that you're live, you can do the following:**

   - Turn off comments by tapping the three dots at the lower right of the screen, as shown in Figure 17-1 (upper right and lower left). However, we recommend that you keep them turned on for more interaction.

   - Add a face filter by tapping the face with stars icon.

   - Turn the camera from the front-facing selfie camera to the rear-facing camera to showcase what you're seeing, rather than showing your face. Tap the curved double arrow (shown in Figure 17-1) to change the camera view.

   - Enter the name of your live broadcast by typing it in a comment and tapping Send. Then tap the comment and choose Pin Comment from the options menu. This pins the name to the top of the comment feed, where it acts like a title.

   - To keep track of your time, tap the pink Live button in the upper right. A timer appears.

   - To see the names of the people who have joined, tap the number to the right of the pink Live button. To kick people out of your Live broadcast, place an X by their name.

7. **When you're finished, tap End, and then tap End Live Video.**

8. **Save the live video by tapping Save at the upper left.**

   The Save button is easy to miss, but you can see where it is in Figure 17-1 (lower right). Your video is saved to your camera roll so you can reuse it elsewhere.

WARNING

You must save your live broadcast immediately after recording (before you agree to share it). After it's shared, there is no option to go back and save it.

9. **To share the live video with your Instagram followers for 24 hours, go to the bottom of your screen and make sure the sharing tab is pushed to the right showing blue; then tap Share, as shown in Figure 17-1 (lower right).**

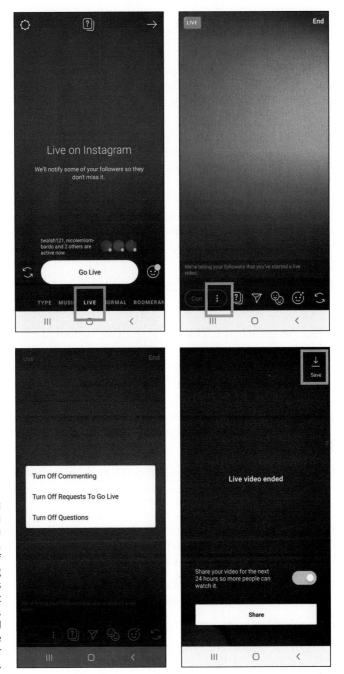

FIGURE 17-1:
Go live on
Instagram
(upper left),
turn off
commenting
or questions
(upper right
and lower left),
and save and
share your live
video (lower
right).

Knowing When to Go Live

TIP

You can go live anytime you want. But it helps to go live when you have plenty of followers online. Pick times of day that work best for you and your followers to ensure more people tune in to the live broadcast.

You may also want to broadcast when you're at an event or experiencing something in your life. Sometimes these can't be planned in advance, and it's okay to go live when the moment strikes you.

WARNING

Instagram Live has a 60-minute time limit. You'll see a 15-second timer countdown when your time is almost up, and then the live broadcast will end. If possible, plan your schedule accordingly so as not to exceed that limit.

Developing a Game Plan

TIP

Now that you know how to physically tap all the buttons to record a live broadcast, it's time to talk strategy. We recommend going on Instagram Live with forethought about what you'll be doing. Here are a few tips to help you execute the best Instagram Live possible:

>> **Think of a topic that will interest your followers.** Some ideas to consider: Showcase your family life, stream your child's rehearsal, show off some of your vacation, share a holiday tradition.

>> **If you plan to talk on the live broadcast, jot down several talking points, but don't memorize or look overly rehearsed.** Live broadcasts are supposed to be a bit off the cuff.

>> **If possible, do a test video on your regular camera app where you plan to do the live broadcast, and at the same time of day.** Check the lighting and the background. Make sure that you can get a decent signal in that location.

>> **Promote your live broadcast ahead of time by posting about it in your Instagram stories, on Facebook, and other social media.**

>> **Be as interactive as possible with your followers during the broadcast.**

>> **Save your broadcast so you can repurpose it to other online media, and then publish your broadcast so it's available for 24 hours.**

TIP

It's often helpful to have a tripod to hold your camera steady and in place while filming live. Arkon Mounts (www.arkon.com) has several tripods available for less than $50.

Interacting with Live Guests

While you're waiting for more people to view your live video, acknowledge the people who are joining you. Use their names or usernames and thank them for participating. Introduce the topic you're sharing on the live video, and after a few minutes of welcoming guests, you can start speaking about the topic at hand.

People will likely comment while you're talking. It's nice to answer questions and comments as they arise, but sometimes it's not practical if you're trying to explain something. In this case, let them know that you're happy to take comments and questions and you'll address them at the end or when you wrap up that current thought.

If you really want to keep the questions organized, you can encourage your viewers to tap the Questions icon — it looks like a question mark — to send you questions. You'll see a numerical notification listed on the Questions icon to let you know someone has posed a question. When you tap the Questions icon, you'll see the list of questions people have submitted (see Figure 17-2). You can tap any one from the list and it will appear on the screen in your live video so that viewers know what question you're answering. Tap the X on the question box on the screen when you're done answering that question.

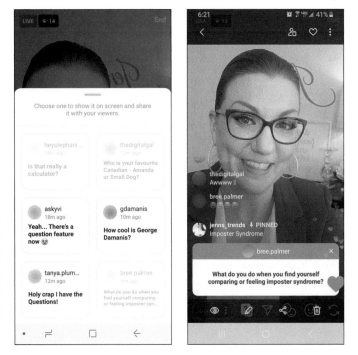

FIGURE 17-2:
Use the Questions feature on live video to collect and select questions to respond to on your broadcast.

Inviting a Guest onto the Live Broadcast

If being live on camera alone makes you nervous, or if you just want to include someone else in your video, Instagram allows you to invite one guest into the live show with you.

Tap the two-face icon (see Figure 17-3) in your live video to invite someone to that video. A screen will appear with a list of recommendations of people to invite into the video, or you can use the search bar to type their name.

Alternatively, someone can request to join your live video when they tap the same button while watching your live broadcast. You'll receive a notification that they want to participate, and you can choose to add them or ignore them.

FIGURE 17-3:
The two-face icon allows you to invite someone into your live video to share the screen with you.

When the guest joins you on the live video, he'll occupy half the screen, sharing his video and audio as well (see Figure 17-4).

FIGURE 17-4:
Guests on a live broadcast will share the screen with you until they leave.

Saving Live Broadcasts and Sharing Them

After you've completed your live broadcast, don't forget to save it! After you've tapped End Live Video, tap Save on the screen that appears (refer to Figure 17-1, lower right). The broadcast is saved to your camera roll on your device.

WARNING

You must have enough storage space on your mobile device to save the full video. If you don't have enough storage space, only a portion or even none of the video will save.

When you save your Instagram Live broadcast, it becomes a regular video that you can use any way you'd like. Here are some places to reuse it:

>> Post it on your YouTube channel, and then share the link to the YouTube video on LinkedIn and Twitter.

>> Post the video on your Facebook page or profile.

>> Post the video on your IGTV channel.

You can also edit the video to create sound bites of 1 minute or less, and upload them directly to Instagram, Facebook, LinkedIn, and Twitter. Or create a graphic about the video for Instagram, and then link to the video (on YouTube or your website) via the link in the bio on your Instagram profile page.

REMEMBER

You can reuse live content in so many creative ways — don't let it go to waste!

5

Becoming a Pro at IGTV

Understand how IGTV operates.

Set up your own IGTV channel and create content optimized for IGTV.

Chapter **18**
Understanding IGTV

GTV was introduced in 2018 as a standalone app that integrated with Instagram. Sound confusing? It is! IGTV was designed to be its own app for viewing and interactions, and yet it's tied directly to your Instagram profile. It's a video-only platform with some unique components.

In this chapter, we show you the various aspects of IGTV, how you can use it, and what makes it different. We also explain why you're seeing what you see in the feed.

Finding IGTV within Instagram

Even though IGTV is a singular component, it's actually accessible from multiple places within the Instagram app:

» **On an account's profile:** If the account is using IGTV and has created videos, you'll see the little IGTV icon just above the images on the user's profile page. Figure 18-1 (left) shows you where to find IGTV from an account's profile.

>> **Within your home feed on Instagram:** In the upper-right corner of the home feed, you see the IGTV icon. Figure 18-1 (center) shows you that location.

>> **On the Explore page (tap the magnifying glass icon in the bottom navigation bar to get there):** On the Explore page, an IGTV tab is at the top of the screen. Figure 18-1 (right) shows you where that's located.

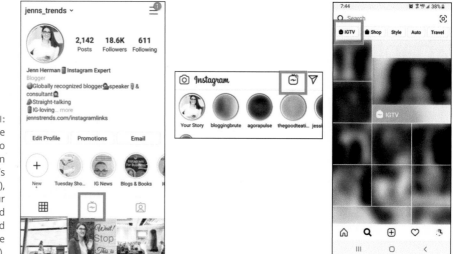

FIGURE 18-1:
There are three locations to access IGTV: on an account's profile (left), within your home feed (center), and on the Explore page (right).

In addition to these three locations, you can also see IGTV videos recommended for you on the Explore page. The videos will appear in the list of suggested content, as shown in Figure 18-1 (right).

If someone you follow creates an IGTV video and shares a preview of that video to Instagram, you'll also see that preview as a post when you're scrolling through your feed (see Figure 18-2, left). It will appear as a regular post, but you'll see the IGTV icon in the lower-left corner of the video. If you tap that icon, you'll be taken to the full IGTV video; if you watch the entire 1-minute preview, you'll be prompted to watch the remainder of the video on IGTV (see Figure 18-2, center). Tapping that option will open the IGTV video and allow you to continue watching (see Figure 18-2, right).

FIGURE 18-2:
Watching an
IGTV video.

Finding IGTV within the IGTV App

As we already mentioned, IGTV is a standalone app. You can install it from the app store for your device by searching for IGTV. After you've installed the app on your device, you can log in as the same account you use on Instagram. All your profile information and followers will transfer to the IGTV app.

**TECHNICAL
STUFF**

If you unfollow or follow someone on IGTV, that same interaction occurs on your Instagram account, and vice versa. The two are linked and you can't follow different people on IGTV than you do on your Instagram account.

After you have your IGTV account set up and you're in the app, you'll be taken to the home feed (see Figure 18-3). This is where the videos of the people you follow and those recommended for you will all appear. You can scroll vertically through the videos and tap any video to play it.

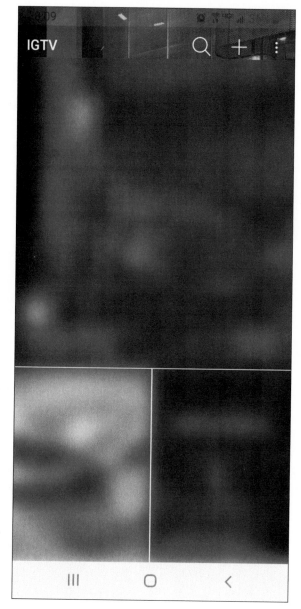

FIGURE 18-3:
The IGTV home feed is full of videos from those you follow and those recommended for you by Instagram.

Understanding How IGTV Videos are Formatted

IGTV was designed to be used only with vertical videos. In addition, the video viewer would not rotate when the mobile device was turned to the horizontal position (as most other video players do).

Instagram wanted to make an impact by forcing content creators to create fresh new content in vertical mode while also adhering to a growing trend for people to shoot and watch videos in a vertical orientation (much like Instagram stories). This different format challenges a lot of content creators because you don't have as much visual real estate to showcase a background or additional content except the object or person in the frame of the video. As more people move toward story content and people become comfortable filming videos in portrait orientations, IGTV will continue to capitalize on that video format.

In 2019, Instagram announced that it would start allowing horizontal videos to be uploaded and that those videos would rotate with the screen. Not all users yet have this functionality, though.

TIP

IGTV videos can be anywhere from 15 seconds up to one hour in length. They encourage longer-form content that keeps viewers watching longer. In contrast to Instagram stories, which only last up to 15 seconds, IGTV videos are meant to share more in-depth content.

Videos from 15 seconds to 10 minutes in length can be uploaded via your mobile device. Videos of 10 minutes to 60 minutes in length can only be uploaded via a desktop computer. We cover the upload procedures in Chapter 19.

Tapping Into Whose Videos You're Seeing

Your IGTV home feed is full of the IGTV videos created by everyone you follow on Instagram. Whenever someone you follow adds another IGTV video, it will appear in your list of videos.

To keep you interested, however, much like the Explore page on Instagram, the IGTV home feed will populate videos that it thinks you'll be interested in. These are not accounts you're following but the video content or the account creators are similar in interest to other content you watch or accounts you follow.

TIP

If there are videos in your IGTV feed that you really don't like or want to see, you can tap and hold that video preview in the feed. An option will pop up to show fewer videos like that in the feed. Additionally, when viewing a video full-screen, you can tap the three-dot button at the bottom of the screen to access a menu that allows you to see fewer posts, report the video, save the video, or copy the link for it. Tapping that menu option to see fewer posts like this one will tell the algorithm to show you less of that type of content.

Chapter **19**

Creating an IGTV Presence

I n the preceding chapter, we show you how IGTV works and where you can find those videos. If you're intrigued by the options in IGTV and you want to create your own videos, this is the next step. In this chapter, we explain how to upload videos and format the videos for better results.

Setting Up an IGTV Channel

In order to upload videos to IGTV, you need to set up your IGTV profile. You can upload via your mobile device or a desktop computer. But you need to have your account formatted on one or both of those platforms to be able to upload.

Using your mobile device to set up IGTV

You can install the IGTV app (separate from Instagram). If you want to upload videos to IGTV on your mobile device and create your own content, you need to have the IGTV app installed. To do this, follow these steps:

1. **Go to the app store for your device (Android or iOS) and search for IGTV.**

2. **Select the IGTV app, click Install, and follow the install procedures for your operating system.**

3. **Open the IGTV app.**

   You see a welcome screen asking you to continue as the username that you're currently logged into on Instagram.

4. **Tap Continue or Switch Accounts to sign in as the appropriate account.**

5. **Tap on the three-dots button or the gear icon (different devices may use one or the other) in the upper-right corner and select View Profile to confirm that your Instagram account information has transferred over.**

Figure 19-1 shows you the steps to log in and confirm your account information with your new IGTV profile.

FIGURE 19-1: Follow the series of prompts to set up IGTV after you've installed the IGTV app on your mobile device.

Using your computer to set up IGTV

If you prefer to use your computer and not install the IGTV app on your mobile device, you can follow these steps to activate your IGTV account:

1. **Go to** http://instagram.com **and log in as your account.**

2. **Go to your profile and click the IGTV tab below your profile info.**

3. **Click Get Started (see Figure 19-2).**

FIGURE 19-2:
Select the
IGTV tab from
your desktop
Instagram
profile and
click Get
Started to
begin setting
up your IGTV
channel.

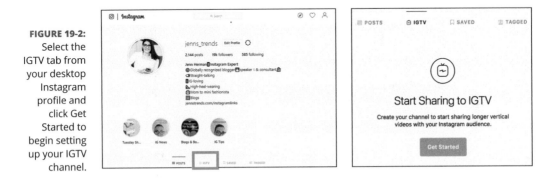

4. **Follow the series of prompts on the screen, clicking Next through some feature information.**

5. **Click Create Channel.**

Uploading Videos to IGTV

Now that you have your IGTV channel all set up for your account, you're ready to start uploading videos!

Using your mobile device to upload

Your mobile device is able to upload videos that are anywhere from 15 seconds to 10 minutes in length. To upload a video, follow these simple steps:

1. **Tap the plus sign (+) icon in the upper-right corner of the IGTV screen.**

   If this is your first time connecting to IGTV, your device may ask you to allow IGTV access to your files. Click OK to allow the access.

Your camera roll will open with all of your video files. Videos over 15 seconds in length appear in full color and are available for upload. Videos less than 15 seconds are grayed out and unavailable to choose.

2. **Select the video you want to upload by tapping it (see Figure 19-3).**

FIGURE 19-3:
Add an IGTV video by tapping the plus sign (+) and selecting a video over 15 seconds from the gallery of videos.

3. **Choose a cover image for the video.**

   The cover image doesn't have to be the first frame of the video. You can drag the slider along the video frames to pick the best cover image as shown in Figure 19-4 (left).

4. **Tap Next.**

5. **Enter the title and description of your video as shown in Figure 19-4 (center).**

6. **If your video is over 1 minute and you want to post a preview in your Instagram feed, tap the toggle button for Post a Preview.**

7. **Tap Post to upload your video to IGTV as shown in Figure 19-4 (right).**

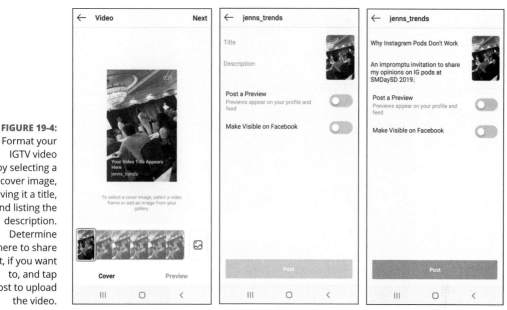

FIGURE 19-4:
Format your
IGTV video
by selecting a
cover image,
giving it a title,
and listing the
description.
Determine
where to share
it, if you want
to, and tap
Post to upload
the video.

WARNING

If your video is less than 1 minute in length and you choose the option to post a preview to Instagram, you'll receive an error message letting you know you can't post previews for videos less than a minute (see Figure 19-5).

Using your computer to upload

If you prefer to use your desktop computer, rather than a mobile device, to upload IGTV videos, or if you want to upload videos over 10 minutes in duration, follow these steps:

1. **Click the Upload button under the IGTV tab on your Instagram profile.**

2. **Drag and drop a video file from your computer to the video box on the upload screen as shown in Figure 19-6.**

   Depending on the size of the video, the upload may take several minutes or longer.

3. **Edit the cover image by choosing a JPG or PNG file from your computer.**

4. **Give your video a title and description.**

5. **Select the Post a Preview check box if you want a preview to appear in your Instagram feed.**

6. **Click Post to upload, as shown in Figure 19-7.**

FIGURE 19-5:
Instagram won't allow previews on your Instagram feed for videos less than 1 minute in length.

FIGURE 19-6:
To add a video
to IGTV via
the desktop,
you can drag
and drop a file
directly onto
the browser
page.

FIGURE 19-7:
Upload your
video to
Instagram via
the desktop
following the
onscreen
instructions.

Creating Quality Content for IGTV

Now that you're ready to upload videos to IGTV, we want to make sure your videos look amazing and perform well. In this section, we provide some suggestions for making your videos even better for IGTV.

Making your videos shine

TIP

If you're looking for some tips to make your IGTV videos look better, sound better, get more views, and longer retention, here are some suggestions for you:

>> **Get right to the point in your video.** Don't waste time with fluff and ramblings. Hook your audience immediately by getting to the meat of the topic.

>> **Make your videos at least one minute in length so that you can load the preview to your Instagram feed.** This will significantly increase views on your videos.

>> **Have a good cover photo that describes the video and looks appealing to those viewing it.** If you're showing up as suggested content to people who don't follow you, it helps to have a good cover photo to draw them in.

>> **Film vertical videos.** Even as Instagram allows more video formats for upload, the vertical video is best formatted for and fits in the IGTV space.

>> **Avoid loud introductions or distracting noises in your videos.** If people are playing the video or it automatically plays after the last one, you don't want people to stop watching because the audio caught them off guard.

>> **Keep your channel content consistent.** Because IGTV is a singular channel, you can't break out types of content. If your videos cover a whole range of topics — from your family vacation, to a recipe, to a business trip, to a party, and more — you probably won't retain viewers. If someone finds you for the recipe you shared, she'll want to see more of the same things, not videos of your dog sleeping. Pick a theme for your channel and keep your content consistent with that.

Using the video description to your advantage

TIP

The description of the IGTV video is a gold mine that most people don't realize is there. Writing a short description about the video may seem simple, but there are hidden tricks to using the description effectively:

>> **Share details about the video and any relevant takeaways, if applicable.** A descriptive caption can appeal to more viewers and increase video views.

- » **Include a URL in the video description.** On Instagram, only business profiles with over 10,000 followers or verified accounts can add swipe-up links to their stories. But on IGTV, any account of any size can add a clickable URL to their video description. Take advantage of this whenever appropriate.

- » **Use hashtags in the description.** Just like Instagram posts, you can include up to 30 hashtags in your IGTV video description. This will help you appear in more searches and have more people find your content. Make sure to follow the same hashtag rules we talked about in Chapter 8.

Responding to Comments on Your Videos

Hopefully, people will love your IGTV videos and want to connect with you via comments to respond to or engage with the videos. When someone responds to your IGTV video, you'll receive a notification in your Instagram notifications. You can reply directly from that notification just as you would any other Instagram post.

Additionally, you can view any comments directly from your IGTV video by tapping the comment icon. The comments screen will open and you can scroll through, view, like, and reply directly to any comments on the video (see Figure 19-8).

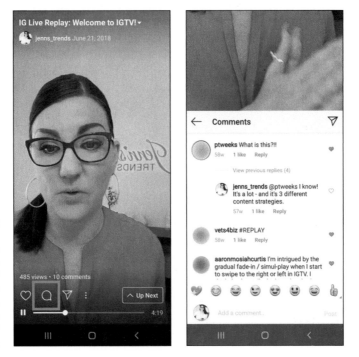

FIGURE 19-8: View, like, and reply to comments on your IGTV video by tapping the comment icon on your IGTV video.

6

The Part of Tens

IN THIS PART . . .

Learn the top ten mistakes to avoid on Instagram.

Find inspiration from types of ideal Instagram photos.

Chapter **20**

Ten Things Not to Do on Instagram

n this book, we provide lots of techniques that will help you do well on Instagram. Sometimes, however, it helps to understand what *not* to do to ensure you create better content or build a better community with your followers.

If you want to make sure you make the best of Instagram, it can help to learn what doesn't work or what will annoy other people so you can avoid those mistakes. With the advice in this chapter, you'll avoid looking like a beginner!

Using the Same Name as Your Username

Nothing says "amateur" on Instagram faster than when your name and username are the same exact thing.

The username is designed to be all lowercase and a string of words, names, or numbers perhaps separated by a period (.) or an underscore (_). The name of the account, however, should be in sentence format, utilizing capital letters, spacing, and even emojis.

If you want your username and your name to both be your *actual name,* your username might be @barackobama while your name would be "Barack Obama." (No pressure or anything.)

TIP

You could include emojis in your name, to add more personality to it. Because the only searchable criteria on Instagram are your name and username, if you want to be potentially found for something in particular (like your career), you might want that keyword to be part of your name. So, while you may keep your username as @barackobama, your name might read "Barack Obama, Former President." Just note that you're limited to 30 characters for your name, so your name can't be, "Barack Obama, Former President, Husband to Michelle, Father to Malia and Sasha." That kind of info is what your bio is for.

Turn to Chapter 3 if you need a refresher on how to set your username and name on Instagram.

Picking an Irrelevant Username

Your username is how you're recognized on Instagram. From posting to liking other content and more, you are your username. Therefore, it should appropriately reflect who you are.

WARNING

A random series of letters and numbers will make you hard to recognize. It will also make you look untrustworthy, and more people will be skeptical that your account is spam or fake, making them less likely to interact with you. An awkward or random username can also make it hard for people to find you if they're trying to spell out your username to find you in search.

You can avoid these issues by picking a username that's easy to recognize and share!

The exception to this rule would be if you wanted to keep your account more private and *not* have it easily found in search. In this case, you might actually want to consider a username that is irrelevant to your actual name.

Using a Bad Profile Photo

One of the downsides to Instagram profile photos is that they get reduced to a very small size in the feed. Even a great full-size photo can look bad or poorly formatted when shrunk down to a circle one-half inch in diameter. In some cases, a perfectly normal photo looks inappropriate or resembles a completely different object when the size is dramatically reduced. Images with a lot of text also tend to look bad on Instagram — the text becomes illegible.

TIP

Choose an image that has good resolution, a clear object of focus, and a simple background. Avoid using a really busy image for your profile photo. If there are lots of people in the photo, or if it has a messy background, the context of the image will get lost when it's shrunk down.

Not Including a Bio

The description in your bio is an easy place to tell new people on Instagram who you are. Leaving this field blank is the equivalent of walking up to someone at a party, telling them your name, and then saying nothing else about yourself.

Your bio can say anything you want about who you are, what you do, what you're known for, and so on. Take the time to write something that will help you to connect with new people who find you on Instagram.

Ignoring Instagram Stories

Instagram stories are currently used by more than 500 million people every single day. With such a large audience and opportunity to connect with new people, you don't want to ignore this part of the app.

Instagram has put a big focus on story-formatted content, and it's expected that this type of content will only continue to grow in its creation and consumption. Ignoring stories means that you won't attract as many followers. Plus, if your existing followers prefer to consume story content and you're not creating that type of content, you'll miss out on the opportunities to connect with those followers.

The tips we gave you in Chapter 14 will help you create content to reach more people and keep your followers engaged with your stories.

Not Using Captions

Instagram is a visual platform, designed around photos and videos, both in the feed and in stories. It wasn't designed for lots of text or long blocks to read through. And although a photo may say a thousand words, a good Instagram caption can actually drive interactions with your followers.

REMEMBER

A photo or video on Instagram without a caption often lacks context. The caption is the opportunity to further convey your message or purpose of the post and connect with your followers. It's a place where you can ask questions, offer a call to action, or simply provide a story and background to the post. These types of interactions are critical to building relationships and driving conversations on Instagram. Don't leave a blank, empty caption on your posts!

Hashjacking

Hashjacking is the act of using trending hashtags on your posts to show up in front of new people. If you're attending New York Fashion Week and use the #nyfw hashtag in your posts, that's okay, because your content is actually related to the #nyfw hashtag. But if your post has nothing to do with New York Fashion Week, then using the #nyfw hashtag would be hashjacking because you're using a popular hashtag just to try to get your image or video in front of a popular audience.

Hashjacking is heavily frowned upon. The content that shows up in trending tags but is completely irrelevant is usually ignored at best. If you're hoping to find new people, chances are, these people aren't going to follow you — plus, now they have a bad impression of you, so using this method can actually *hurt* your reputation. You may even find your content getting reported for spam by people who don't think your content belongs. And getting flagged for spam content will punish your account for at least 24 hours because you won't show up in other hashtag searches.

With the consequences of hashjacking, it's not worth using these hashtags unless, as we said, you actually have content related to the topic.

Tagging People Who Are Not in the Photo

You can easily tag other accounts in your Instagram posts. Tagging people is so easy, in fact, that people often take advantage of it! You should only tag people or brands that actually appear in the post itself.

For example, if you share a photo of you and your friends at a local restaurant, you could tag each of the people in the photo. You could also tag the restaurant's Instagram account because you're eating there. And you could even tag the brands for the clothing you're wearing in the photo. All of that would be acceptable because those accounts are in the photo you uploaded.

What you *don't* want to do is tag a bunch of other accounts of famous people, or influencers you want to connect with, or brands that aren't in the photo, or people you follow. Some people do this to try to grab the attention of these other accounts, but the kind of attention you'll get is negative at best.

Another common tactic some people use is to post a motivational quote or similar content and then tag a bunch of people they want to "inspire." Unless these people are your friends, most people don't want to be tagged in your photos.

WARNING

These tagging tactics can often be viewed as spam and may get your account flagged for bad behavior. If you're regularly tagging people inappropriately, they may also unfollow you or block you. So, avoid these tactics and only tag the people or accounts who actually appear in the post.

Following Everyone Who Follows You

Instagram is a heavily engaged platform, and you'll see a lot of reciprocity where people follow you back if you follow them. But there is no expectation of reciprocal following. You don't need to follow everyone who follows you.

TIP

Instagram is meant to be fun. But it will only *be* fun if the content you see in your feed is content that you want to see. If it's full of your friends, family, favorite celebrities, brands you love, and accounts that inspire you, then you'll enjoy it, which means you'll log in more often, interact with more content, and enjoy the whole experience.

In contrast, if you follow hundreds of people you don't know simply because they followed you, your feed will include those people's posts, with their families, musings, random content, and whatever else they choose to post. Chances are, this content won't be relevant to you and you won't want to see it or interact it with it.

REMEMBER

There's no need to fill your feed with things that don't matter to you! If someone follows you and you like her content, follow her back. But don't feel any obligation to follow everyone who follows you.

Using Automated Tools to Follow or Like Others

As you get deeper into the Instagram experience, you'll likely discover a variety of tools that offer services to augment your Instagram experience. Many of these apps or websites are legitimate tools that properly integrate with Instagram and will help you get more value out of Instagram.

WARNING

Tools that offer to automate the process of liking posts, leaving comments, or following people for you are *not* these approved tools. In fact, any tool that does this is violating the Instagram application programming interface (API) and violating the terms of use you agreed to when you signed up for Instagram. Using any of these tools can put your account at risk of various penalties, up to and including your account being shut down. So, don't rely on any tool that automates the interactions on Instagram for you!

You can, however, use a tool or app that helps you manage your Instagram account. Tools like Hootsuite (http://hootsuite.com) allow you to connect your Instagram account so that you can post to it from a desktop and manage your comments and other notifications. Most of these dashboard tools, like Agorapulse (www.agorapulse.com), Sprout Social (https://sproutsocial.com), and Tailwind (www.tailwindapp.com), only integrate with Instagram Business profiles though. Again, this is due to the way the Instagram API is set up. If you're using a personal profile on Instagram, you'll find most tools limited in their ability to integrate with your account.

Chapter **21**

Ten Types of Great Instagram Photos

There are so many things you can do with Instagram and so many things you can photograph! But what works best on Instagram? What types of photos typically get more engagement?

In this chapter, we give you ten examples of content that will generally perform better on Instagram.

The Human Element

People connect with people and Instagram is no exception to that rule. If you can include a person, or a part of a person, in your Instagram post, chances are, it will perform better with your audience.

The photo doesn't always have to be a full-body shot or even include the face of the person. Simply including a hand holding a product, or the back of a person's head reading something, or a shot from the knees down to show a pair of shoes is enough to convey the human component and connect with your audience (see Figure 21-1).

Look for creative ways to incorporate yourself or other people into your posts.

FIGURE 21-1:
Instagram user @ maine_blonde does a great job of including human elements in her photos to highlight various products of focus, like jewelry or accessories.

Adorable Animals

Everyone loves puppies, right? We're all suckers for a cute baby animal. But all animals typically perform well on Instagram. Including a pet or animal in your photos can generate more likes for your posts.

Even if your post isn't specifically about the animal itself, just their presence in the image can boost your like counts. Of course, it doesn't hurt to make the post about the cutie pie, does it? Lots of people even create Instagram accounts exclusively for their pets (see Figure 21-2)!

FIGURE 21-2: @canadasmall-dog is a feature account based entirely on the life of a dog and his travels around North America.

Bold Colors

You may want to find unique ways to stand out on Instagram. Instagram has a lot of content, and people are scrolling fast. One way to catch people's attention can be with the use of bold colors in your images (see Figure 21-3).

You can rely on well-staged scenes with bold colors, but don't forget to take advantage of photo-editing tools within Instagram to add more saturation and boldness to your images.

White Space

An alternative way to stand out in the feed, is to focus on plenty of white space in your image (see Figure 21-4). With lots of white space, the object of focus will stand out more in the feed and better attract people's attention.

A recent study by AdEspresso showed that photos with good white space performed 29 percent better than those images without white space.

Including lots of white space isn't always easy to achieve and it can make your images much more muted in general contrast. If you choose to go this route, make sure it aligns with your style of photography.

Make It Blue

According to that same study by AdEspresso, images with the color blue as a dominant color perform 24 percent better than images where the dominant color is red.

Fortunately for you, there's plenty of blue in the world! From the sky, to the water, to clothing, and plenty of other everyday objects, there are lots of creative ways you can bring more blue into your posts (see Figure 21-5).

FIGURE 21-4:
This image from @tickletreestudio includes plenty of white space in both the décor and the wall itself, allowing the print to stand out as the object of focus.

FIGURE 21-5:
In this image from author Jenn Herman, there is plenty of blue to work with, from the water to the sky to the clothing.

Flat Lays

Flat lays are formatted when the image is taken from directly above the objects. A camera is usually mounted above a table or flat surface and the objects are laid out on the table (see Figure 21-6). This is very common for food photos, as well as accessories and even clothing.

FIGURE 21-6:
In this image, Cleveland Kraut created a great flat lay for @ therealdillco to showcase food, in addition to the product.

These images provide a fun way to showcase an object from a different viewpoint than straight in front of the camera.

Long Angles

Unique angles and long lines are very appealing visually and can stimulate more engagement on your Instagram posts. A great way to find these long angles in your everyday world is to look at roads, bridges, buildings, architecture, and even flooring!

When taking these photos, position yourself to maximize the length of the object across your plane of focus to make the lines look more accentuated or longer. In Figure 21-7, the photo has the building at the full height of the image on the left side of the screen and it's elongated across the image to a vanishing point on the right.

Lifestyle

There's a whole lifestyle component on Instagram. The rise of the influencer came from the perceived lifestyle images and styling that many people used to create content on Instagram.

You can tap into this with well-staged photos that show you at home, at work, on vacation, or wherever your lifestyle takes you. Figure 21-8, from @joselynmartinez, hits the high notes on lifestyle as she stands in her New York apartment with the city in the background. She also incorporates the pop of bold color in her dress, and there is a dominant blue hue to maximize her image performance.

FIGURE 21-7:
A great example of architecture and long lines is this sample from @kylenekaelin.

FIGURE 21-8:
This image
from @jose-
lynmartinez
plays up the
photographer's
lifestyle.

Rule of Thirds

The Rule of Thirds is a classic photography technique that breaks your field of vision into thirds, creating nine squares in the image. You can turn on the grid on your mobile device in your camera settings so that this grid is easily aligned for your photos.

The idea is to put objects of focus at the intersection points of the lines or in one of the major third quadrants: left or right, or top or bottom. This creates visual appeal and removes the standard placement of putting the object of focus in the center (see Figure 21-9).

Organic Environments

One of the keys to success on Instagram is to put things in their "organic" environments. Simply putting a product on an empty shelf or in a box won't appeal to many people because the context of the item is removed. Instead, place items in the environment in which you would find them (see Figure 21-10).

TIP

Put a coffee cup on a counter or cute table. Put a book on a desk or a bed or a chair with a comfy blanket. This makes the object more relatable and will usually result in more engagement for you.

FIGURE 21-9: Strategically placed items in this photo from @ theyachtstew shows how the flowers hit specific points in the various quadrants for strong visual appeal.

FIGURE 21-10:
This photo from @ yorkelee_prints puts the product, their framed print, in an actual living space, surrounded by furniture and décor, making it more appealing than just hanging on a blank wall.

Index

Symbols

+ (plus) icon, 78
#follow4follow hashtag, 149
#tbt (throwback Thursday) hashtag, 93
@ mention. *See* tagging people

A

Abusive Comment option, 164
accounts
  disabled, 67
  hacked, 64
  Instagram and IGTV, 303
  linked, resetting, 68–69
  private
    overview, 39–40
    requesting to follow, 140
    usernames for, 320
    using hashtags in, 128
  professional
    dashboard tools for, 324
    upgrading to, 37–39
    using calls to action (CTA), 124
    web addresses and, 315
  public, 39
  spam accounts
    overview, 149
    reporting, 164
    usernames and, 320
Accounts feature
  finding new accounts to follow,
    145
  searching with Explore page, 50
activating IGTV account, 309
AdEspresso study, 329
Adjust tool, 85
Adobe Photoshop, 285
ads, in stories, 203
Agorapulse social media management
    software, 324

algorithm for Instagram
  Explore page and, 47
  hashtags, 132
  IGTV home feed and, 306
  Instagram suggestions for following, 145
  overview, 44–46
Allow Message Replies setting, 212
Allow Sharing setting, 212
Android devices
  bio on, formatting, 34
  comments, deleting, 161–162
  installing Instagram on
    issues with, 58, 63
    overview, 15
  notifications on, 69–70
  predictive text for hashtags, 132–133
  problems, reporting, 71
  storage space on, 60–63
angles, long, 334
animals, 326–327
API (application programming interface), 324
App Store, 12
Apple iPads, 8
  deleting comments, 160–161
  finding storage space on, 60
  installing Instagram on, 12–14
  reporting problems on, 70–71
  setting notifications on, 69
Apple iPhones, 8
  deleting comments, 160–161
  finding storage space on, 60
  installing Instagram on, 12
  reporting problems on, 70–71
  setting notifications on, 69
  using Notes app for captions, 123
Apple Mac computers
  installing on, 17–19
  uploading photos from, 96
Apple Support, 63
application programming interface (API), 324

apps. *See also specific apps*
  App Store, 12
  Continual app, 208
  CutStory app, 208
  Flume app, 18
  Google Play Store, 15
  IGTV app, 303–304
  Instagram
    installing, 11–19
    starting, 21–24
  Later app, 218
  Notes app
    storing hashtags on, 133–134
    writing captions in, 123
  Planoly app, 218
  Storeo app, 208
  StoryCutter app, 208
  Tailwind app, 134, 324
  Uplet app, 18
archived stories
  adding content to highlight galleries,
    285–287
  saving, 241–243
Arkon Mounts tripods, 294

B

before and after stories, 221
behind-the-scenes stories, 218–219
bios, 32–37
  adding web address to, 35–37
  advantages of, 321
  formatting, 34–35
  hashtags in, 34
  including information, 32–34
  layouts for, 35
  overview, 32
Bitly link shortener, 36
blocking
  commenters, 165
  hashtags, 132
blue as dominant color, 329, 331
Boomerang camera option,
    223, 230–233
Boomerang icon, 96–97
Brightness tool, 85

broadcasts, 291–298
  general discussion of, 10
  interacting with live guests, 295
  inviting guests onto, 296–297
  overview, 291–293
  planning tips, 294
  saving, 298
  scheduling, 294
  sharing, 298
business profiles. *See* Professional Accounts

C

calls to action (CTA), 123–124, 322
camera roll
  saving to
    live videos, 298
    stories, 238
  uploading from
    photos, 96–97
    videos, 234–236
cameras
  accessing for stories, 210–215
    changing camera mode, 215
    editing settings, 212–214
  grid, turning on, 336
  options, 228–234
    Boomerang, 230–233
    Focus, 233
    Hands-Free, 233–234
    Rewind, 230–233
    SuperZoom, 230
  selfie mode, 215, 223, 227
  tripods for, 294
Canva graphic-design tool website, 285
captions, 119–124
  adding to photos, 89–91
  adding to videos, 111–112
  advantages of, 322
  formatting, 122–123
  including calls to action (CTA), 123–124
  length of, 119–121
channels on IGTV, setting up, 307–309
Chat stickers, 254–256
cheat sheet, for this book, 3
Close Friends list, 268–271

Color tool, 87
colors
  blue as dominant color, 329, 331
  bold, 328–329
  options for location stickers, 246
commenting. *See also* direct messages (DMs)
  blocking commenters, 165
  error messages, 71–72
  hashtags, 128–129
  replying to, 158–163
    deleting comments, 160–163
    on IGTV, 315
    from Notifications tab, 158–159
    from posts, 160
  reporting commenters, 164
  turning on and off
    for photo posts, 94
    for video posts, 111–112
  using automated tools for, 324
communities, 149–153
  finding, 150–151
  Instagram pods, 152–153
  overview, 149
Community Guidelines
  filtering words or phrases, 72
  flagged for spam content, 322
  resolving disputes, 163
  tagging people, 92
Compass icon, 20
compatibility error messages, 58
contact list, syncing, 140–141
Continual app, 208
Contrast tool, 85
conversations, using direct messages, 167–195
  cultivating communities through, 150
  declining, 194–195
  group conversations, 186–187
  inbox, 191–194
    deleting messages, 193
    overview, 191–192
    searching in, 194
  overview, 9
  replying to, 188
  sending in response to stories, 205
  sharing GIFs via, 181–183

sharing photos and videos via
  overview, 173–177
  sending disappearing, 177–180
sharing stories via, 267–268
starting new, 168–172
using Live Chat in, 188–191
using voice messages, 184–185
Countdown stickers, 238, 256
cover images
  for highlight galleries, 282–285
    custom, 282–285
    overview, 282
  for IGTV videos, 310, 314
  for videos, 110–111
Create setting features, 237–238
creating
  content for IGTV, 314–315
    tips for, 314
    using video description, 314–315
  hashtags, 134–135
  stories, 217–243
    photo, 221–226
    planning tips, 217–218
    reasons for, 218–221
    text posts, 236–238
    video, 227–236
Creator accounts, 38
CTA (calls to action), 123–124, 322
CutStory app, 208

D

declining direct messages, 194–195
Delete button, 108
deleting
  comments
    Android device users, 161–162
    error messages, 72
    iPhone and iPad users, 160–161
    website users, 163
  direct messages (DMs), 191–193
  stickers, 258–259
  stories from highlights, 287–288
  text posts, 263
  video clips, 108

devices
  Android devices
    bio on, formatting, 34
    comments, deleting, 161–162
    installing Instagram on, 15, 58, 63
    notifications on, 69–70
    predictive text for hashtags, 132–133
    problems, reporting, 71
    storage space on, 60–63
  iPads, 8
    deleting comments, 160–161
    finding storage space on, 60
    installing Instagram on, 12–14
    reporting problems on, 70–71
    setting notifications on, 69
  iPhones, 8
    deleting comments, 160–161
    finding storage space on, 60
    installing Instagram on, 12
    reporting problems on, 70–71
    setting notifications on, 69
    using Notes app for captions, 123
Direct icon, 168
direct messages (DMs), 167–195
  cultivating communities through, 150
  declining, 194–195
  group conversations, 186–187
  inbox, 191–194
    deleting messages, 193
    overview, 191–192
    searching in, 194
  overview, 9
  replying to, 188
  sending in response to stories, 205
  sharing GIFs via, 181–183
  sharing photos and videos via
    overview, 173–177
    sending disappearing, 177–180
  sharing stories via, 267–268
  starting new, 168–172
  using Live Chat in, 188–191
  using voice messages, 184–185
disabled accounts, 67

disappearing
  photos or videos, 177–180
  stories
    highlight galleries, 287–288
    saving, 238
disputes with commenters, 163–165
  blocking others, 165
  reporting, 164
DMs (direct messages), 167–195
  cultivating communities through, 150
  declining, 194–195
  group conversations, 186–187
  inbox, 191–194
    deleting messages, 193
    overview, 191–192
    searching in, 194
  overview, 9
  replying to, 188
  sending in response to stories, 205
  sharing GIFs via, 181–183
  sharing photos and videos via
    overview, 173–177
    sending disappearing, 177–180
  sharing stories via, 267–268
  starting new, 168–172
  using Live Chat in, 188–191
  using voice messages, 184–185
doodles, 259–262
double-tapping
  in Explore function, 142
  interacting by, 9
  overview, 156
  using automated tools for, 324
drawing tools, 259–262

E

editing
  camera settings for stories, 212–214
  photos tools for
    multiple photos in one post, 102
    overview, 83–89
  privacy settings, 39–40

email, storing hashtags in, 134

emojis
  in captions, 122
  stickers, 252–253

error messages, 71–73
  adding comments, 71–72
  deleting comments, 72
  following users, 73
  refreshing feed, 72–73

Explore page, 47–53
  following friends, 142–143
  IGTV on, 302
  searching with, 47–53
    Accounts feature, 50, 51
    Places feature, 50, 53
    Tags feature, 50, 52
    Top feature, 48–49
  viewing, 47

F

face filters, 223–224

Facebook
  Instagram business profiles and, 38
  logging in with, 19
  promoting live videos on, 294
  sharing photos on, 92–93

Fade tool, 87

feed, home
  defined, 8
  Instagram algorithm, 44–46
  interacting from, 155–157
  overview, 41–44
  refreshing, errors with, 72–73
  sharing posts as stories, 272–274

sharing stories as posts, 274–275

Filter screen, 79–80

filters
  applying to photos
    multiple photos in one post, 101–102
    overview, 81–83
  applying to videos, 110
  in direct messages (DMs), 168
  face filters, 223–224

flagging messages, 191–193

flash icon, 79

flat lays, 332–333

Flume app, 18

Focus camera option, 233

follower list, 147

following, 139–153
  communities, 149–153
    finding, 150–151
    Instagram pods, 152–153
  error messages with, 73
  finding new friends, 141–146
    Explore page, 142–143
    Instagram suggestions, 145–146
    Search feature, 143–145
  following back, 147–149
    followers, 147–148
    guidelines for, 323
    reasons for, 148–149
  overview, 9
  syncing contact list, 140–141
  unfollowing
    cleaning up feed by, 149
    overview, 45–46
  using automated tools for, 324

Following tab, 56

font options for text posts, 262–263

food photos, 332

formatting
  bios, 34–35
  captions, 122–123
  for IGTV videos, 305
  profile photos and, 320–321

frames, cover, for videos, 110–111

G

galleries of highlights, 277–289
  adding content to, 285–287
    from active stories, 285
    from archived stories, 285–287
  creating, 279–285
    from active stories, 279–281
    cover image for, 282–285

galleries of highlights *(continued)*
    naming, 282
    from profile, 279
  deleting stories from, 287–288
  overview, 277–279
  suggestions for, 289
GIFs
  stickers, 251
  via direct messages (DMs), 181–183
Giphy, 181
Google Analytics, 36
Google Play Store, 15
Google Play troubleshooting wizard, 63
Google URL Shortener, 36
grid in camera settings, 336
group conversations, via direct messages (DMs), 186–187
guests
  interacting with on live videos, 295
  inviting onto live videos, 296–297
Guidelines, Community
  filtering words or phrases, 72
  flagged for spam content, 322
  resolving disputes, 163
  tagging people, 92

H

hacking, 64
Hands-Free camera option, 223, 233–234
harassment, 163
hashjacking, 322
hashtag stickers, 250–251
hashtags, 128–135
  #follow4follow hashtag, 149
  #tbt (throwback Thursday) hashtag, 93
  algorithm for Instagram, 132
  in bios, 34
  choosing, 130–132
  creating, 134–135
  expanding reach with, 130
  in IGTV video description, 315
  limitations, 250
  placement of, 128–129
  saving, 132–134
  searching by, 50, 52, 130–132
  for stories, 218

Heart icon, 9, 20, 156. *See also* double-tapping
Hide Story From setting, 212
Highlight button, 279, 281
highlights, 277–289
  adding content to, 285–287
    from active stories, 285
    from archived stories, 285–287
  creating galleries, 279–285
    from active stories, 279–281
    cover image for, 282–285
    naming, 282
    from profile, 279
  deleting stories from, 287–288
  overview, 277–279
  suggestions for, 289
Highlights option, Color tool, 87
Highlights tool, 87
home feed
  defined, 8
  Instagram algorithm, 44–46
  interacting from, 155–157
  overview, 41–44
  refreshing, errors with, 72–73
  sharing posts as stories, 272–274
  sharing stories as posts, 274–275
Hootsuite social media management
    platform, 324
human element, in posting,
    325–326
hyperlinks
  copying IGTV, 306
  sharing, 156
  shortening, 36

I

icons
  Boomerang icon, 96–97
  Compass icon, 20
  Direct icon, 168
  flash icon, 79
  Heart icon, 9, 20, 156
  IGTV icon, 302
  Instagram Direct icon, 168
  Layout icon, 96–97
  paper airplane icon, 156, 272

Person icon, 20
plus (+) icon, 78
Questions icon, 295
speech bubble icon, 156
switch cameras icon, 79
used in this book, 2–3
IGTV
  content for, creating, 314–315
    tips for, 314
    using video description, 314–315
  defined, 9
  finding with IGTV app, 303–304
  home feed, 305–306
  on Instagram app, 301–303
  overview, 10
  responding to comments, 315
  setting up channel, 307–309
  uploading videos to, 309–313
    live, 298
    using computers, 311–313
    using mobile devices, 309–311
  videos on, formatting for, 305
IGTV app, 303–304
IGTV icon, 302
images
  GIFs
    stickers, 251
    via direct messages (DMs), 181–183
  photos
    adding captions to, 89–91
    adding location to, 92
    improving, 79–89
    pixelated, 32
    posting, 94–95, 98–102
    for profile, 30–32
    sending in response to stories,
      205–206
    sharing, 92–94, 173–180
inappropriate activity, 132
inbox, direct messages, 191–194
  deleting messages, 193
  overview, 191–192
  searching in, 194
influencers
  lifestyle photos, 333
  overview, 217

Instagram, 7–10
  Explore page, 47–53
    searching with, 47–53
    viewing, 47
  feed
    algorithm, 44–46
    overview, 41–44
  following on, 9
  IGTV on, 10, 301–303
  installing app, 11–24
    on Android, 15
    on iPad, 12–14
    on iPhone, 12
    on Mac, 17–19
    on Windows PC, 15–17
  issues with, 57–73
    disabled accounts, 67
    error messages, 71–73
    installation, 57–63
    logging in, 64–67
    notifications, 69–70
    reporting, 70–71
    sharing, 67–69
  notifications, 53–56
  posting, 119–135
    captions, 89–91, 119–124, 322
    creating galleries from profile, 279
    hashtags, 128–135
    locations, adding, 92, 111–112, 126–127
    overview, 8–9
    photos, 94–95, 98–102
    preview of IGTV videos, 310–311
    replying to comments, 160
    suggestions for content, 325–338
    tagging people, 91–92, 124–126
    turning on notifications for, 45–46
    videos, 113–114, 310–311
  smartphones for, 7–8
  starting app, 21–24
  stories
    overview, 10
    posting, 265–275
  terms of use, 324
  tools for managing
    approved, 324
    Tailwind app, 134

Instagram *(continued)*

website users

deleting comments, 163

overview, 19–21

Instagram Direct

cultivating communities through, 150

declining direct messages, 194–195

group conversations, 186–187

inbox, 191–194

deleting messages, 193

overview, 191–192

searching in, 194

overview, 9

replying to direct messages, 188

sending direct messages in response to stories, 205

sharing GIFs via direct messages, 181–183

sharing photos and videos via

overview, 173–177

sending disappearing, 177–180

sharing stories via, 267–268

starting new, 168–172

using Live Chat in, 188–191

using voice messages, 184–185

Instagram Direct icon, 168

Instagram Direct inbox, 191–194

Instagram Live

general discussion of, 10

interacting with live guests, 295

inviting guests onto, 296–297

overview, 291–293

planning tips, 294

saving, 298

scheduling, 294

sharing, 298

Instagram Live screen, 291, 293

Instagram pods, 152–153

Instagram stories

accessing camera for, 210–215

changing camera mode, 215

editing settings, 212–214

before and after, 221

behind-the-scenes, 218–219

of candid shots, 220

creating, 217–243

photo stories, 221–226

planning tips, 217–218

reasons for, 218–221

text posts, 236–238

video stories, 227–236

defined, 8

highlight galleries, 277–289

adding content to, 285–287

creating, 279–285

deleting stories from, 287–288

overview, 277–279

suggestions for, 289

ignoring, 321

limitations for, 207–209

recording time, 208–209

uploading, 208

overview, 10, 199–203

pausing, 205

personalizing, 245–264

with doodles, 259–262

with stickers, 245–259

with text, 262–264

promoting live videos on, 294

reacting to, 205–206

rewatching, 204–205

saving, 238–243

accessing archives, 241–243

after publishing, 238

automatically, 238–241

before publishing, 238

series, 221

sharing, 265–275

another story to own story, 265–267

posts from feed, 272–274

as posts on feed, 274–275

to select people, 267–271

skipping through, 204

Instagram suggestions, 145–146

Instagram's Community Guidelines

filtering words or phrases, 72

flagged for spam content, 322

resolving disputes, 163

tagging people, 92

installing Instagram, 11–24

on Android, 15

IGTV app, 308

on iPad, 12–14

on iPhone, 12
issues with, 57–63
  with Android device, 63
  compatibility error messages, 58
  finding missing apps, 63
  storage issues, 58–63
  unfreezing, 63
on Mac, 17–19
on Windows PC, 15–17
interacting on Instagram, 155–165
  from home feed, 155–157
  with live guests on live videos, 295
  replying to comments, 158–163
    deleting comments, 160–163
    from Notifications tab, 158–159
    from posts, 160
  resolving disputes, 163–165
    blocking commenters, 165
    reporting commenters, 164
inviting guests onto live videos, 296–297
iPads, 8
  deleting comments, 160–161
  finding storage space on, 60
  installing Instagram on, 12–14
  reporting problems on, 70–71
  setting notifications on, 69
iPhones, 8
  deleting comments, 160–161
  finding storage space on, 60
  installing Instagram on, 12
  reporting problems on, 70–71
  setting notifications on, 69
  using Notes app for captions, 123
issues with Instagram, 57–73
  disabled accounts, 67
  error messages, 71–73
    adding comments, 71–72
    deleting comments, 72
    following users, 73
    refreshing feed, 72–73
  installation, 57–63
    with Android device, 63
    compatibility error messages, 58
    finding missing apps, 63
    storage issues, 58–63
    unfreezing, 63

logging in, 64–67
  checking username, 64
  fixing password issues, 64–67
notifications, 69–70
reporting, 70–71
sharing, 67–69

L

Later app, 218
Layout icon, 96–97
layouts, for bios, 35
lifestyle, 333, 335
liking posts. *See* double-tapping
limitations
  for bio, 32
  for following users, 9
  IGTV
    hashtags, 315
    length of, 305
  for live videos, 294
  for stories, 207–209
    hashtags, 250
    recording time, 208–209
    uploading, 208
  video length, 103
links
  copying IGTV, 306
  sharing, 156
  shortening, 36
Live camera setting, 223
Live Chat, in direct messages (DMs), 188–191
live videos, 291–298
  general discussion of, 10
  interacting with live guests, 295
  inviting guests onto, 296–297
  overview, 291–293
  planning tips, 294
  saving, 298
  scheduling, 294
  sharing, 298
location
  adding to photos, 92
  adding to videos, 111–112
  posting, 126–127

location *(continued)*
  searching by, 50, 53
  in stories, 218
location stickers, 246–249
logging in, issues with, 64–67
  checking username, 64
  fixing password issues, 64–67
long angles, 333
Lux tool, 86–87, 102
lyrics, for Music stickers, 256

M

Mac computers
  installing on, 17–19
  uploading photos from, 96
Manage Filters screen, 81–82
Mention stickers, 249–250
mentioning people. *See* tagging people
messages, direct, 167–195
  cultivating communities through, 150
  declining, 194–195
  group conversations, 186–187
  inbox, 191–194
    deleting messages, 193
    overview, 191–192
    searching in, 194
  overview, 9
  replying to, 188
  sending in response to stories, 205
  sharing GIFs via, 181–183
  sharing photos and videos via
    overview, 173–177
    sending disappearing, 177–180
  sharing stories via, 267–268
  starting new, 168–172
  using Live Chat in, 188–191
  using voice messages, 184–185
messages, error, 71–73
  adding comments, 71–72
  deleting comments, 72
  following users, 73
  refreshing feed, 72–73
micro-blogs, 121
microphones, allowing access to, 104
Microsoft, 15

Music stickers, 256
muting
  posts, 45–46
  video chats, 190

N

names
  choosing, 29–30
  as username, 319–320
Normal camera setting, 223
Notes app
  storing hashtags on, 133–134
  writing captions in, 123
notifications
  from being tagged, 126
  checking on app, 53–56
  issues with, 69–70
  overview, 22–23
  push notifications, 55
  turning on post, 45–46
Notifications tab, replying to comments from, 158–159

O

online resources
  Agorapulse social media management software, 324
  Apple Support, 63
  Arkon Mounts tripods, 294
  Bitly link shortener, 36
  cheat sheet for this book, 3
  Community Guidelines, 164
  filing trademark violation claims, 28
  formatting captions, 91
  Google Play troubleshooting wizard, 63
  Google URL Shortener, 36
  Hootsuite social media management platform, 324
  Instagram limits, 73
  Instagram website, 19
  Macworld UK website, 18
  Rebrandly link shortener, 36
  securing accounts, 64
  Sprout Social social media management software, 324
  Tailwind app, 324
organic environments, 336, 338

P

Painter, Lewis, 18

pages
  Explore page, 47–53
    following friends, 142–143
    IGTV on, 302
    searching with, 47–53
    viewing, 47
  Profile page
    seeing saved stories from, 242
    viewing current stories from, 199–200

paper airplane icon, 156, 272

passwords, issues with, 64–67

pausing stories, 205

people, tagging
  for calls to action (CTA), 123–124
  Mention stickers for, 249–250
  overview, 124–126
  in photos
    overview, 91–92
    spam and, 125, 322–323
  sharing stories and, 265–267
  in stories, 218

Person icon, 20

personal profiles, 25–32
  choosing name, 29–30
  choosing username, 27–29
  profile photo, 30–32

Photo screen, 78

photos, 77–102
  adding captions to, 89–91
  adding location to, 92
  improving, 79–89
    applying filters, 81–83
    with editing tools, 83–89
    saving changes, 89
  pixelated, 32
  posting, 94–95
  for profile, 30–32
  sending in response to stories, 205–206
  sharing
    on Facebook, 92–93
    on Tumblr, 93–94
    on Twitter, 93
    via direct messages (DMs), 173–180

stories, creating
  from camera roll, 225–226
  with candid shots, 220
  overview, 221–224
suggestions for
  animals, 326–327
  blue as dominant color, 329, 331
  bold colors, 328–329
  flat lays, 332–333
  human element, 325–326
  lifestyle, 333, 335
  long angles, 333, 334
  organic environments, 336, 338
  Rule of Thirds, 336–337
  white space, 329, 330
tagging people in, 91–92
taking, 77–79
uploading
  from camera roll, 96–97
  multiple photos, 98–102

Photoshop, 285

picture-in-picture stickers, 256

pixelated photos, 32

Places feature
  finding new users to follow, 145
  searching with Explore page, 50

Planoly app, 218

plus (+) icon, 78

pods, 152–153

Poll stickers, 238, 254

posting, 119–135
  adding locations, 92, 111–112, 126–127
  captions, 119–124
    adding, 89–91, 111–112
    advantages of including, 322
    formatting, 122–123
    including calls to action (CTA), 123–124
    length of, 119–121
  content suggestions, 325–338
    animals, 326–327
    blue as dominant color, 329, 331
    bold colors, 328–329
    flat lays, 332–333
    human element, 325–326
    lifestyle, 333, 335

posting *(continued)*
    long angles, 333, 334
    organic environments, 336, 338
    Rule of Thirds, 336–337
    white space, 329, 330
  creating galleries from profile, 279
  hashtags, 128–135
    choosing, 130–132
    creating, 134–135
    expanding reach with, 130
    placement of, 128–129
    saving, 132–134
  overview, 8–9
  photos
    multiple, 98–102
    overview, 94–95
  preview of IGTV videos, 310–311
  replying to comments, 160
  stories, 265–275
    another story to own story, 265–267
    posts from feed, 272–274
    as posts on feed, 274–275
    to select people, 267–271
  tagging people, 91–92, 124–126
  turning on notifications for, 45–46
  videos, 113–114
privacy settings, 39–40
private accounts
  choosing usernames for, 320
  overview, 39–40
  requesting to follow, 140
  using hashtags in, 128
profanity, 72
Professional Accounts
  dashboard tools for, 324
  upgrading to, 37–39
  using calls to action (CTA), 124
  web addresses and, 315
Profile page
  seeing saved stories from, 242
  viewing current stories from, 199–200
profile photos
  choosing, 30–32
  tips for, 320–321

profiles, 25–40. *See also* accounts
  bios for, 32–37
    adding web address to, 35–37
    formatting, 34–35
    including information, 32–34
    layouts for, 35
  business, 37–39
  personal, 25–32
    choosing name, 29–30
    choosing username, 27–29
    profile photo, 30–32
  privacy settings, 39–40
public accounts, 39
Push Notifications, 55

Q

Questions icon, during live videos, 295
Questions stickers, 237, 253–254
Quick Reaction emojis, 205–206
Quiz stickers, 254

R

reacting to stories, 205–206
Rebrandly link shortener, 36
Record button, 107
recording bar, 104
recording videos, 103–109
  deleting clips, 108
  limitations
    length of, 103
    for stories, 208–209
  multiple clips, 108
  reviewing, 108–109
  with smartphone or tablet, 104–107
  for stories
    camera options, 228–234
    filming with stories camera, 227–228
refreshing feed, 72–73
reinstalling, 60
replying to comments, 158–163
  deleting comments, 160–163
    Android smartphone and tablet users, 161–162
    iPhone and iPad users, 160–161
    website users, 163

in direct messages (DMs), 188
  on IGTV, 315
  from Notifications tab, 158–159
  from posts, 160
reporting
  commenters, 164
  IGTV videos, 306
  inappropriate messages, 194
  issues with Instagram, 70–71
resolution, photo, 94, 208
resolving disputes, 163–165
  blocking commenters, 165
  reporting commenters, 164
rewatching stories, 204–205
Rewind camera option, 223,
    230–233
Rule of Thirds, 336–337

S

Saturation tool, 87
saving
  changes to photos, 89
  hashtags, 132–134
  IGTV videos, 306
  live videos, 298
  stories, 238–243
    accessing archives, 241–243
    after publishing, 238
    automatically, 238–241
    before publishing, 238
Saving setting, 212
scheduling live videos, 294
"seamless" videos, 228
Search feature
  finding new accounts to follow,
    143–145
  search queries with, 27
  stickers and exposure on, 246
selfie mode, 215, 223, 227
selfies
  adding captions to, 119
  as stickers, 256
series stories, 221

settings
  Allow Message Replies setting, 212
  Allow Sharing setting, 212
  camera
    for camera access, 212–214
    grid in, 336
    Live camera, 223
    Normal camera, 223
  Close Friends list, 268–270
  Create setting features, 237–238
  Hide Story From setting, 212
  notifications
    on Android devices, 69–70
    on iPads, 69
    on iPhones, 69
  privacy, 39–40
  Saving setting, 212
Shadows option, Color tool, 87
Shadows tool, 87
sharing. *See also* posting
  GIFs, 181–183
  issues with Instagram, 67–69
  links, 156
  live videos, 298
  photos
    on Facebook, 92–93
    on Tumblr, 93–94
    on Twitter, 93
    via direct messages (DMs), 173–180
  stories, 265–275
    another story to own story, 265–267
    posts from feed, 272–274
    as posts on feed, 274–275
    to select people, 267–271
  videos via direct messages (DMs), 173–180
Sharpen tool, 89
shutter button, 79
skipping through stories, 204
Slider stickers, 251–252
smartphones
  for Instagram, 7–8
  recording videos with, 104–107
  uploading videos to IGTV from, 309–311

social media influencers, 217, 333

social media traffic, Google Analytics tracking, 36

spacing in captions, 122

spam

  accounts

    overview, 149

    reporting, 164

    usernames and, 320

  content

    general discussion of, 125

    hashjacking and, 322

Spam or Scam option, 164

speech bubble icon, 156

Sprout Social social media management
    software, 324

starting app, 21–24

stickers, 10, 245–259

  adding

    Chat, 254–256

    Countdown, 256

    emojis, 252–253

    GIF, 251

    hashtag, 250–251

    location, 246–249

    Mention, 249–250

    Music, 256

    picture-in-picture effect, 256

    Poll and Quiz, 254

    Questions, 253–254

    Slider, 251–252

  deleting, 258–259

  overview, 245

storage issues, 58–63

Storeo app, 208

stories, 199–215

  accessing camera for, 210–215

    changing camera mode, 215

    editing settings, 212–214

  before and after, 221

  behind-the-scenes, 218–219

  of candid shots, 220

  creating, 217–243

    photo stories, 221–226

    planning tips, 217–218

    reasons for, 218–221

    text posts, 236–238

    video stories, 227–236

  defined, 8

  highlight galleries, 277–289

    adding content to, 285–287

    creating, 279–285

    deleting stories from, 287–288

    overview, 277–279

    suggestions for, 289

  ignoring, 321

  limitations for, 207–209

    recording time, 208–209

    uploading, 208

  overview, 10, 199–203

  pausing, 205

  personalizing, 245–264

    with doodles, 259–262

    with stickers, 245–259

    with text, 262–264

  promoting live videos on, 294

  reacting to, 205–206

  rewatching, 204–205

  saving, 238–243

    accessing archives, 241–243

    after publishing, 238

    automatically, 238–241

    before publishing, 238

  series, 221

  sharing, 265–275

    another story to own story,
      265–267

    posts from feed, 272–274

    as posts on feed, 274–275

    to select people, 267–271

  skipping through, 204

Story Controls page, 212

StoryCutter app, 208

Structure tool, 87

SuperZoom camera option, 230

switch cameras icon, 79

syncing contact list, 140–141

T

tablets, 7, 104–107

tapping, double
  in Explore function, 142
  interacting by, 9
  overview, 156
using automated tools for, 324

tagging people
  for calls to action (CTA), 123–124
  Mention stickers for, 249–250
  overview, 124–126
  in photos
    overview, 91–92
    spam and, 125, 322–323
  sharing stories and, 265–267
  in stories, 218

Tags feature. See also hashtags
  finding new accounts to follow, 145
  hashjacking and, 322
  searching with Explore page, 50

Tailwind app, 134, 324

text posts
  creating in stories, 236–238
    Create setting features, 237–238
    overview, 236–237
  font options, 262–263
  removing, 263

throwback Thursday (#tbt) hashtag, 93

Tilt Shift tool, 88–89

timers for live videos, 292

tools
  for managing Instagram
    approved, 324
    Tailwind app, 134
  for photo editing
    Canva graphic-design tool website, 285
    multiple photos in one post, 102
    overview, 83–89
    Photoshop, 285

Top feature
  finding new accounts to follow, 145
  searching with Explore page, 48–49

trademark violation claims, 28

travel photos, 218

tribes. See communities

Trim screen, 116–117

tripods, 294

Tumblr, sharing photos on, 93–94

Twitter, sharing photos on, 93

U

unblocking, 165

unfollowing
  cleaning up feed by, 149
  overview, 45–46

unfreezing app installation, 63

upgrading to business profiles, 37–39

Uplet app, 18

uploading
  photos
    from camera roll, 96–97
    screenshots of stories, 267
  videos, 114–118
    to IGTV, 309–313
    multiple, 116–118
    overview, 114–115
    for stories, 234–236

URLs. See web addresses

usernames
  changing, 28–29
  choosing, 27–28
  irrelevant, 320
  issues with logging in, 64
  searching for, 50, 51
  using name as, 319–320

V

vertical videos, 314

Video screen, 104–106

videos, 103–118
  creating story
    camera options, 228–234
    with candid shots, 220
    filming with stories camera, 227–228
    talking to camera, 219–220
    uploading video from camera roll, 234–236

videos *(continued)*
  IGTV, 301–306, 307–315
    creating content for, 314–315
    finding with IGTV app, 303–304
    formatting for videos on, 305
    home feed, 305–306
    on Instagram app, 301–303
    responding to comments, 315
    setting up channel, 307–309
    uploading videos to, 309–313
  improving, 109–114
    adding details, 111–112
    applying filters, 110
    changing cover frame, 110–111
    posting, 113–114
  live videos, 291–298
    general discussion of, 10
    interacting with live guests, 295
    inviting guests onto, 296–297
    overview, 291–293
    planning tips, 294
    saving, 298
    scheduling, 294
    sharing, 298
  recording, 103–109
    deleting clips, 108
    multiple clips, 108
    reviewing, 108–109
    with smartphone or tablet, 104–107

  sending in response to stories, 205–206
  sharing via direct messages (DMs), 173–180
  sound for, 108
  uploading, 114–118
    multiple, 116–118
    overview, 114–115
  vertical, 314
Vignette tool, 87
violence, 163
voice messages, 184–185

W
Warmth tool, 87
web addresses
  adding to bios, 35–37
  for calls to action (CTA), 123–124
  on IGTV videos, 315
  for Instagram accounts, 27
  link shorteners, 36
website users, Instagram
  deleting comments, 163
  exploring, 19–21
white space, 329, 330
Windows PC, installing Instagram on, 15–17

Y
You tab, 54–55

About the Authors

Jenn Herman: Jenn is a social media consultant, speaker, and globally recognized Instagram expert. She is a popular blogger on Instagram marketing, and her blog, Jenn's Trends (www.jennstrends.com), has won the title of a Top 10 Social Media Blog in 2014, 2015, and 2016. Through her blog, consulting, and speaking, Jenn provides tips, resources, and training for organizations of all sizes that need to structure their social media strategies.

Jenn has been featured in *Inc.*, *HuffPost*, *The Verge*, CBS Radio L.A., Fox News, Yahoo! Finance, and numerous other podcasts and publications. She is the author of the self-published books *The Ultimate Beginner's Guide to Instagram* and *Stop Guessing: Your Step-by-Step Guide to Creating a Social Media Strategy*, as well as *Instagram For Business For Dummies* (Wiley). Jenn's Instagram username is @jenns_trends.

Eric Butow: Eric is the owner of Butow Communications Group (BCG) in Jackson, California. BCG offers website design, online marketing, and technical documentation services for businesses. He has written 31 computing and user experience books. His most recent books include and *Samsung Gear S2 For Dummies* (Wiley), *Instagram For Business For Dummies* (Wiley), and *Pro iOS Security and Forensics* (Apress).

When he's not working in (and on) his business or writing books, you can find Eric enjoying time with his friends, walking around the historic Gold Rush town of Jackson, and helping his mother manage her infant and toddler day-care business. Eric's Instagram username is @ericbutow.

Corey Walker: Corey is the owner of The Marketing Specialist in El Dorado Hills, California. The Marketing Specialist offers social media strategy, content, ad management, and analytics, with a concentrated passion for Instagram and Facebook. She has managed the social media accounts of hospitals, medical groups, real estate agents, online businesses, and publications. She is also coauthor of *Instagram For Business For Dummies* (Wiley).

When she's not online, you can find Corey with her husband, cheering on her daughters at a volleyball tournament or a soccer game, or gathering with friends and neighbors for a night of good food and wine. Corey's Instagram username is @coreycwalker.

Dedications

To my daughter, who has taught me so many amazing things.

—Jenn Herman

To everyone who never stopped believing in me.

—Eric Butow

To my husband, Les, and daughters, Kendall and Cameryn.

—Corey Walker

Authors' Acknowledgments

We would like to thank the team of people who made this book happen. Our agent, Carole Jelen, was a huge help in getting this book off the ground. The team at Wiley, especially Executive Editor Steve Hayes, made this book possible. Hannah Partridge offered lots of useful suggestions as our technical editor. Our families and friends supported us through all our late-night writing sessions. And a final thanks to you, for buying this book and being a part of the Instagram community we love!

Publisher's Acknowledgments

Executive Editor: Steven Hayes

Technical Editor: Hannah Partridge

Sr. Editorial Assistant: Cherie Case

Production Editor: Magesh Elangovan

Cover Image: © Tim Robberts/Getty Images